DA BEARS!

STEVE DELSOHN

CROWN ARCHETYPE   NEW YORK

DA BEARS!

HOW THE 1985 MONSTERS OF THE MIDWAY

BECAME THE GREATEST TEAM IN NFL HISTORY

Published in the United States by Crown Archetype, an imprint of the

Crown Publishing Group, a division of Random House, Inc., New York.

www.crownpublishing.com

Crown Archetype with colophon is a trademark of

Random House, Inc.

Insert and title-page photographs copyright © 2010 by Bob Baer

Library of Congress Cataloging-in-Publication Data

Delsohn, Steve.

Da Bears! : how the 1985 monsters of the midway became the greatest team

in NFL history / Steve Delsohn.—1st ed.

p.   cm.

Includes index.

1. Chicago Bears (Football team)—History.

2. National Football League—History.   I. Title.

GV956.C5D45 2010

796.332'640977311—dc22

2010016775

ISBN 978–0-307–46467–5

Printed in the United States of America

Design by Leonard W. Henderson

1 3 5 7 9 10 8 6 4 2

First Edition

For Eilene Delsohn, my mother, a true Chicagoan

||||||||||||||||||||||||||||||||||||||||||||||||||||||||||||||||||||||||||||||||||||||||||||||||||||||||||||||||||||||||

CONTENTS

DA BEARS!

||||||||||||||||||||||||||||||||||||||||||||||||||||||||||||||||||||||||||||||||||||||||||||||||||

CHAPTER 1

||||||||||||||||||||||||||||||||||||||||||||||||||||||||||||||||||||||||||||||||||||||

UP AND THEN WAY DOWN IN '84

Aggression was a weapon which Mike Ditka believed in. During the 1960s, he had been a relentless tight end for the Chicago Bears. Now, at age 45, he was in his third year as their combative head coach. Thus he viewed the next football game as more than a game. It was a litmus test to see just how ferocious his 1984 Bears were.

It was the first week of November and they were getting ready to play the Los Angeles Raiders. Even in a league understood to be violent, the Raiders were historically the biggest bullies. They were also the defending NFL champions, having dismantled the Washington Redskins 38–9 in the previous Super Bowl. The 1984 Bears were a pretty good football team trying to figure out if they could be great.

"If you want to defeat your opponent, you got to out-hit him," says Ditka. "People say, 'Well, you need to out-think him.' No! You gotta out-hit him. That's what football players understand. It's like a boxer. You hit him in the nose enough times he's gonna respect you. The Raiders were always a physical football team, and that's what we talked about before the game. I said, 'We're going toe to toe with these guys. It's gonna be a heavyweight match, and we're gonna slug with them.'"

On November 6, 1984, the Bears mauled the Raiders 17–6. This being Chicago, it was windy and cold on that Sunday afternoon at Soldier Field. This being the 1984 Bears, the offense did just enough, led by its beloved warrior Walter Payton, who gained 111 yards and scored both of his team's two touchdowns. On defense, the Bears made the Raiders look weak and confused, forcing 3 interceptions and 2 fumbles and sacking the Raider quarterbacks 9 times. Read that again—9 times—because it doesn't happen too often. The single-game NFL record is 12, which is held by five different teams, including the '84 Bears, who did it later that season against the Lions.

Against the Raiders, it seemed as if the Bears competed against *each other* to see who could beat the snot out of the quarterback first. First they fractured Marc Wilson's arm and knocked him out of the game. Then they knocked out his replacement, David Humm, with a knee injury. Wilson was forced to reenter the game and found himself getting knocked out a second time. Curry Kirkpatrick, writing for *Sports Illustrated* during his heyday, was deeply impressed. "So brutal was the Bear onslaught that Al Davis was seen covering his face with his hands. Just breathe, baby."

The NFL's closest observers were also starting to see that the Bear offensive line had become increasingly nasty in its own right. Kurt Becker started that game at right guard for Chicago. A six-foot-five, 280-pound Michigan graduate with a maniacal streak, he frequently tangled that Sunday with future Hall of Fame lineman Howie Long, who later told *Sports Illustrated* he finally screamed at Becker, "I'm going to get you in the parking lot after the game and beat you up in front of your family!"

Becker says Long tried to follow through on his threat.

"Howie was out of his mind by the end of the game," he recalls. "He tried to come into our locker room and confront me. Then he wouldn't get on their team bus. He was looking for me in the parking lot."

Years later, Emery Moorehead, Chicago's multitalented tight end, ran into the great Raider running back Marcus Allen, and they began reminiscing about the day the '84 Bears made the '84 Raiders look soft.

"Marcus said, after we knocked out both of their quarterbacks, they wanted to put in Ray Guy, their punter, because he was supposed to be their emergency quarterback," says Moorehead. "But Guy refused to go in. Then all of them were arguing at halftime about who was going back in—was it gonna be David Humm or Marc Wilson? *Nobody* wanted to go back in. That's how intimidating our defense was then. You can't even hit guys today the way our defense hit them. You'd be suspended."

Ditka, who doesn't joke about this kind of thing, says the 1984 win against the Raiders "was the most brutal football game I've ever watched. Did you see how many guys they were carrying off the field for both teams?"

In the second quarter, the Bears lost their own starting quarterback, Jim McMahon, when he scrambled away from the pressure and ran for a first down before getting pinned between two Raiders. On the CBS telecast it looked fairly benign, but in reality one of the Raiders had struck McMahon in his side with a helmet. His offensive teammates told him to leave the game. He refused and remained for three more plays, but at halftime he had trouble breathing. McMahon tried to play again in the third quarter, and this time his offensive linemen ordered him to the sideline.

"Jim got hit in the kidney, and it came over the bone in his rib cage and his kidney got lacerated," says McMahon's long-time agent Steve Zucker. "I was in the stands, and I met him in the locker room. He was pissing blood, I mean pure blood, and he was in intense pain. He was in agony."

When asked now if he was scared, McMahon doesn't say yes, and maybe he wasn't. According to several teammates, McMahon was never afraid of anything. But he does say, "I could have died. It was an internal organ, so it ain't no joke."

Adds McMahon, "They wanted to remove it, but I knew my career would be over. The bottom part of it was gone, and it was cut in about five places. It was bleeding for two days. The doctor told me, 'Look, you're gonna die if we don't cut it out.' I said, 'You can't cut this out, you cut it out and I'm finished. Just keep giving me the morphine and leave me alone.'

"That's what he did. I told him I'd sign a waiver, he wouldn't be responsible, but he wasn't cutting that out of me. On Tuesday night, they came in and gave me a transfusion because they said they had to operate on Wednesday. I said, 'Just give me until the morning, and if it's still bleeding you do what you have to do.' Overnight this thing just started closing up by itself. The doctor still doesn't know how the hell it happened. I've had my knees, my shoulders, my ribs, and everything else blown up. But I never felt anything like that in my whole life."

McMahon spent the next ten days in the hospital. Right after the Raiders game, Bears trainer Fred Cato told reporters, "At this point, I will say he will play again this season. But he will miss four weeks. There was no rib damage, no other organs were injured, but there was a lot of pain, and he did urinate blood. On the positive side, he didn't rupture the kidney, which could have ended his career."

Cato turned out to be wrong about McMahon returning

after a month. For McMahon, the '84 season had just ended. And just that abruptly the Bears lost their momentum. They were 7–3, but now it seemed less likely that they would keep winning enough to make the playoffs. If they did qualify for the postseason, their quarterbacks would be Steve Fuller and Rusty Lisch.

"That [injury] was significant," says Ken Valdiserri, the Bears' director of public relations. "We were just coming into our own, and this put us in a position of not having any continuity. It was symbolic of Jim's career from an injury standpoint, and it was symbolic of his reckless play. I think what we saw there was a guy who was reckless with the way he played the position."

Nobody ever questioned the toughness of Jim McMahon. While the Raider quarterbacks were trying to stay on the sidelines, he had internal bleeding and was arguing with his linemen to stay in the game. But questions about why he was injured so often persisted throughout his eight seasons in Chicago. Was he truly reckless during games? Or, at six-foot and 190 pounds, did he simply sustain the injuries that came inevitably from playing such a hazardous position? Off the field, did he drink too much, take poor care of his body, not get enough rest?

"That was the rumor, that he lived too wild," says his agent Zucker. "I don't think that was real. Jim was not a big guy, and he played like a wild man. That's why his teammates loved him. He threw everything out there. He had no fear."

"Jimmy Mac was a linebacker playing the quarterback position," says All-Pro safety Dave Duerson. "He would win at all costs, including giving up his body. If we needed a yard to get a first down, Mac was going to get that yard. He wouldn't run out of bounds. He wouldn't slide. He laid it on the line."

And yet, Valdiserri says, "if McMahon took better care of himself, he would have been on the field more. It was a combination of the way he played the game, recklessly, and living his life recklessly off the field. He was reckless in every phase of his life. When he was in good shape, he was in good shape. But he wasn't in good shape for a long portion of his Bears career."

Different people saw different things in McMahon—and he himself will weigh in later on this—but everybody agreed that his health had an enormous impact on Chicago's chances of winning from week to week. In one remarkable stretch from late 1984 through 1988, the Bears went 35–3 in regular-season games with McMahon as their starter. But during that same span, he was sidelined for a month or more four different times.

Thus, going into the 1985 season, this was one of the NFL's prominent story lines: if Jim McMahon could stay healthy, the Chicago Bears could go to the Super Bowl.

For now, in '84, after the Raiders game, he was replaced by his sometimes efficient, always cautious, mostly boring backup, Steve Fuller. If Fuller went down, the third-string quarterback was Rusty Lisch, who had once started at Notre Dame in front of Joe Montana until Irish coach Dan Devine came to his senses. Lisch was quiet, sensitive, pious—the anti-McMahon. Once, when Chicago played on *Monday Night Football,* Ditka went ballistic as Lisch returned to the sideline after an interception. McMahon and Fuller were used to Ditka's profane eruptions, but Lisch, who rarely got playing time, seemed offended. The next time Chicago's offense went on the field, Lisch stayed there on the sideline, looking miffed. "I don't think I can go back in after the way you talked to me," he told Ditka. Rather than pummel his quarterback in prime time, Ditka unballed his fist and told Lisch he had only been kidding.

By early November 1984, especially coming off the big physical win against the Raiders, Ditka should have felt more secure in his job. The Bears were now 7–3, and the *way* they won, says offensive tackle Keith Van Horne, "started to set the foundation for '85. The Raiders were the defending Super Bowl champions, and it was a statement game. Let's see if you really belong. That game showed we belonged."

But Ditka did *not* feel safe. In the final year of his three-year contract, he still couldn't tell where he really stood with management. In 1982, his first year as a head coach at any level, the Bears had gone 3–6 during the shortened season when the NFL players walked out on strike. In 1983 Chicago went 8–8 and won five of its last six games to narrowly miss the playoffs. Nonetheless, in 1984 McMahon told *Sports Illustrated* before the first game, "We all know Mike's job is on the line."

By then the legendary George Halas had died. Ditka had been hired by the Bears' longtime owner and president, who had also been Ditka's coach when Ditka ran people over as a fire-breathing tight end in Chicago. Halas died of cancer at age 88 on October 31, 1983. His 39-year-old grandson, Michael McCaskey, was announced as the team's new president 11 days later. By the time the 1984 season started, McCaskey was telling reporters that he wouldn't "review" Ditka's status until the season ended.

On November 19, 1984, two weeks after the Bears beat up the Raiders, Ditka blurted out on his local radio show, "You've got to understand that I didn't come here hired by the people who own the ball club now. And there probably is a good chance that I probably won't be back next year."

Many Chicago fans scoffed, figuring it was just Ditka being

Ditka by calling out Mike McCaskey in front of the entire god-damn city. There were other fans who believed Ditka might actually not return and suspected that McCaskey, a graduate of Yale and later a Harvard professor, wanted someone more corporate and polished than the hot-tempered SOB currently roaming the sidelines in Chicago.

"I can honestly tell you from the bottom of my heart, I never worried for one minute about my job with the Chicago Bears," Ditka says. "I was gonna come, I was gonna go. That never bothered me. I wasn't coaching for money at that time. When I took the job, I was one of the lowest-paid coaches in the league. When I quit, I made good money, but that wasn't what it was about. The most important thing was to be the Chicago Bears coach and fulfill a dream, an ambition."

That's what Iron Mike says now. In his 1986 autobiography, *Ditka,* he wrote that "winning and not knowing anything started bothering me a little bit." As for McCaskey, he later told *Sports Illustrated,* "Mike was my grandfather's choice as coach. I wanted the future coach to be my choice. I needed time."

The Bears finished the 1984 regular season at 10–6, winning their first division title since 1963, which was also the last time they won a NFL championship. Then, on December 30, 1984, Chicago went into deafening RFK Stadium and upset the Washington Redskins 23–19 in the first round of the NFC playoffs. Payton ran for 104 gritty yards, threw a touchdown pass on a reverse, and delivered a crushing block that broke cornerback Curtis Jordan's shoulder. Fuller played well for three quarters before the entire offense took a siesta. The game was saved by Chicago's attacking 46 defense, which frustrated John Riggins, flustered Joe Theissman, and bailed out the faltering Chicago offense by repeatedly holding off Washington in the fourth quarter.

After the Bears had won their first playoff game since 1963—back in the glory days when Ditka played for Halas—Ditka grandly told the press, "I just think it's time for the city of Chicago to take a bow."

The next week McCaskey announced that he would extend Ditka's contract by three years. Given that the Bears were now preparing for the NFC title game in San Francisco, Ditka calls McCaskey's timing a "distraction." He says he told McCaskey they should just wait until after the season. But suddenly the boss seemed eager to prove how much he valued the coach, and the new deal was inked on January 2. Did that make McCaskey a front-runner? Of course it did, but it was still an important moment in Ditka's career. The three-year contract extension—along with the momentous wins over the Raiders and Redskins—helped quiet the critics who had questioned his inexperience and self-control.

Next came the team's biggest game in a generation. If the Bears could win at San Francisco in the NFC championship on January 6, they would advance to the team's first Super Bowl.

But the 1984 Bears weren't ready for that.

They weren't ready yet for that type of big-game pressure. They were also without McMahon.

The 49ers trounced them, 23–0.

The defense played impressively up until halftime, when the Joe Montana–led Niners were ahead only by 6–0 on two field goals. But because the Chicago offense was so pathetic, the defense finally wore down after spending too much time on the field. Fuller got sacked a humiliating nine times and passed for an absurd 37 yards. Receiver Willie Gault was thrown only one ball the entire game, he bobbled it, and an interception ensued. Then Gault got humbled, again, after the game by San Francisco safety Eric Wright.

"Gault kept his head on a swivel, looking for the guy who was going to take a shot at him," Wright told reporters.

Wright was known for his talent *and* his big mouth. Still, he told the truth. Gault had been a track star in college at Tennessee. In Chicago his great speed stretched out the defense, taking some pressure off Payton since other teams couldn't put eight players up in the box. But Gault *was* concerned about getting hit. You could see it in his body language.

Says Kurt Becker, the crazed Chicago right guard, "The 49ers stomped us pretty good that day. The message was, we were good, but we weren't really that good. We had to come back and work harder."

Getting shut out in the NFC championship game was embarrassing. Getting punked on national television by Bill Walsh made the Bears start thinking immediately about payback. The legendary 49ers coach waited until the fourth quarter to insert Guy McIntyre, a 264-pound guard, into the offensive backfield as a blocker down near the goal line. With the game already a blowout, this was hardly some sort of tactical thing.

This was a "fuck you" thing.

Says Hall of Fame defensive lineman Dan Hampton, "When they put Guy McIntyre, this guard, into the backfield late in the game, I thought it was just Bill Walsh being a jagoff. But Ditka didn't forget."

"I remembered it the next time we played them in '85," says Ditka. "People said, 'Well, that's kind of small.' I don't give a shit if people think it's small. I remembered. I remember a lot of things."

The long flight back to Chicago was subdued. McMahon stayed behind that week in San Francisco, visiting his wife's family and feeling as if he might vomit every time he picked up a Bay Area paper. "Their players were making it sound like we didn't belong on the same field with them," says McMahon. Specifically, they were now saying publicly what a few of them had said as the Bears trudged off the field at Candlestick: "Next time, bring your offense."

"That really stuck with me," says Chicago's All-Pro left tackle Jimbo Covert, who wasn't a guy you'd really want to insult. At the University of Pittsburgh, the six-foot-four, 280-pounder was charged with protecting Dan Marino's blind side. Covert did it so well, he didn't allow any sacks his senior year and only three in his last three college seasons. In Chicago, he protected McMahon's blind side and opened holes for Payton, and Covert did that so well, he was later voted to the NFL's Team of the '80s by the Pro Football Hall of Fame's Board of Selectors.

"They were saying it on the field right after the game," says Covert. "I think it was Randy Cross and a few other guys on their defense. They were saying, 'Come back next time and bring an offense.' "

There were guys on Chicago's defense who seemed to feel the same way. Safety Gary Fencik, a big hitter even by the NFL's sick standards, told reporters in the postgame locker room, "We really needed something from our offense. They had a tough day and couldn't generate any points. I thought if we could have just gotten one touchdown in the third quarter, we would have them on edge and guessing, but we never got in that position."

It was an ancient dynamic in Chicago—the defense feeling the offense let it down, the offense getting sick of hearing about it, the defense and offense *divided*—but now that Ditka was head coach and de facto offensive coordinator, and Buddy Ryan was the defensive coordinator, the split between the two units had never been more apparent.

Their laundry list of grievances included:

Ryan thought *he* should be the Bears head coach. He thought Ditka was in over his head. Ditka thought Ryan cared too much about taking the credit when things went well. He thought Ryan was too snide—and too public—when he criticized the players in the media. In the NFL, that wasn't supposed to be a coordinator's role.

Ditka hadn't even picked Ryan to be on his staff in the first place. Ditka inherited Ryan when Ditka was hired by Halas in 1982. Ryan was already there, and Halas told Ditka that Ryan was staying there.

Today nobody from the 1985 Bears even goes through the motions of trying to sugarcoat it. The players say Ditka and Ryan ranged from ignoring each other to cursing each other.

"I came there in 1981," says Van Horne. "That was the year before Ditka. The team was very fractured. It was an offense-defense thing. And you could kind of see why they hadn't done so well. The defense for many years had been a strong point, and the defense really had no respect for the offense. Everything was just fractured. And that continued to exist just because of the Buddy and Mike thing. Ditka did get us to focus more on becoming more of a team. Ditka did try and do that. But that never really went away."

Against the 49ers in the 1984 NFC championship, says Van Horne, "I just know we got our ass kicked. Then again, it's a team sport. So Gary Fencik can stick it up his ass. He may be right. I'd have to look at the statistics and all that. Maybe we didn't perform as well as we should have. But I can say that about the '85 season and the Miami game. The defense that game—where were you? But that [Fencik's postgame comments] illustrates the divide that did exist, and that had a lot to do with the coaches. It was like having two head coaches. I remember Ditka stuck his head into their defensive meeting room once. Buddy threw an eraser at him and said, 'This is my team, get out of here.' "

As the game clock wound down on that grim afternoon at Candlestick Park, Payton appeared to be limping on the sideline. He had gained 92 yards, but he had been ganged up on by the 49er defenders because they had no respect for Chicago's passing game without McMahon. With a few minutes left in the 23–0 debacle, Payton sat down by himself at the far end of the bench and lowered his head to his hands. Payton was ten years into his career, all of them with the Bears, who had often been lousy, and now he believed he might never play in a Super Bowl. Even if the Bears somehow got there, Payton feared he wouldn't be around. The people in Chicago feared it too. They thought Payton might become the city's next Ernie Banks, who played 19 years for the Cubs and never made it to the World Series.

At the same time, Mike Singletary, Chicago's All-Pro middle linebacker, stood a few feet behind the bench trying to ignore the nonstop heckling from the gleeful 49er fans. They screamed "Teddy Bears!" and "Cubbies!" and their own team's next destination—"Super Bowl, Super Bowl!"

"I remember it like it was yesterday," says Singletary. "I remember watching the clock go down. The score was 23–0. I remember losing my shoe and screaming at the top of my voice, 'Why can't I get shoes that work?' And their fans were yelling and singing, and I got up on the stands and I yelled, *'We'll be back next year! Just watch and see! We'll be back!'* "

Maybe they would, but that was hardly certain. Getting humiliated in the NFL playoffs could set a franchise back the following season. Over the next several months, the Bears would still be coping with their failure, not knowing if they would prove strong enough to overcome it.

CHAPTER 2

|||||||||||||||||||||||||||||||||||||||||||||||||||||||||||||||||||||||||||||

THE '85 CIRCUS IS OPEN

O n April 30, 1985, the Bears chose a defensive tackle
from Clemson in the first round of the NFL draft.
Taking William Perry with their number one was
a controversial move and major gamble. Paul Zimmerman,
Sports Illustrated's top pro football writer, appeared on ESPN
the day of the draft and thoroughly trashed the pick when it
was announced.

"I had scouts legitimately say that he will not go before
the fifth round, that he's going to get the shock of his life on
draft day," Zimmerman said. "I've heard nothing but nega-
tives about William Perry. The only team that really showed
a great interest was the Raiders, but not as a first-rounder.
They all felt he was a knight in armor, that if he fell down
he'd never get up again. I heard he really made an effort to
trim down for the draft. Maybe it's just cosmetic for the draft.
He's in the sauna doing all these things and probably got his
weight down to 500 or something."

Harsh.

Zimmerman wasn't alone in thinking the Bears had
screwed up. On the other hand, it was difficult to second-guess
them when it came to their recent number-one picks. In 1982
they chose McMahon, who after years of Payton right and

Payton left, finally gave the Bears a legitimate passer capable of diversifying their offense. In 1983 they selected Covert, the dominating left tackle who would help transform a good offensive line into a great one. In 1984 they took linebacker Wilber Marshall, whose career started slowly in Ryan's complex 46 defense, but who would soon become an All-Pro.

The 1983 draft, from top to bottom, is still perceived in Chicago as "the Turning Point." The Bears chose seven players who by 1985 would all be starters: Covert and wide receiver Willie Gault in the first round; cornerback Mike Richardson in the second; safety Dave Duerson in the third; guard Tom Thayer in the fourth; and defensive end Richard Dent and defensive tackle Mark Bortz in the eighth.

By 1985 Bortz would be switched to left guard, and he, Covert, and Thayer (after Kurt Becker got injured) would combine with left tackle Keith Van Horne and center Jay Hilgenberg to give the Bears the league's most physical offensive line. Gault provided tremendous speed and a deep threat for McMahon when other teams keyed on Payton. Dent developed into one of the premier pass rushers in the game, while Richardson and Duerson were quick cover guys. Duerson could also step up and deliver a punishing blow.

Years later, the NFL Network ranked the Chicago draft of 1983 as the third best in league history.

"And it wasn't just the guys at the top of the draft," says Dan Hampton. "You get Richard Dent and Mark Bortz in the eighth round, you're doing something right."

Bears assistant PR man Brian Harlan says the '83 masterpiece was mostly rendered by Ditka, general manager Jim Finks, and, above all, personnel director Bill Tobin.

"We had a very small scouting department," recalls Harlan. "Bill Tobin was on the road scouting all the time, and his track record was unbelievable. Finks and Ditka had input, but it was mostly Tobin who put that '85 team together. He didn't get the credit because Ditka was visible and Finks was visible and the owner, Mike McCaskey, wanted to be visible. So Tobin got overlooked. And it wasn't just the '83 draft. Tobin got Steve McMichael off waivers. He drafted Hampton, Singletary, Otis Wilson, Matt Suhey. I mean, a lot of those great players came in before '83. Tobin rarely missed in the first two rounds, and that was the key."

Just how small was Chicago's scouting department? With only three men, including Tobin, responsible for scouting the entire college football landscape, it was the second-smallest department in the NFL. The smallest one belonged to the even-more-thrifty Cincinnati Bengals, who amazingly had only one college scout.

For all of the important input from Tobin and Finks, it was Ditka who had the most say when it came to those final, fluid, critical draft-day decisions.

"I think that was one of the things that most people don't realize about Ditka," says halfback Thomas Sanders, himself a ninth-round pick in '85 who wound up playing seven years in the NFL. "He was good at evaluating college players, and he was committed to building his team through the draft. Ditka used to say he wanted his own guys, he didn't want to depend on other teams' rejects."

By 1985, Finks had left the Bears to become executive vice president of the Cubs. Jerry Vanisi had replaced him as general manager. Ditka and Vanisi were normally united, but in this case Ditka and Tobin wanted to draft William Perry in the first round, while Vanisi and McCaskey favored Florida State wide receiver Jessie Hester. Ditka and Tobin won, but many questioned their sanity. Paul Zimmerman, who had already blasted the pick on ESPN, took another shot in his annual NFL preview in *Sports Illustrated.*

"Picking Perry was an arrogant move by the Bears," Zimmerman wrote. "They were saying, we're so good we can go for a gamble, a project. A fleet cornerback would have made more sense or maybe a wideout to give their talented young quarterback Jim McMahon an extra target. Willie Gault, the flyer, has been a disappointment."

Zimmerman also made a crack about Perry going on a diet of "sunflower seeds and alfalfa sprouts," the writer's way of saying Perry was fat. Perry was not only fat but completely out of shape when he finally arrived at camp after missing the first two weeks because of a contract dispute. Ditka said Perry weighed about 330 when he practiced for the first time, but Hampton nicknamed him "Biscuit," figuring he was one biscuit short of 350. After seeing Perry with his shirt off, some of his teammates started calling him "Mud Slide."

Perry picked up his most famous nickname, "the Refrigerator," at Clemson, where he weighed 315 pounds as a freshman and later ballooned to a dangerous 380. Perry wasn't the most cerebral college athlete. When the NCAA imposed a two-year TV and postseason ban on the Tigers, he said, "What makes it hard is that we can't watch television for two years." Perry may have been kidding, but nobody seemed to think so.

But he was round. He was easy to like. He had a great smile, with a big gap in his grin where a cousin shot out his front tooth with a pellet gun. When Perry arrived in Chicago, he had a 22-inch neck, a size 58 coat, and a self-effacing humor the fans and the media appreciated.

"I was born to be big," he told *Sports Illustrated* his rookie year. "And I ain't disappointing nobody."

Still, the NFL is a business, and number-one picks are crucial. So why draft an overweight defensive lineman when your defense is already loaded—particularly on the line where in 1984 Hampton and Dent had gone to the Pro Bowl and McMichael had 10 of the team's NFL record 72 sacks?

"Ditka put his foot down and said, 'We're drafting Fridge,'" says Hampton. "Was it a smart move? We already had the best pass rush in the history of pro football. And go back and look at a picture of us. There was not a fat guy on that damn defense. We all did a hundred up-downs every day. We did line drills. We were in shape. No bad bodies at all. So what did Ditka do? Go and draft a damn 350-pound guy that is basically ideally suited to play nose tackle. We don't play nose tackle in our defense. Everyone has a two-gap and rushes the passer. Slouches need not apply. But he's a first-round pick, what are you gonna do? You can't kill him."

"Honestly?" says Ditka. "When I watched him play in college, I didn't think we had anyone who could block him, and I had a pretty damn good offensive line. I thought he was one of the most dominant college players I watched. He could dunk a basketball. He had a great vertical leap. He had great explosion. He was fast for 20, 30 yards. He had no endurance to go and run a mile or anything like that, but he could do those other things pretty damn well. Quickness, strength—I loved him. Buddy Ryan didn't like him."

Ryan didn't like any rookies. He didn't trust them to run his complex 46 defense.

He also resented that Ditka rarely consulted with him on draft picks, even though Ryan *was* defensive coordinator. When the Bears took Perry, Ryan was even more irked than usual, believing that Perry would soon be drummed out of the league.

Says starting right cornerback Leslie Frazier, "I remember

Bill Tobin saying that the Fridge would be a good player. But Buddy Ryan is saying he's not going to get on the field, he's just a big fat slob, so you wondered if Fridge would ever *really* be good. But Fridge was a fun-loving guy, so everyone just enjoyed being in his company, even though he was getting killed every day in training camp by our defensive coordinator."

Tyrone Keys was a defensive lineman who could have been threatened by Perry but ended up his best friend on the team. Keys said Ryan made his feelings apparent on Tuesday, August 6, Perry's second day at camp in Platteville, Wisconsin.

"It was our second practice of the day," remembers Keys. "We were in the locker room, and the guys on the defensive line were always the last guys to go outside. We told Fridge it was time to go, and he said, 'Man, I can't go.' I kind of stayed back with him and said, 'It's time to go practice, man.' And he sat on that stool and he didn't go. He said, 'Man, I lost 22 pounds just this morning. I can't go back out there. If I go back out there, at the rate I'm losing weight, they might have to move me to running back or wide receiver.'

"So we go out there, and Buddy Ryan is saying—and not this politely—'Where is Perry?' We said, 'Fridge isn't coming.' That's when the friction started. That's when Ryan called him a wasted draft pick."

Ryan made his famous comment later that day, a few hours after Perry didn't participate in the afternoon workout.

"He's just a big overweight kid," Ryan told the reporters covering the Bears in Platteville. "He hasn't shown me anything since he's been here. He was a wasted draft choice and a waste of money."

Ryan wasn't done. He also said that night on a radio talk show, "We should have given the money to [training-camp holdout] Todd Bell and the pros we know who can play and brought them into camp. We should have forgotten about him. He's an overweight kid and a helluva nice kid, but you know, I got twin boys at home that are nice kids, and I don't want them playing for me."

The story broke in Chicago, went over the wire, and turned into national news.

Ron Rivera understood what it felt like to pick up the morning paper and be castigated by Ryan a few days into your first NFL camp. In July 1984, the rookie middle linebacker from Cal slammed into a blocking sled and pinched a nerve in his back. Rivera didn't tell anyone he was suffering, but when the pain in his back shot all the way down through his legs, he was diagnosed and wound up in traction. When Rivera returned to practice three days later, Ryan rode him mercilessly and then told the media that the team's second-round draft pick was "slow." After Ditka and Ryan publicly squabbled over Ryan's remarks, Rivera barely got on the field that season.

In 1985 the drafting of rookie kicker Kevin Butler was also derided by Ryan. This time, Ryan was hardly alone. Just as Paul Zimmerman wrote in *Sports Illustrated* that picking Perry in the first round "was an arrogant move by the Bears," taking a kicker in the fourth round was also thought to be hubris. It turned out more like genius when Butler beat out veteran kicker Bob Thomas in training camp and then went on to make 28 of 29 field goal attempts from inside the 40-yard line, 31 of 38 overall, and all 51 of his extra-point kicks. His 144 points set an NFL record for rookies.

Eventually, Butler says, Ryan came around, especially when he saw that the pugnacious Butler could actually make a tackle when necessary on kickoffs. But the first time he met Ryan, a few days after the '85 draft, Butler says his "jaw dropped open."

"I came into Halas Hall with our special teams coach, Steve Kazor," Butler recalls. "The first person I walked into upstairs was Buddy Ryan. Steve introduced me and said, 'Hey, this is Kevin Butler, our fourth-round pick. Buddy looked at me and goes, 'Are you the kicker?' I said, 'Yes, sir.' He said, 'You were a wasted draft pick.' He turned around and walked off, and it was kind of a punch in the gut. Here's one of my coaches, he doesn't want me there, what am I doing here? But then Ditka came up behind me and tapped me on the shoulder. Ditka said, 'Don't listen to that guy ever. He doesn't know what he's talking about.' "

It was one thing for Ryan to privately call Butler a wasted pick. When he told the public the same thing about the Refrigerator, Rivera says it defied an NFL adage: "What happens here, stays here. What you see here, do here, say here, keep it inside the locker room." Adds Rivera, who is now the defensive coordinator for the San Diego Chargers, "I think that was something Mike Ditka and Buddy Ryan disagreed on."

"I think you gotta consider the source and the reason," says Ditka when asked about Ryan's public dig at Perry. "I think he was lashing out. He had his own reason for his disappointment and anger, and I can't control that. I never responded to any of that. I thought it was childish. Here we are, we're a football team, we're trying to get better, and all the sudden we're saying we wasted a draft pick on this guy? I just never paid much attention to what he was saying."

Ditka paid *some* attention, of course, but managed to rein in his temper, merely telling reporters he was "kinda surprised" by Ryan's comments, which "kinda makes me look like an idiot because I'm the guy who picked him."

But then, on August 8, Bill Tobin blasted directly back at Ryan. "If he were a scout, he would have to write his reports in pencil because he changes his mind so often," said Tobin. "If we win, it's because he's a genius. If we lose, it's because there's no talent here. Sometimes when you read the papers, you think we have co–head coaches. To my knowledge, that hasn't been true since the war. We have too many spokes-men."

The Chicago media was doing cartwheels. Two weeks into camp and already an unexpected controversy! And the circus was just beginning.

Perry was hardly the only holdout that summer. As training camp opened on July 23, several key veterans were also missing.

Strong safety Todd Bell was one of the Bears' biggest hit-ters and thus one of Ryan's favorites. Bell sat out the entire camp, and it didn't seem like he'd be coming in anytime soon. His agent, Howard Slusher, was gruff, unbending, and widely despised by the NFL owners. As training camps convened in 1985, Slusher represented 18 holdouts.

And with Slusher you never knew: he might hold out a player indefinitely if he thought a team was sticking it to his client. His nickname was "Agent Orange."

In 1984 Bell had gone to the Pro Bowl while earning $77,000 in the last year of his contract. In 1985 Slusher asked the Bears for $1.65 million for three years. The Bears coun-tered with $1.6 million for four years. Slusher said no and asked for a trade, which the Bears refused. Then McCaskey went on the offensive in the papers. "I deplore his negotiating tactics," he said. "I think he tries to grab a club by the throat and choke them. He's trying to so badly damage the team that in the end he wants to force you to agree to his terms."

Though Bell and starting outsider linebacker Al Harris

both wound up missing all of training camp, Van Horne, McMichael, Dent, and Keys eventually filtered in late. One of the last to arrive in camp was Singletary, who surprised a lot of people by holding out in the first place. When most athletes say, "It's not about the money," the fans roll their eyes. When Singletary said it in 1985, he tended to receive the benefit of the doubt.

Singletary was a wild man in college, but only on the field, where he broke 16 of his own helmets in his four seasons at Baylor. Chicago's second-round pick in the 1981 draft, he later became the ideal middle linebacker—a man with a 20-inch neck, an analytical brain, and an endless desire for self-improvement.

"Nobody studied more film than Mike Singletary," says his fellow linebacker Cliff Thrift. "Nobody worked harder than Mike, tried harder than Mike, and nobody was harder on Mike than Mike was. Mike Singletary was Buddy Ryan's godsend. I think Buddy considered Singletary an ally and basically an extension of him on the field."

Singletary's large eyes would widen just before contact, sometimes the final thing a running back remembered before Singletary knocked him senseless. But for all the rattling hits he was capable of, he was known in Chicago to be a stand-up guy and thoughtful leader. Several of his teammates say they were not surprised when he became a head coach in San Francisco.

In 1985 Singletary held out through almost the entire month of August. He wanted his contract renegotiated, which he says the front office promised if he made All-Pro or was named Defensive Player of the Year. He had signed a six-year contract before the 1984 season that would pay him an average of $276,000 a year. Six years was forever in the NFL, but

Singletary says he was willing to do it because "I wanted to be with the Bears. I knew I didn't want to go anywhere else."

In 1984 his six-year deal put him among the top-paid linebackers in the NFL. But the United States Football League changed that. The USFL began play in 1983 and finally gave pro football players some leverage—another open market—which dramatically albeit briefly pushed up salaries in the NFL. In fact, in the first two years of the USFL, the average annual increase in NFL salaries nearly doubled.

In 1984 Singletary made All-Pro *and* was voted NFC Defensive Player of the Year by UPI. By 1985 he was widely considered the best linebacker in football—even better than the Giants' Lawrence Taylor—but at least 15 other linebackers had bigger contracts. One of them was his young teammate Wilber Marshall, whom the Bears had signed in 1984 for $1.6 million over four years during a bidding war with the USFL. In 1985 Marshall was scheduled to earn $493,000 to Singletary's projected $200,000.

So Singletary asked the team to keep its word.

"They had said they would make it right if certain things happened," he says. "But when they really happened, they told me they couldn't renegotiate. I don't think they knew how serious I was. So I held out. It was that simple."

"It was an ominous way to start a new season," says guard Tom Thayer. "I remember at the first meeting when all the veterans were in camp except for the guys who were still holding out. Ditka said to us, 'Fuck it. I'm ready to go to work with the guys in this room.' But Ditka knew we needed everyone."

Thayer had just joined the Bears directly from the now-crumbling USFL. He played his last USFL game on a Saturday night in Tempe, Arizona, drove straight through to Platteville, Wisconsin, and took part in a full-blast workout with the Bears on Monday morning. Over the course of one year, between the USFL and NFL, he would play in 27 pro football games, earning the respect of even his most jaded teammates.

"But I was scared to death at first," says Thayer. "I went from playing USFL games to practicing against the best defense in the NFL at a lightning pace because of the competitiveness between Buddy Ryan and Mike Ditka."

By August 1985, the USFL was in rapid demise, thanks largely to Donald Trump, the flamboyant owner of the New Jersey Generals, who had urged his fellow owners to move to a fall schedule to compete directly against the NFL. What Trump really wanted to do was force a merger, and the USFL wound up filing an antitrust lawsuit claiming the NFL had built a monopoly. The USFL won the case, but not really. A jury in New York awarded it one stinking dollar instead of the $1.69 billion in damages it sought from the NFL. Shortly after the verdict was announced, the league's remaining eight owners said the 1986 season was on hold. The USFL never returned.

Bad news for NFL players, great news for NFL owners. In 1985, with the upstart USFL in the process of failing, the 28 NFL teams were taking a hard-nosed stand in their contract negotiations. "We're rolling back because the competition isn't there," the Bears' GM Vanisi candidly told the *Chicago Tribune.* "The same thing happened after the World Football League folded."

This was also the era before NFL free agency, one big reason, says tight end Emery Moorehead, why the '85 Bears, though located in a city with severe winters, had no indoor practice facility of their own. Except for Tampa Bay, which didn't need to worry about cold weather, the Bears were the only team in the NFC Central Division without one.

"We practiced all over the place," remembers Moorehead.

"We practiced outside on this grass field at Lake Forest College. But when it rained and froze and turned into ice, then we had to go to this neighborhood park. We would walk over there in our cleats. And then when that wouldn't work, we had to get on a bus and practice indoors at Morton East High School [in Cicero]. Then we would bus back to Lake Forest at rush hour on the Eisenhower Expressway in full uniform like a high school football team.

"But, hey, that was the way it was back then. Once there was free agency, then you *had* to have good facilities. You had to compete if you wanted to sign free agents. But there was no reason to compete before free agency. You drafted a player and you kept him his whole career until you didn't want him anymore."

So with all their contract disputes in 1985—some of which lasted *all season*—were the Chicago Bears simply like the other 28 teams, holding all the cards in their financial dealings with the players? Or were they especially stingy?

According to an NFL Players Association survey conducted in 1985, the Bears ranked 24th in the league in payroll.

None of which was lost on the Bear players.

"Let me put it this way," says Jim Covert. "We had to get on a bus when the weather was bad and go to Morton East High School to practice and then come back on the bus in rush hour. I don't think [owner] Eddie DeBartolo was doing things like that with the 49ers."

"I don't think anyone can shy away from saying the Bears were cheap," says tight end Tim Wrightman.

In 1982, after an All-American senior year at UCLA, Wrightman became the first college player to sign with the USFL, rather than sign with the Bears for what he considered to be a lame offer. He finally came to Chicago in 1985 when the USFL faltered and the Bears still owned his NFL rights.

Says Wrightman, "When I first went to the Bears, I said, 'This is the NFL?' The locker rooms and the facilities at UCLA were ten times better. The Bears were notorious for being that way, going all the way back to Mike Ditka when he played there. Ditka said George Halas threw nickels around like manhole covers. Hey, that's Bear football!"

At first, Van Horne is slightly more diplomatic, calling the Bears "notoriously frugal." Then the offensive lineman picks up steam. "Mike McCaskey had taken over from Halas by that time, and I think maybe McCaskey was trying to make a statement to the other owners. And it worked out for him because we went to the Super Bowl. So that made him look like a genius, but trust me, he's cheap. There was no free agency back then either. That's why we went on strike in '82, and that's why we went on strike in '87. That's why I like to call him Gene Fuckshaw. And I know that's disrespectful to the dead. Gene Upshaw was a great player, Hall of Famer, deserves all that, but as a union leader? Well, the current players love him because now there's free agency and they make a lot of money, and of course Upshaw made a lot of money too. But he turned his back on the players who made it happen, and of course all the guys who came before us as well. With the strikes in '82 and '87, Upshaw told us, you guys do this and we'll take care of you and the pension and all. And then he was quoted as saying, once we retired, 'Hey, I don't work for those guys.' "

Fencik has heard all the grumbling about the Bears being cheap. He grew up in Chicago and played all 12 of his NFL seasons there. But if the guys on the team were underpaid, he says, at least they were playing in a great city.

"It was such a devoted Bears town," says Fencik. "Even when we had bad teams, the fans were still loyal. And I was from Chicago, so where else would I want to go? I didn't want to do it in San Francisco. I wanted to be a Bear. I wanted to play for George Halas."

George Halas had been a Bear since the beginning of time, it seemed, but really just since the beginning of the franchise. A gifted all-around athlete, he grew up on Chicago's West Side and attended the University of Illinois, where he played basketball, baseball, and football and was named one of the most valuable players in the 1919 Rose Bowl. After Halas became a commander in the navy, he briefly played right field for the New York Yankees before injuring his hip and yielding the position to Babe Ruth. Halas later took a job in Decatur, Illinois, as a railroad worker for A. E. Staley, a self-made millionaire whose semipro football team, the Decatur Staleys, was used as a sales tool for the corn products Staley sold. Staley named Halas head coach, but Halas soon ran the entire operation. On September 17, 1920, he was one of the pioneers who attended the historic meeting in an automobile showroom in Canton, Ohio, to found the organization that soon became the National Football League. "We only had two chairs at that meeting," Halas was fond of saying. "Everybody else sat on the running boards or the fenders."

In 1921 Halas moved the Staleys to Chicago, where he renamed them the Bears in an effort to link them to the popular Cubs. Between 1921 and 1963, Halas won seven championships while serving as Bears head coach as well as owner.

Was Halas stubborn and vengeful? It was during a contract dispute after the 1966 season that Ditka told the press that Halas "throws nickels around like manhole covers."

See you later, Iron Mike.

Halas traded Ditka to the lowly Eagles, where his playing days nearly ended before they were resurrected by Tom Landry's Cowboys.

Would Halas do anything to get an edge? He would put the band behind the visitors' bench and tell them to keep playing loudly.

Would he sneak a few sips from his flask in the *middle of games?* Some of his players said they could smell the booze on his breath.

He was also a forward thinker who helped revolutionize the NFL. Halas introduced training camps, game films, daily practice sessions, assistant coaches, modern scouting techniques, and broadcasting NFL games on radio. During the 1960s, he and Pittsburgh Steelers owner Art Rooney threw all their clout behind Commissioner Pete Rozelle's radical plan for every NFL team to share television revenue equally, one of the major reasons the NFL is still the most prosperous and stable sports league.

Halas was often called the father of pro football. In Chicago he was known as "Papa Bear," or "the Old Man," not always affectionately. By 1968 Halas was 73, and for all his visionary contributions, critics said the game had now passed him by. Led by the electric halfback Gayle Sayers and the maniacal middle linebacker Dick Butkus, "the Monsters of the Midway" could still "ground and pound"—run the ball effectively and play tough defense. But even in a city that made throwing the ball difficult once winter set in, a modern NFL team needed a passing attack to be successful. The Bears' passing attack, when they employed one at all, resembled something out of the 1950s. It was time for the Old Man to give up some control.

In 1968, when Halas stopped coaching, his record including the playoffs was 326–150–31. He refused to concede that criticism played even the slightest role in his move from owner-coach to just plain owner. He attributed it to his arthritic hip, the one he had first injured while playing for the Yankees. "I knew it was time to stop coaching," he said. "I started to go after an official walking along the sideline and I couldn't keep up with him."

Ditka still gets impassioned when the conversation comes around to Halas.

"There are very few people in history like George Halas," he says. "His whole life was football. He owned it, general-managed it, coached it. He was the equipment guy when he wanted to be. He weighed in every player every season. He signed every contract. Where do you find that today in any business? George Halas was everything. There was nobody else like him in the history of the game."

Between 1968 and 1981, the Bears had two winning seasons during the 14 years after Halas stopped coaching. His successors were Jim Dooley, Abe Gibron, Jack Pardee, and Neill Armstrong, who all had losing records when Halas told them to move on.

In 1982 Halas flew Ditka into Chicago from Dallas, where he coached special teams on Landry's staff. They discussed the job opening at the Halas kitchen table, where Halas began grilling Ditka on what type of offense and defense he would run. "I don't know and you don't care. I just want to win," Ditka told him. There inside his kitchen, Halas anointed Ditka to restore the reputation of the franchise.

Halas died of pancreatic cancer in late October 1983. The team's new president (and later the chief executive officer) was his grandson Mike McCaskey, who was named to his position one month before his 40th birthday. McCaskey was very young to be running an NFL team, and some of the players thought his only qualification was his last name. His father was Ed McCaskey, the Bears' chairman of the board, who never had much power while Halas was alive. Halas had first brought Ed into the family business when Ed married Halas's daughter, Virginia.

Ed and Virginia McCaskey had 11 kids of their own. Their oldest child, Mike, went to Notre Dame High School in the Chicago suburbs, graduated from Yale, spent two years with the Peace Corps in Ethiopia, joined the faculty at the Harvard Business School, wrote a book on management, and ran his own management consulting firm with his wife, Nancy. In 1983, when Halas died, McCaskey was still running his firm in Boston when he returned to Chicago to be team president. This decision had been made by Virginia and Ed, not Halas. Although fond of his grandson Mike, Halas didn't think he cared enough about football to run the Chicago Bears.

A lot of the 1985 players agree. One after another says the same thing: Mike McCaskey wasn't a football guy.

"I think that's what he had to overcome, and he never really quite overcame it," says tight end Emery Moorehead. "He was a guy from Yale who the family put in charge of a team that had been around for 75 years."

But although his résumé screamed corporate and Ivy League—and, to his critics, elitist—Mike McCaskey *was* a football guy. At least, he had been in his formative years. He had grown up around his grandfather's Bears. He worked summers as a ball boy at training camp. He played football in high school. He lettered for two years at Yale as a wide receiver.

The players were not impressed. Players don't like owners as a rule, and clearly this was true in 1985, before free agency, when players were paid a fraction of what they are today. Furthermore, there was labor unrest as the next strike in '87 approached. All this anti-management feeling was intensified in McCaskey's case because he simply did not fit in. On a rough-and-tumble team in a blue-collar city, he was the archetypal yuppie with his pompous vocabulary, array of spiffy blue blazers, and penny loafers polished to within an inch of their lives.

Plus, McCaskey was thought to be cheap.

Halas himself had been a notorious tightwad. Why jump on his grandson for maintaining the family tradition? McCaskey didn't believe in rewriting contracts, making loan arrangements with players, or awarding them guaranteed deals. His goal was to make the organization solvent. Halas strived for that too. But the players knew that McCaskey was also pushing agendas that Halas never had. In 1985, still getting his feet wet as a member of the NFL's long-range planning committee, McCaskey urged his fellow executives to cut rosters from 53 to 45. In other words, profit margins mattered more than the players. And yet, when the '85 Bears started winning and drawing attention, the players thought McCaskey took too much credit for *their* accomplishments.

Jim McMahon says, "McCaskey had no clue."

Dave Duerson says, "He wasn't very well liked, and he did it to himself."

Mike Tomczak says, "He didn't have the athletic mind-set. He didn't realize how much we gave up our bodies or how hard we prepared."

Clift Thrift has a more sympathetic point of view. "When you play for three different NFL teams, you find out the business side is the same everywhere. They're gonna try to get you to play as great as you can for the least amount of money that you will do it for. It's not even, what have you done for me lately? It's, what can you do for me tomorrow? The one thing about the Bears, it's still the original family. It's Virginia McCaskey and her sons, but it's still the descendants of Papa Bear. It's still a business to them, but they're a lot more family-oriented than a lot of teams in the NFL. I still get a Christmas card every year from the Bears. I don't get anything from the Rams or Chargers. When I go back to Chicago, it feels more like a family reunion."

In 1983 the Bears still trained in the summer at their home base in Lake Forest, but Ditka wanted a camp with fewer distractions. In 1984 Ditka moved camp to the far western edge of southwestern Wisconsin. There, in dairy country, the players worked out twice a day under the searing sun at the University of Wisconsin–Platteville, an extension of the main campus in Madison. Platteville was a small college town, population 9,708, but a college town nevertheless, which meant there were plenty of bars for the big thirsty Bears to frequent.

"It was a brutal camp in '85," says Dan Hampton. "Ditka wasn't going to let up. We were close, he could smell it, he had his foot on the throttle. When we used to train in Lake Forest, the wives would come with the babies and the ice chests, and after practice all the guys would run over to their wives, and the babies were all screaming and blah-blah-blah. The guys never really came together. When we went to Platteville, it was three or four hours away, and at the end of the day the only people to hang out with were your teammates. And every single night at five to eleven, we would all race back to the dorm to make the curfew."

"That training camp was out of control," says Kevin Butler, who, even though a rookie, was a really crazy rookie and soon became drinking buddies with McMahon. "We all drove these little red scooters around. We would jump on our scooters right after practice and head straight up to Freddie's in Platteville and then throw down a few beers before we went back to our meetings. It was really the close of an era, when football players were still a little bit raw and when having a personality was still okay. Everything was okay, as long as we won. That was kind of our unwritten rule.

"So, yes, that team pushed the envelope the night before games. But I have *never* seen a team with that much confidence. I remember in mini-camp—in mini-camp!—we had our first team meeting, and then Singletary stood up and asked Ditka and all the coaches to leave the room. You had Singletary, Payton, Hampton, McMahon, all these great players, and they basically started calling people out. They were saying, 'If you're not in this room to win the Super Bowl, you can walk out right now. We got embarrassed out in San Francisco. We *are* going to win the Super Bowl.' "

Butler says he left that meeting, called his fiancée Kathy, and said they needed to change their wedding date. Butler says she asked if he'd met another woman. Butler assured her he hadn't, but they simply could not get married on January 25, 1986.

"I told her the Super Bowl was scheduled on the 26th," says Butler. "Kathy said, 'You just got there. You haven't even made the team.' I said, 'We're going to the Super Bowl. That's what they're saying, and I believe them.' "

A lot of the bars in Platteville were densely concentrated on Second Street. The Super Bowl was scheduled for New Orleans; thus their rallying cry became "From Second Street to Bourbon Street." Ditka didn't mind when he found out. He loved it. He *wanted* a team with the balls to be talking about the Super Bowl in July.

"We were definitely not a Vince Lombardi–type of team,"

says Fencik. "We were much looser. We had all types of personalities. And Ditka was one of them. And he didn't make any attempt to try and temper us. It's tough for a coach to do that because they want to control everything.

"But with Ditka, it would have been the pot calling the kettle black. He was one of the wild guys of his era. Back then, you heard all these stories about this hard-partying guy, but he showed up on the field every single Sunday. I heard Roger Staubach talking once about Ditka. He was talking about when Ditka punched some guy in the Cleveland game. Staubach respected Ditka because he was the real deal. Ditka could tell us, 'I've been there,' and it wasn't just bullshit. He *had* been there. So as an ex-player, he was very relaxed about anything you did with your own time."

Ditka still liked drinking a beer or glass of wine. He still lived for his cigars. He was the only NFL head coach with a mustache and still had the powerful build of a tight end. Ditka was 45, 13 years removed from his playing days, but Ron Rivera recalls him constantly jumping in and demonstrating drills to show the players how *he* wanted it done.

"I played the game," says Ditka. "I *played* the game, don't forget. I understood what players went through. Be there on time and practice hard, pay attention, all those things had to happen. But I wasn't going to stand there and be a nanny, and I wasn't going to be a policeman. I found out later, hey, they went out a lot more than I thought they went out, but so what? Did it change anything? I don't know. I don't believe in going out the night before a game. I *did* when I was a player. Was it right? I don't know if it was right. I played and caught four touchdown passes one game when I was out late. So what?"

Says McMahon, "When Ditka played, those guys went out all the time. That's the way it was back in the day. Everybody went out together and had a good time. That's what we were able to do in '85. So, to answer your question, yeah, we did go out the night before games. We always had a few the night before. Not a big deal. Had Ditka and I been teammates, he would have understood me a lot better. I think he thought I just did stuff to piss him off."

Although nobody was thrilled, no one was too pissed off when the '85 Bears went 1–3 in preseason, with three straight losses to the Cardinals, Colts, and Cowboys before a victory against the Bills. For one thing, exhibition games were mostly a way for the teams to judge personnel while holding their breath that no one important got injured. For another, poor preseason records hadn't meant much lately in the NFL. The last three Super Bowl champions (1984 49ers, 1983 Raiders, 1982 Redskins) had gone a combined 3–9 in their exhibition games. Even the Bears themselves had gone 1–3 in the 1984 preseason and then had their best season in 20 years.

The biggest issue by far as training camp ended was that Todd Bell and Al Harris were still demanding more money and management was still refusing to budge. Even Singletary had sat out the first two preseason games—one headline read "Singletary: I Might Be an Ex-Bear"—before ending his 27-day holdout. When he finally arrived, he raced out onto the field and saw Buddy Ryan, who noted that Singletary was still "small and fat."

Jeff Fisher played cornerback and punt returner that season before getting injured and moving straight into coaching as an assistant with the Eagles. Today he is the respected head coach of the Tennessee Titans, but back when he was still an '85 Bear, he says he viewed management purely from the perspective of a player.

"If some of our defensive players felt closer to Buddy

Ryan than to Mike Ditka and the front office, it was partly because Todd Bell and Al Harris weren't there," says Fisher. "Todd Bell and Al Harris, in Buddy's eyes and in our eyes, were starters and a big reason why we had gone to the [NFC] championship game the year before. And so what kind of commitment—and these are players talking now—did the front office really have? The players are saying, 'They're not gonna sign these guys. They don't want to win. *They don't want to win.*' I remember sitting around with Fencik and Buddy and the other guys, and everybody is saying, 'This is bullshit. We need these guys.' "

So in certain important respects, the 1985 Bears were a fragmented NFL team—the players vs. the front office, Ditka vs. Ryan, the offense vs. the defense—as they prepared to open at home against Tampa Bay. Furthermore, Chicago couldn't sneak up on anyone after reaching the NFC title game the last season. Thus Ditka had told his players all the way back at the start of training camp: "Put a chip on your shoulder in July and keep it there until January."

Coming from him, it was an order, not a request.

CHAPTER 3

||||||||||||||||||||||||||||||||||||||||||||||||||||||||||||||||||||||||||||||||

THE MIKE AND BUDDY SHOW

Booing is as old as professional football itself. Every player on the team had been the recipient of it, maybe even as far back as Pop Warner. But the 1985 Bears were getting booed *already* . . . at halftime . . . of their regular-season opener . . . at home? This was how they were starting their alleged run to the Super Bowl? By rolling over and playing dead for the pedestrian Tampa Bay Buccaneers?

No one could blame it on McMahon's being sidelined. With his lacerated kidney fully healed, he was making smart reads and putting the ball in tight spaces. And no one could blame it on the overall offense, which had already scored 17 points in two quarters. This time it was the heralded Chicago defense that seemed to have its collective head up its rear.

As early as the first quarter, the CBS announcers wondered aloud how much the Bears would miss Todd Bell and Al Harris. In fact, the entire defense seemed confused as Tampa Bay's receivers kept getting wide open and halfback James Wilder kept running through massive holes. By halftime, Wilder had gained 105 yards, quarterback Steve DeBerg had thrown three touchdown passes, and the NFL's top-ranked defense the last two seasons had already allowed 28 points.

Thus the Bears were booed, at home, as they went to their locker room losing 28–17.

It was Sunday, September 8, a sweltering fall afternoon at Soldier Field, where the artificial turf still registered 133 degrees at halftime. But rather than wilt in the heat, the defense came charging back after spending the intermission mostly insulting itself.

"At halftime a lot of the players were saying we stunk," Hampton said later.

"We were embarrassed," said Singletary. "What we want to do and what we want to be was not exemplified by that first half."

"We could lift our dress up like a girl or go out like a man," said Dent.

Tampa Bay didn't score a point in the second half. The biggest play of the game and arguably the whole season was made by cornerback Leslie Frazier. Two plays into the third quarter, Dent tipped a sideline pass into Frazier's hands, and he ran 29 yards for a touchdown. But Frazier made such a great break on the ball, he would have intercepted it even if Dent never touched it.

"From that point on, man, it was an avalanche. We just crushed them," says Frazier.

Outscoring Tampa Bay 21–0 in the second half, Chicago won 38–24. It was the most the Bears had scored in a season opener since 1948, when they beat the hated Packers 45–7.

Not everyone on the Bears' offense played well. Early in the second quarter, a CBS camera isolated on Gault as the graphic on the screen showed his stats from 1984—only 34 receptions, ranking him 83rd in the NFL. The announcer said Gault still "feels somewhat demeaned" and "not fully accepted as a football player," a reference to the fact that he had been a track star at Tennessee. As the ball was snapped on that very play, Gault sprinted by the defense, and McMahon threw him a perfect pass in the end zone; Gault dropped it, however, without being touched by a defender. After he dropped another pass in the third quarter—this one over the middle, where the top NFL receivers have to make plays—Ditka pulled Gault out for the rest of the game.

Still, Payton ran for 120 yards, and McMahon completed 23 passes for 274 yards and two touchdowns. McMahon's 23 completions broke his personal NFL record of 20. When he starred in college at pass-happy BYU, McMahon would often have 20 completions by halftime. But maybe times were changing in Chicago. Hadn't the offense just bailed out the defense as the Bears began their season 1–0?

Though the defense would receive most of the glory, the '85 Bears were loaded on both sides of the ball. They were also the youngest team in the NFL—average age 25.1—which promised a dominant future *if* they could hold things together. These were their starting lineups for the opener against Tampa Bay as well as their second game against New England:

OFFENSE

Wide receiver	Willie Gault
Wide receiver	Dennis McKinnon
Tight end	Emery Moorehead
Right tackle	Keith Van Horne
Right guard	Kurt Becker
Center	Jay Hilgenberg
Left guard	Mark Bortz
Left tackle	Jim Covert
Quarterback	Jim McMahon
Halfback	Walter Payton
Fullback	Matt Suhey

DEFENSE

Right end	Richard Dent
Right tackle	Dan Hampton
Left tackle	Steve McMichael
Left end	Mike Hartenstine
Right linebacker	Wilber Marshall
Middle linebacker	Mike Singletary
Left linebacker	Otis Wilson
Right cornerback	Leslie Frazier
Left cornerback	Mike Richardson
Safety	Gary Fencik
Safety	Dave Duerson

They were talented, they were young, and to a degree, the players on offense and defense were divided. This wasn't anything new for the Chicago Bears. In 1963, when the Bears won the championship with Ditka playing tight end, defensive end Ed O'Bradovich would berate his offensive teammates as they reached the sidelines after another feeble possession. In 1970, when a reporter asked middle linebacker Dick Butkus if he thought the Bears could beat the Vikings that week, Butkus said, "Yeah, the defense can beat them. I don't know if the offense can score any points." In 1982, when Ditka became head coach and made a public plea for team unity, safety Doug Plank replied, "This year I'm going to learn the names of all the guys who play on offense. This year we might even cheer each other."

"I think it was really bad up to that point because the defense had carried their ass for the past ten years," says McMahon. "When I got there in '82, I noticed a lot of it, and I said, 'We're on the same team. You guys can't do shit without us, and we can't do anything without you guys. Once we figure that out, we'll be a lot better.' "

In 1985 the primary instigator was Buddy Ryan, who believed so religiously in "us against them" that it didn't matter if them happened to wear the same uniform as us. It also didn't matter if the person in charge of the offense was Mike Ditka, who on paper was Ryan's boss.

"In Richard Dent's rookie year in 1983, it was a cold game at Soldier Field," remembers safety Jeff Fisher. "I had broken my leg and was helping Buddy on the sidelines with defensive substitutions. Mike walked up and saw Richard and said, 'Why aren't you on the field?' Richard gave him this blank stare. Buddy said, 'He's a pussy, he's cold, and he's not playing.' Mike said, 'Get in there.' Buddy said, 'No, stay.' Now Richard's kind of moving back and forth. Buddy said, 'No, he's not playing.' Mike said, 'This is my fucking football team, and I said, get his ass in here.' Buddy said, 'This is my fucking defense and he's staying right here.'

"So Singletary is out there just jumping up and down because he's waiting for the call. Buddy finally gets the call in and the guy playing for Dent, Tyrone Keys, has a sack. Buddy says, 'Here, hold this,' and he takes off his headphones and gives them to me. He walks up to Mike and pulls him on the shoulder and turns him around, and he said it again, 'This is my fucking defense.' Mike said, 'This is my fucking football team, and your ass is gone tomorrow.' Then it was over. Buddy was still around, and they were still Mike and Buddy."

Buddy Ryan was born on February 17, 1934, in Frederick, Oklahoma. He grew up poor on his family's small farm, his parents and their six children crammed into a four-room house with no indoor plumbing. Buddy's job every morning was milking the cows.

Linebacker Cliff Thrift was a fellow Oklahoman who signed with the Bears in 1985. Thrift says Ryan liked him because of their common background and because Thrift was willing to play through pain. In his eight NFL seasons, he says, he had two torn rotator cuffs, two torn biceps, three separated shoulders, seven surgeries, at least seven concussions, and thirteen broken bones. Says Bear punter Maury Buford, who hails from Texas, "Ryan admired Thrift because they were both old-school. And because they were both tough sons of bitches."

"Buddy was a product of where he came from," says Thrift. "One time I was shaving in the locker room, and I turned the water on and used my razor, and then I turned the water immediately back off. Well, some of our other guys just left the water running the whole time. Buddy came over and said, 'You grew up on a farm. Probably had well water.' I said, 'Yeah, that's right, Buddy.' He said, 'Me too. You learn early on you don't leave that water running because you might run the well dry. Then you gotta go and reprime the pump.' So it was just little things, but I could see early on that his upbringing on a farm had shaped the person he was. Buddy was like a good farmer. Not real showy and not real loud. But very confident. And dumb like a fox."

Ryan played football in high school and then fought in Korea, arriving there on Christmas Day 1951. Ryan was 17 but he was farm-boy strong and had a presence. The army promoted him from private to master sergeant, Ryan has said, "because the old guy we had there before me was getting a little scared." After playing on the Fourth Army championship football team in Japan, he came home and played guard at Oklahoma State from 1952 to 1955. He began his coaching career as head coach at Granville High School in Texas, his last head coaching position for the next 25 years. He moved up to the college game as defensive coordinator at the University of Buffalo. Ryan got married there to his fiancée, Joanie, and they ended up having three sons, one of them named Rex, who would someday become head coach of the New York Jets.

Two more college jobs followed before Buddy broke through to the pros, joining the Jets as their defensive line coach in 1968. That year Ryan won his first Super Bowl, which everyone would remember for Joe Namath's bold guarantee that the AFL's Jets would upset the NFL's Colts. But it was Ryan's defensive linemen who helped shut down Baltimore in New York's 16–7 victory.

Ryan spent seven more years as an assistant with the Jets under Weeb Ewbank, then two years under Bud Grant as a line coach for the Vikings' Purple People Eaters. Ryan had already been to a second Super Bowl—this one a defeat, with Minnesota—when George Halas hired him in 1978 to be Chicago's defensive coordinator. Ryan was 47 and this was the first pro defense that was all his.

Halas also brought in Neill Armstrong as Chicago's new head coach that season. From 1978 to 1981, the Bears went 7–9, 10–6, 7–9, and 6–10. In 1982 Armstrong lost his job with one year left on his contract. Then Halas surprised the entire NFL by replacing Armstrong with Ditka, a special teams coach with the Cowboys who had never been a head coach or a coordinator at any level.

A few weeks before Halas fired Armstrong, the players could see it coming, and frequently when the head coach gets his pink slip, so does a lot of his staff. Fencik says this was why he and Alan Page, a Hall of Fame defensive end playing out his last years in Chicago, wrote this letter to Halas on Ryan's behalf. It was dated December 8, 1981.

Dear Mr. Halas:

We the undersigned members of the Bears defensive team football team are concerned about the future of our team. We recognize that with the disappointing season the Bears have had this year there may be changes in our coaching staff and/or the administration of the team. Our main concern is over the fate of Buddy Ryan and the other defensive coaches. . . .

Buddy has maintained the discipline, morale, pride, and effort we need in order to play well defensively, in spite of the fact that we haven't had much help from our offensive team. It would be easy for us to fold our tent and play out the season, but Buddy and his staff wouldn't let that happen.

Our concern centers on the fact that if Buddy and his staff were replaced, it would set our defensive team back a minimum of two years, and possibly more, by the time we learn a new system and adjust to new coaches.

We feel that if there is to be a change in the coaching staff, Buddy Ryan and his staff should be retained in order to avoid a setback to our defense. We feel we are a good defensive team and that with their help we can be a great defensive team in the near future.

Thank you for considering our request.
Sincerely,
The Chicago Bears Defensive Team

"Alan Page and I wrote the letter, and then we covered our butts by having all the defensive players sign it," says Fencik. "By that time, George Halas never came to practice, and then all the sudden he shows up. I'm thinking, *Oh God, it's the letter.* We had already broken up offensively and defensively, and Halas told all the coaches to take a walk. He said, 'I got your letter. Your coaches will be back next year.' That was a big deal, because we thought Buddy was a great coach and we thought his job might be in danger. Then, sure enough, Neill

Armstrong got canned. And Ditka inherited Buddy and some other defensive coaches."

That moment was later described by the sensational magazine writer Gary Smith. In a 1994 *Sports Illustrated* profile of Ryan, Smith asked his readers to "consider the collision of feeling inside Buddy, the relief of knowing that the old man isn't discarding him, the pain of wondering why the old man is overlooking him and naming Ditka, a man eight honest years younger than Buddy, a man with no head coaching experience, to run the Bears."

In 1982, Ditka's first year as head coach, McMahon also joined the Bears as their number-one draft pick. Almost immediately, he says, Ditka's and Ryan's hard feelings were clear to the players.

"Buddy was upset that he didn't get the job," remembers McMahon. "Plus, Halas had hired Buddy, so he knew Ditka couldn't fire him. So Buddy pretty much did what he wanted to do."

By the 1985 season, McMahon continues, "our sidelines were a joke during the games. I bet if people really knew what was going on back then, they would have been amazed that we could win. They were fighting each other all the time. Ditka would yell at him to run a certain defense, and Buddy would say, 'Fuck you, I run the defense, get outta here.' It would happen in practice too. We would look at each other and go, 'These are our two leaders, and they bitch at each other every day.' But we had the best team, so it was hard for us *not* to win."

"Mike Ditka was a notorious hothead," says Dan Hampton. "Tearing up cards, tearing up card rooms and shit, breaking all his golf clubs—and for someone to come at him like Buddy Ryan did? In Ditka's mind, Buddy was subordinate. But in Buddy's mind, Ditka was subordinate. It was always this titanic clash of wills and egos. Now listen, I loved Ditka. He meant everything to us. He said, 'I've been there, I've done it, I'll show you how.' We couldn't have gone to the Super Bowl without him. But the real leader of our bunch was Buddy Ryan."

Frazier, who is now the defensive coordinator for the Vikings, says he has never seen another situation quite like the one he experienced in Chicago.

"Buddy never seemed to respect Ditka, although he was his boss," says Frazier. "And remember, Mike Ditka was a very prideful guy. He had a lot of success in the league as a player, and Buddy never played in the NFL. And now being a first-time head coach, to have a defensive coordinator on your staff totally disrespecting you?

"But Buddy played on all that to bond our defense. He would disparage the offense to us, just be negative about them. 'The only good guy they got is Walter Payton.' It really was like we *weren't* on the same team. That was how Buddy approached it, and our defensive guys bought into it. 'Hey, we're going to win the NFL championship in spite of our offense, which means in spite of Mike Ditka.' It was a weird way to approach it, but it was effective."

With the players already aware of the dark undercurrent flowing between their two coaches—and the fans in Chicago catching on as well, what with Ditka and Ryan sparring from time to time in the local papers—the first time the national press got a collective close look was the week before the Bears lost to the 49ers in the 1984 NFC championship. By then, Ryan's defense had just led the NFL for the second straight time and set a league record with 72 sacks. That week the *New York Times* began a profile of Ryan this way:

Almost every season, a new genius emerges. Don Shula became one in 1972, when his Miami Dolphins won every game they played, including the Super Bowl. When Bill Walsh matched up a spiffy pass offense with Joe Montana and Dwight Clark a few years ago, the San Francisco 49ers won a Super Bowl, and Walsh was a genius. He even looked the part, tall, with his white hair and professorial manner.

Buddy Ryan is the latest, although he would clearly never be mistaken for Walsh. Ryan is this slightly paunchy, bespectacled, gray-haired, fingernail-biting career assistant coach who became the Chicago Bears defensive coordinator in 1979, three years before Mike Ditka was hired as head coach.

At a news conference in Chicago later that week, Ditka told the large national media throng, "There's no sign on my door that says Genius at Work. Maybe there's one on Buddy's door."

In 1985, with all pretenses of civility abandoned, the put-downs through the media continued, and most of the time it was Ryan making the digs. "Does McMahon audible most of his touchdown plays?" Ryan was fond of asking reporters. "At least that's what they tell me." For his part, Ditka once snapped at a press conference, "I don't ask him [anything], I *tell* him."

Meanwhile, on the sidelines, Duerson says, the two coaches routinely screamed at each other during the games.

"If something went wrong on defense," recalls Duerson, "Ditka would yell at Buddy, and Buddy would yell back, 'Don't worry about it, I got it, just put some fucking points on the board.' They were always F-ing each other. That was their vernacular."

Ditka says today, with his trademark bluntness, "Ryan thought he should have been head coach. That was something *he* had to deal with. I didn't have to deal with that. I just wanted the opportunity to be the head coach of the Bears. Halas could have told me I needed to keep Genghis Khan as my defensive coordinator. I wouldn't have given a damn, that didn't matter to me. Anybody that knows me, whether you like me or don't like me, I'm fair, I'm honest, I can work with anybody. Don't bullshit me, that's all, don't lie to me, don't bullshit. I think everybody understood that pretty good. As for us having two different teams that year, that's bullshit. We were all together. But if you're saying, was there a chasm, yeah, there could have been a chasm, if people let it grow. I wouldn't let it grow. I stopped it every chance I got."

Ryan appreciated some of the players on offense, particularly Payton and McMahon. "Jim is like a defensive guy. He'll spit on you," Ryan once said. But generally speaking, says tight end Tim Wrightman, "we were kind of useless in Buddy's eyes. He would never even bother with us unless we ran the wrong formation or the wrong play when we were running a scout team. Then he'd yell at us. It's strange, but really the whole team that year was somewhat divided. You had Buddy and Mike at odds. You had Ditka kind of at odds with Mike McCaskey. As the season went on we used to joke that we were the most unhappy unbeaten team in the country. But I think it kind of worked for us. Other teams were probably saying, 'We don't want to play those guys, they even hate each other. Just think what they think about us.' "

Although it could not go on this way forever, the Ditka-Ryan tension *did* work for the 1985 Bears. As they engaged in their psychological warfare, they created an edge that raised the intensity level of their players. Practice fights were commonplace that season, mostly on Wednesdays and Thursdays, when the offense and defense went live.

"Obviously our defense had an attitude about it," says guard Kurt Becker. "So our offense developed its own attitude. I mean, there's no question the defense didn't respect us. They thought they were the nuts and bolts of the organization and if it wasn't for them we would be nothing."

Most of the fights were between the offensive and defensive linemen. Several of them involved Hampton, one of the biggest (six-foot-five, 270 pounds) of the Bears' defensive linemen—and when angered, maybe the most frightening. Unlike most NFL stars, he didn't start playing football until his junior year of high school, but then Hampton worked on his game with a frenzy that took him to the Hall of Fame. His nickname on the Bears was "Danimal," and Ryan often called him the best defensive tackle in pro football. On a team with a number of men willing to play through pain, he was known as one of the Bears with the highest tolerance for it. During the six-year stretch from 1979 to 1984, he had four knee surgeries and one on his finger, which ended up severely and permanently bent at the middle knuckle. While almost all ex-football players are disfigured, Hampton's fingers, as a group, are especially gnarly symbols of the physical price the NFL exacts.

"Here is the deal on our offense and defense," says Hampton. "It started in training camp. In training camp they couldn't block us, so they would chop-block us. You know, you could tear up a knee. So we would basically say, 'Hey, pinhead, don't be chopping us or we're really gonna start kicking the shit out of you,' tackling the backs and Walter [Payton] and everything. So it would escalate through the course of practice, day after day after day. Buddy did nothing to slow it down. Ditka did nothing to diffuse it. The defense knew we were lead dogs, the offense knew they were second fiddle, and they didn't like it. But they had guys like Payton and Covert and Hilgenberg and Van Horne, who weren't about to be subservient. So they said, Bring it on."

No one can remember the exact day, but within one or two weeks after beating Tampa Bay 38–24 in the opener there was a serious practice fight between defensive tackle Steve McMichael and offensive tackle Jim Covert. McMichael was known for trash-talking the offense, taking borderline cheap shots on the younger running backs, while easily leading the Bears in practice brawls. Covert rarely spoke during practice, and no one recalls him fighting except for this time.

"I like Steve a lot, but at the time Steve was Steve," Covert remembers. "That day I was blocking Richard Dent, and we were engaged, and then the play was over, and Steve barrels into me from the side pretty hard. I said, 'What's your problem?' He used a couple expletives, and he said, 'Your own guy pushed you into me. What the hell are you gonna do about it?'

"It was a real hot day, so I just picked him up and body-slammed him. I wrestled in high school and I was pretty good, so I got him down and gave it to him pretty good. And it was a football fight, so they let it go for a while, and he got it pretty good. Then he stood up, and I tried to get his helmet off him so I could give him a couple of good shots in the head. His chin strap was over his mouth, so you couldn't really hear him. But I think he said, 'You want this helmet so bad? You can have it.' He threw it at me, and I just punched him and dropped him. Then I hit him again."

Says offensive tackle Van Horne, "Those guys on defense liked to talk a lot. Jimbo just picked him up and basically planted him straight into the ground. McMichael didn't say much after that."

"Jimbo Covert was out of Pitt," says guard Tom Thayer. "Ditka was out of Pitt. Jimbo was Ditka's draft pick. So that's Ditka's guy. When Jimbo picked up McMichael and body-slammed him, Ditka was like a proud papa. You want to draw that line in the sand, us against them? Okay, fine, then *boom*."

"Nobody loved Steve McMichael more than I did, because he was my kind of player," says Ditka. "He gave you everything he had. But what happened at practice is, you're trying to run an offense, and you're trying to get ready to play a football game, and the defense is throwing our guys around like Ping-Pong balls; there's not much we can get out of that. We got to be able to get some timing down and work on things. Well, I guess Steve said something, and Covert was a wrestler, and I have never seen anybody on top of anybody that quick in my life. Then it ended. They were good friends. But I think what happened at that moment, the defense understood that the offense was not taking shit off anybody. And maybe it took Jim Covert to get it done. I don't know. But it got done. We practiced a lot better after that, that's all I can tell you."

On Sunday, September 15, at Soldier Field, the Bears beat the Patriots 20–7 to improve to 2–0. This time Chicago's defense, which had allowed 28 first-half points against Tampa Bay, took over from the beginning. The Bears sacked young quarterback Tony Eason six times, intercepted him three times, and harassed him all afternoon. Running back Craig James carried seven times for a measly five yards. The Patriots as a team rushed for just 27. New England, amazingly, spent only 21 seconds on Chicago's side of the field.

"We were humbled," said a bruised Eason afterward.

"They beat us physically," said Patriot guard Ron Wooten.

"Eason was getting confused," said Mike Singletary. "First a guy came from the right, then the left, then up the middle. I don't care how good you are, if you haven't been in the league that much and you haven't played against the Chicago Bears, it's pretty tough."

That was the genius of Ryan's 46 defense: it not only created pressure on quarterbacks but also disguised it. And now, 25 years later, the 46 is still revered and remembered. What most people don't realize is that Ditka didn't initially want to use it.

In 1982, when Halas retained Ryan before he hired Ditka, Ditka wanted the Bears to switch to a 3–4 "Flex" resembling the one the Cowboys had run during Ditka's nine years there as an assistant. Linebacker Brian Cabral says Ditka announced this to the entire team during one of his first meetings as Chicago's new head coach.

"Then the defensive players broke up for our own meeting," recalls Cabral. "And Buddy told us it wasn't going to happen. He said, 'No one is telling me what defense to run. I'm running my own stuff.' "

Ryan wanted to stick with the 46, the defense he had dreamed up when he arrived in Chicago in 1978. Ryan kept tweaking it, and by 1981 it was the Bears' base defense. Ryan had named it after his legendarily tough safety Doug Plank, who wore number 46 while racing around the field and smashing into people with his helmet. Thus Plank was nicknamed "the Human Missile."

"Doug was one of my mentors," says Fencik. "Once, we were playing St. Louis, and near the end of a play this wide receiver came in and cleaned my clock. Then he got in my face and went 'Boo!' I said, 'Doug, can you help me out with this guy?' Then, a while later, we got an interception, and I'm looking for this guy to lay him out. But he was already spread-eagle. I took the guy's chin strap off—he was laid out—and I went 'Boo!' I didn't *see* Doug get him. I just *knew*

Doug got him. There was no question in my mind that Doug had laid him out."

Plank led with his helmet so often, before this was outlawed by the NFL, he always gobbled aspirin before games and put smelling salts into his pants for the collisions he knew would rattle his brain. But while Plank epitomized the pure aggression that Ryan valued so highly, he also had a high defensive IQ, another trait prized by Ryan. Because, in the 46, the ideal player was smart *and* thirsted for blood.

In the 46, the Bears often gave the terrifying appearance of an eight-man front, with Otis Wilson and Wilber Marshall shoulder-to-shoulder over the tight end, Dan Hampton, Steve McMichael, and Mike Hartenstine tying up the center and two guards, Richard Dent controlling the outside away from the tight end, and Mike Singletary and Dave Duerson positioned as linebackers inside the box.

With its constantly changing tactics and alignments, it is hard to boil down the 46, but in essence, on running plays, it tried to force ball carriers to run east or west, which made them appealing targets for Singletary, Marshall, and Wilson, the most fearsome linebacking trio in the league. In passing situations, the 46 created blitzing schemes that limited double-team blocking, meaning that the Bear defenders were frequently one-on-one—a matchup, with their vast talent, that they were inclined to win. This in turn created pressure on quarterbacks, who had the depressing option of holding on to the ball and getting drilled or throwing the ball before they were ready to. Hence, the 46 also put extreme pressure on Leslie Frazier and Mike Richardson, the cornerbacks often left to cover speedy receivers one-on-one. When safety Gary Fencik wasn't rushing up to pulverize runners, he was back there to help, reading the quarterback's eyes, but he was the *only* deep help since the other safety, Duerson, was typically up near the line.

In time the West Coast offense came along, with its short-passing game that allowed quarterbacks to throw the ball quickly before the pressure arrived. Later there was "the Spread," which spaced the offensive players from sideline to sideline so the defense *couldn't* put eight players inside the box and then have them take turns mauling the quarterback. To a significant degree, it was Ryan's 46 that created these changes in pro football.

"The 46 definitely made the offenses in the NFL evolve," says Cabral. "In 1985 nobody knew what to do with the 46. It was a pressure defense, we came at you from every direction, and no one had ever seen that scheme before. And no one knew how to be effective against it."

Says Cabral's fellow linebacker Ron Rivera, "Buddy used to say, 'If the cornerbacks can just give me two and a half or three seconds of coverage, we can get to the quarterback.' The whole idea was to attack, to attack, to attack."

Really, this also summed up Ryan's worldview. Whenever the defense broke off for its own meetings, he could be brutally hard on his own players, particularly the Bear rookies. But once Ryan trusted a player—even one he still ripped from time to time—he made that player believe he would always protect him.

"Buddy had this grading system when we watched film," says Jeff Fisher. "He either said nothing about you, which meant you did your job. Or he said you were horse shit, a dumbass, or an asshole. If you were horse shit, you missed a tackle. If you were a dumbass, you made a mental error and let up a big play. If you were an asshole, you were probably going to be on the streets pretty soon.

"We went to Minnesota my first or second year, and our

starting cornerback, Reuben Henderson, said in the pregame warm-up he couldn't play. So Buddy threw me in as part of the nickel package, and I ended up on Sammy White twice in the red zone, within the five-yard line, on two different series, covering him all by myself with no help in blitz. I gave up two touchdowns.

"Buddy sent for me on the plane. He said, 'Don't worry about it, that's not your fault. It was Reuben's fault because he couldn't play, and my fault 'cause I put you in there.' The next day we sat down and watched the tape, and that was one tape I didn't want to see. But Buddy had our video guy leave those two plays out. They didn't show them. That kind of thing made players feel loyal to Buddy."

Now an NFL head coach with the Tennessee Titans, Fisher is asked to describe the defensive meetings held by the '85 Bears.

"In this day and age, I would be appalled," he says, laughing. "Buddy sat by the projector smoking his pipe. Singletary sat next to him, because Mike was making the defensive calls. Buddy sat Otis Wilson next to him too, because Otis would sometimes get confused in the scheme. Buddy didn't care what anybody else did. Guys would find their spots on the floor and pull their sweatshirts over their heads and go to sleep. And it didn't even matter, because the guys who were sleeping all knew what they were doing."

"Buddy served in Korea," says Singletary. "He was a big military guy. And the NFL didn't have limitations then as to what a coach could do. So he would break a man down of everything he had, and then allow him to build himself back up again. There is something psychologically brainwashing about that process. Underneath it all, you knew he loved you, and this was the only way he knew how to do things—the military way. So he had a bunch of guys he broke down together, and they became a family because they were all they had—and he was the bad guy."

Ryan was so committed to breaking down rookies, he even rode Singletary, who was so hard on himself he didn't need to be ridden. Taken in the second round of the 1981 draft, Singletary was not the player Ryan had wanted. Ryan thought the Bears should have used that spot instead to draft a fast cornerback. Thus the great Mike Singletary, who along with Fencik would become an extension of Ryan on the field, was brutalized in his first few months in Chicago.

Singletary was black and Asian. He was six feet tall and 228 pounds. Ryan called him short, stupid, a dog, little fat guy, fat Jap, an embarrassment to the defense, but never by his given name. Mostly, he was called by his number, 50, as in "You're nothing, Fifty, I can't believe we drafted a nothing this high." Ryan made most of these digs during practices and meetings. During games Ryan ignored him.

"I would be bugging him," says Singletary. "I'd be like, 'Let me go in, let me go in, let me go in.' And he would be telling me five or six times a game, 'Go sit down. We are trying to *win* the game.' It was very frustrating and humiliating. Then I'd draw up enough confidence to ask him again the next week, and Buddy would say the same thing."

Seven games into his rookie season, Singletary never played as the Lions dismantled the Bears, 48–17, on *Monday Night Football.* The next week Ryan told him he would get his first NFL start against the Chargers. However, Ryan warned his rookie middle linebacker: Only do what I tell you and nothing more.

"So I go in the game, and he calls the first play, and I was in on the first tackle," remembers Singletary. "I get up, and we're jumping around, and Buddy calls the next play and he calls 2-Z. I get in the huddle, and I get everybody together, and then Fencik comes in the huddle and says, '3-Z.' I said, 'No, it's 2-Z.' Gary said, 'No, it's 3-Z.' So in wanting to make sure that I did only what Buddy told me to do, I called time-out, because I didn't want to make a mistake. I'm on my way to the sideline, and Buddy is swearing at me all the way over there. He said, 'You idiot, no rookie calls time-out! You go over there and sit on the bench!' So I sat on the bench and I didn't get up. He didn't play me again the rest of the day."

Says fellow linebacker Brian Cabral, "Buddy wasn't afraid to stand up to Ditka. He wasn't afraid to stand up to management. He wasn't afraid of anyone. We were in the weight room once, and Buddy walked by this big strong defensive guy who was getting ready to lift a bunch of weight. Buddy said to our strength coach, 'It doesn't matter. The guy can't play.' "

"When it came to belittling players, Buddy was like a bull in a china shop," says Thrift. "He was just as bad as Ditka. Except Ditka did it with anger and physical outbursts, and Buddy did it with sarcasm. I wasn't sure how to take the guy at first. The other players said, 'He's just trying to get a rise out of you.' Of course, we ended up being very close."

But what about those defensive players who never made it inside Ryan's circle? What about the way he treated Dave Duerson?

"He was extremely hard on Duerson," says Leslie Frazier. "Dave had replaced Todd Bell, who was holding out. Buddy loved Todd Bell, so Dave was in his doghouse just for that reason. Not because he wasn't good enough. Dave was more than good enough as a player."

Duerson had come to Chicago from Notre Dame as the team's third-round pick in its classic 1983 draft. But it was Ditka and Tobin who wanted him, not Ryan. Even worse for Duerson, the Bears made room for him by cutting safety

Lenny Walterscheid, Fencik's veteran backup and one of Ryan's favorites.

Says Duerson, "Buddy told me when I got there, 'I had to let a good man go because of you.' That was my introduction to Buddy Ryan. Lenny wore number 23, which was my Notre Dame number, and that was the number I wanted. But I figured, shit, I just took the guy's job, I better not take his jersey. So I took 22."

In 1985 Duerson took the place of another Ryan favorite, this time stepping into the starting lineup during Bell's highly publicized contract dispute. Asked how much pressure he felt replacing an All-Pro safety, on a team that had designs on the Super Bowl, Duerson says, "The only pressure and stress I felt every day in '85 was from Buddy. He made no bones about it. Every other day he would tell me, '22, I'm just waiting for you to fuck up one time so I can bring Todd back.' "

Adds Duerson, "I never showed any emotion. And I think it was that, more than anything, which incited Buddy. I never showed that he was getting to me."

Nobody knew it yet, but Duerson would end up playing in four straight Pro Bowls. Bell would sit out the entire 1985 season, and Ryan would continue pining for him, while seeming in some strange way as if he blamed Duerson for Bell's absence. Ryan made his feelings public before the season opener against Tampa Bay when he appeared on Chet Coppock's popular radio show. Coppock wanted to know if the '85 defense would be a work in progress with Bell and Al Harris still unsigned.

"You want to know how bad Duerson is?" said Ryan. "If Todd Bell shows up tomorrow, I'm going to start him on Sunday."

Duerson soon heard what Ryan said about him. A lot of people in Chicago did. Still showing no emotion 25 years later, Duerson says, "Buddy Ryan was rooting for me to fail."

CHAPTER 4

||||||||||||||||||||||||||||||||||||||||||||||||||||||||||||||||||||||||||||

JIMMY MAC BLOWS UP IN MINNESOTA

After defeating New England 20–7, the Bears faced Minnesota on Thursday, September 19, at the Metrodome in Minneapolis. It was ABC's special edition of *Monday Night Football*—a big national TV game and a sign of the Bears' success in 1984. The last time they had been invited to play on a Thursday was in 1981 against the Cowboys, who beat the Bears 10–9 in a Thanksgiving snoozer.

This week's game featured two NFC Central rivals with 2–0 records. And while Chicago–Minnesota could never be as hateful as Chicago–Green Bay, there was still ill will between the Bears and Vikings. Minnesota coach Bud Grant wasn't enamored of Ditka, who had replaced Grant's former assistant Neill Armstrong as the Bears' head coach in 1982. It was well known around the league that while Ditka was still an assistant with the Cowboys he wrote a letter to Halas saying he would love to come home and one day become head coach of the Chicago Bears—while Armstrong still held that job, if tenuously.

"It's not what you know, it's who you know," Grant said when Halas hired Ditka, who never forgot the public insult.

The Bears' hard feelings were also rooted in envy. Minnesota was often the class of the NFC Central, and sometimes the entire NFC, with four trips to the Super Bowl to Chicago's none.

Playing on Thursday night meant a short week of preparation, especially for the Bears, who would lose part of their Wednesday for travel. Worse, Jim McMahon was now hurting. He had an infected right shin, where he had been kicked in the opener against Tampa Bay. McMahon also had muscle spasms in his upper back, which he said had started before the New England game from "sleeping wrong" in his waterbed.

In the week before the Vikings game, he spent Sunday and Monday nights in and out of traction at Lake Forest Hospital. On Tuesday he was released, equipped with an enormous collar that looked like a life preserver around his neck. McMahon didn't work out on Tuesday and barely even watched practice. Instead, he sat in the bleachers with Joe Namath, who was part of the ABC broadcasting team. Like many kids who grew up in the 1960s, McMahon had identified with the cocky quarterback who played for the Jets.

"He got to be in New York," says McMahon. "He was a bachelor. He seemed to live the lifestyle I kind of liked. He was brash, and he said what he thought, and he backed it up."

Namath came to Chicago a few days before the Minnesota game to work on a feature story about how the Bear quarterback was healthy again. But ABC killed the piece because, apparently, now McMahon wasn't.

"I assume Steve [Fuller] probably will be starting," Ditka told reporters on Tuesday night. "I think you have to practice to play. If Jim's capable of working Wednesday, we'll take a look at it. If not, we'll go with Steve and back-up with Mike [Tomczak] and don't look back."

"There is no possibility I won't play," replied McMahon.

Then he backed off a little, at least as much as McMahon was capable of. "If it was up to me, I'd play," he said. "But I read in the paper he doesn't like playing guys who don't practice. We'll have to see."

From Pop Warner to the pros, McMahon says, football coaches have been telling their players forever, "You play like you practice." McMahon says, "I never understood that, because I could never get up for practice. It's not the same. When it's Sunday afternoon or Monday night, it's a whole different ball game."

The McMahon drama played out all week in the Chicago papers. In 1984 he had missed nine regular-season games and the two games in the playoffs with a broken hand, a bruised back, and a lacerated kidney. Now it was only game three and the "Will McMahon play this week?" questions were already spreading doubt across the city.

Ditka made it semi-official after Wednesday's practice in Lake Forest, telling reporters Fuller would start and the chances for McMahon to even get in the game were "very remote." Late Wednesday afternoon, the Bears flew to Minnesota, where McMahon kept bugging Ditka anyway, telling him all he needed was the game plan.

"Jim didn't think he was going to play," says Tom Thayer. "So I think he went out that Wednesday night before the game and had a few beers and in the morning maybe didn't have all his wits about him. But it was a night game, and he came around, and he kept needling Ditka to let him play."

Tomczak, the third-string rookie quarterback from Ohio State, thought he might see some action with McMahon on the sidelines. But he says he changed his mind after speaking to McMahon at the mandatory pregame meal on Thursday.

"Jim told me, 'I'm starting to feel pretty good, man,' "

Tomczak recalls. "He said, 'I may have to take my medication and get on the field and help this team out.' I kind of had this feeling that he was going to do something spectacular. Then, even in pregame, Jim was in Ditka's ear, saying, 'Hey, if you need me, I'm here.' Ditka said, 'No, you're not cleared.' "

When the Bears went back inside for their final pregame talk, Cliff Thrift says that Ditka told the players, " 'I don't care who you are, if you don't practice, you don't play.' Well, everyone knew who he was talking about. So our backup, Steve Fuller, started the game."

With Namath, O. J. Simpson, and Frank Gifford all wearing their yellow blazers up in the booth, the telecast was only a few seconds old when ABC made its main story line crystal clear. As the Bears lined up for the opening kickoff, the camera shot switched to McMahon, standing on the sideline without his helmet.

"There is Jim McMahon," said Gifford. "They would love to have him in there tonight. But again, he had trouble in last Sunday's game, he was in traction right after the game, he has not worked out this week. Mike Ditka has told us that he will only see action if there is a catastrophe at quarterback."

McMahon remained off-camera through a dreadfully boring first quarter that ended 3–3. At first, the three announcers were as stiff and lifeless as the game they covered. Gifford provided concrete information, but he wrapped it up in clichés, and twice he called Buddy Ryan "Buddy Curry." Namath was too folksy and too careful; he seemed to have misplaced his swagger now that he was announcing instead of playing. Simpson spoke hardly at all and stated the obvious the few times he did.

The second isolated shot of McMahon came in the second quarter, prompting this exchange between Gifford and Namath:

GIFFORD: I think he really genuinely felt he·was gonna play tonight, Joe.

NAMATH: He told me that nothing would keep him from playing in this football game tonight. Well, he must have forgot about Coach Mike Ditka. Obviously, Mike has other ideas. Mike is a firm believer that the man has to practice during the week to be ready for the game. And Jim simply couldn't practice.

With the score still 3–3 early in the second quarter, Fuller threw a terrible interception, tossing it straight to one Minnesota defender who was part of a double-coverage on Gault. Instantly after this play, ABC showed McMahon a third time on the sidelines.

"I just have to believe that Jim McMahon would make a difference in this game, and I'm sure the Chicago Bears feel that way," said Namath. "They're certainly not gonna give up on Fuller, but McMahon has a way of making things happen out there, good things, positive things."

By now even the dumbest American viewer understood that ABC would pay big money to Ditka if he would just put McMahon into the goddamn game.

The Vikings scored a touchdown to go up 10–6 just before halftime. Chicago had only two Kevin Butler field goals. Fuller had already thrown two interceptions and had been penalized three times, twice for intentional grounding and once for throwing a pass after crossing the line of scrimmage. He had also completed one pass to Payton while Payton, unfortunately, stood several feet out of bounds.

Instantly after *that* boneheaded play, McMahon appeared on-camera a fourth time. Simpson, who had fallen silent for long stretches of the broadcast, evidently awakened, talking about how McMahon had led the Bears onto the field for pre-game warm-ups and then looked good throwing the ball.

"I mean, he looked sharp," said Simpson. "He looked *ready to play.*"

During the first half, Simpson also called a pass to fullback Matt Suhey "the most imaginative play that I've seen out of Chicago in the two games that I've watched them." Given that it was an utterly basic screen pass, this remark begat a mild feud between the Bears and the *Monday Night* crew that season. As Ditka later wrote in his 1986 autobiography, "I think what O. J. Simpson knows about football I threw up in a bar in Dallas in 1968."

McMahon Camera Shot Number Five came midway through the third quarter. But it wasn't just ABC that was fixating on McMahon. By then, according to linebacker Cliff Thrift, "it was like all of us started looking at Ditka, thinking, *Okay, you made your point. But what about putting Jimmy Mac in and let's win this game?*"

By this time, says McMahon, he was all but stalking Ditka on the sidelines.

"I kept telling him, 'Things aren't going right. We gotta make a move,' " McMahon remembers. "I could see the body language of our players. It wasn't the same confidence we had going into that week. It wasn't like Steve Fuller was playing poorly, it was just what was going on. Ditka was telling me, 'Get out of my face, leave me alone, you're not playing.' I'm convinced that's the only reason he put me in—to get me out of his face."

McMahon finally entered the game with the Bears behind

17–9 and 7:22 remaining in the third quarter. On his first play, the Vikings blitzed, thinking, *Let's kick this guy's ass before he gets his bearings.* But Payton, the best blocking NFL halfback who ever lived, recognized what was happening and ran up and knocked the first blitzer off to the side. McMahon stumbled while pulling away from center, but he regained his balance and spotted something much better than the screen pass to Suhey that Ditka had called. McMahon got crunched as he threw a bomb to Gault for a 70-yard touchdown.

Namath yelled, *"I love it!"*

"That play tells you a lot about McMahon," says Jim Covert. "Gault was running deep to spread the defense and open up the screen pass. But when Gault ran right by the cornerback, McMahon threw him the ball. A lot of quarterbacks would never have done that. They would have thrown the screen pass. That's just how capable a quarterback Jim was. And that's why we performed at such a high level when he was in there."

"It was a screen pass, and they blitzed," explains McMahon. "Well, when you got a blitz, you know it's man-to-man coverage, which is not usually good for the screen because the linebacker can usually dodge the lineman who is out there and he can get to the running back one-on-one. Luckily, Walter picked up his man on the blitz. I looked downfield, knew it was blitz, so knew it was man-to-man. And as I looked down there, Willie was behind his man by ten yards. So I just let it go.

"After the play I came to the sideline, and Ditka was screaming at me about what play did I call. I said I called a screen, and he said, 'Why did you throw it to Willie?' I said, 'Well, because he was open.' I mean, what the hell? We just scored."

Now it was 17–16, Minnesota, and anyone watching the game sensed something was brewing. The next time the Bears got the ball, again on the very first play, McMahon rolled to his left, took a few more steps back away from the pressure, and threw a 25-yard strike over the middle to Dennis McKinnon in the end zone. McMahon was two-for-two for 95 yards and two touchdowns. Even Ditka seemed stunned, turning his back on the sidelines as if he hadn't seen what he just saw. McMahon ran back to the bench yelling, *"Screw them all!"* Gifford called him "colorful, fun, and rather skillful."

After the Bears got the ball back on a punt, McMahon completed two of his next four passes, and then, with 33 seconds left in the third quarter, he dropped straight back in the pocket, scrambled to his left, and lofted a 43-yard touchdown pass to McKinnon. In the span of 6:40, McMahon was five-of-seven with three touchdowns and the Bears had gone from trailing 17–9 to leading 30–17.

Namath screamed, *"He makes things happen!!!"*

The only guy who looked as upset as the Minnesota fans was poor Steve Fuller. Unable to resist, ABC focused on Fuller, without his helmet on, right after McMahon's third touchdown pass. Forget all that propaganda you've heard all your life about team spirit. The camera rarely lies, and Fuller looked pissed.

When it ended, Chicago had won 33–24, McMahon was an overnight rock star, and the country had a gut feeling that the 1985 Bears might be very, very interesting.

"My world changed after that Thursday night game," says Ken Valdiserri, the Bears' public relations director. "That catapulted the team into the limelight. The national reporters started seeing not just the performance, but the characters behind it and some of the side antics that were happening. Everyone could tell that something was going on."

"It was a wild night," says Valdiserri's assistant, Brian Harlan. "And that Minnesota game in some way epitomizes a lot of what McMahon was. You never knew if he was going to be able to play because he was hurt a lot. His head coach doesn't want to start him. Then he gets the coach to let him into the game. And then he saves the team."

The only dark note of the night was a serious injury to Kurt Becker, the hard-nosed starting left guard, who damaged his right knee without even being touched by another player. Becker was devastated but not entirely surprised. This was not the first time something like this had occurred at the Metrodome, universally despised by NFL players for its dangerous artificial turf.

"Their middle linebacker blitzed, and I came out of my stance," says Becker. "I went to push off to engage him, and to cut him, as he was blitzing through the hole. My right foot stuck in the turf, and I felt a sharp pain in my knee.

"Minnesota probably had the worst turf in the league. But there were a lot of bad ones. The first product of turf was terrible. It was laid on a hard surface, which was usually asphalt or concrete. It was just a synthetic, tightly woven fiber, which would wear out. And as the turf got used, there were seams that came up, and guys got caught. The other thing is, when turf first came out, they didn't have the shoes to match the product. So guys were experimenting with everything you can imagine. Obviously, through that experimentation, guys were getting hurt.

"You know how it got into the NFL? The people who made the turf sold it to the owners and TV. Late in the season, most teams in the Midwest and the Northeast had no grass left. In Minnesota, come November, the field was all dirt. They would spray-paint it green for the games, and then they'd paint white lines on top of that. So TV wanted a better-looking game, and the NFL owners said okay."

Becker had knee surgery after the Vikings game, went on injured reserve, and started his grueling rehab. He would not even practice again until week eleven. And yet, in 1985, there were no signs that the league was addressing its obvious problem. To the contrary, 17 of the NFL's 28 teams still had artificial turf on their home fields. All these original turfs were hazardous to the players; the only difference was in the degree.

It's hard to imagine today, with the mega-success enjoyed by the NFL, but before the '85 Bears barged onto the scene, the league was still stuck in the doldrums. A three-year decline had begun in 1982 when the ugly player strike cut the season to nine games and alienated millions of fans. In 1983 the league still felt the hangover from the strike as the fans, media, owners, general managers, coaches, and players kept bringing it up.

In 1983 and 1984 the bidding wars with the USFL created a talent drain as Jim Kelly, Reggie White, Steve Young, Herschel Walker, Sam Mills, Joe Cribbs, Mike Rozier, Anthony Carter, Bobby Hebert, and other good players were all in the upstart league.

By the end of the 1984 season, all three networks (CBS, ABC, and NBC) showed an alarming drop in their NFL ratings, the print media pondered how the league could escape its malaise, and there was a sense of gloom at NFL headquarters on Park Avenue.

In 1985 the NFL began its recovery. By season's end, TV ratings were rising, people were talking about pro football again, and the dour old NFL suddenly seemed refreshing. The primary reason was the roguish and rollicking Chicago Bears.

"I think if anybody remembers one thing about that football team," says Ditka, "they will remember this: they played hard, they had fun doing it. Now, sometimes you look at teams today, they might play hard, but it doesn't look like it's much fun anymore. I'm just saying, that's the way we played—we had fun doing what we were doing. And we did it pretty well. As a result, I think the league benefited from it. But they benefited from the 49ers too and Bill Walsh, and they benefited from the Miami Dolphins and Don Shula, and the Cowboys and Tom Landry, and Lombardi and the Packers, and Halas and the Bears. But at that time, yeah, we probably were a jolt of energy for the league. We had a cast of characters who got after you."

Their legend began to blow up on that Thursday night in Minnesota. The star of that live, prime-time show was the player the other Bears called Jimmy Mac. Beginning with his electric, implausible performance on national TV against the Vikings, McMahon became a pop culture hero that season. Even people who didn't like pro football became intrigued with "the punk-rock quarterback who sneered at authority." And according to his head coach, that anti-authority thing was very real.

"I never saw too many people play the quarterback position the way Jim McMahon did," says Ditka. "He had no regard for his body. He played it hard. Yet I think he had a problem with authority. I think he had a problem with his father, with his coach at BYU, with me. He didn't want to be a conformist. He wanted to be the guy that was a little bit defiant all the time. And I guess that could be good or that could be bad. That's who he was. You're asking me who he was. Are you asking me would I rather have someone else on my football team? No, not at that position."

What about McMahon? Does he think he had a problem with authority figures?

"I don't think I had trouble with them," says McMahon. "I questioned them sometimes. I don't think there's any problem with questioning authority. Especially when you think the authority doesn't know what the hell he is talking about. Why are they the authority anyway? Just because they're older?"

What about his other famous label? Was Jim McMahon a punk rocker or wasn't he? With the blue mirrored wraparound sunglasses he always wore and that sketchy semi-Mohawk, which evolved into that gelled-up, spiked-up crew cut, people said he *must* be a punk rocker. In fact, if you have Nexis, type in "Jim McMahon" and "punk rock" and you'll get 47 hits. All of which makes Steve Zucker, his close friend and longtime agent, chuckle.

"That all started in Platteville in '85," says Zucker. "They were in training camp, and they had nothing to do, and Jim decided to give himself a haircut with one of those electric shears. Gault finished the job, and he cut his hair in some kind of Mohawk. It was all an accident. None of it was true. Punk rocker? The punky QB? He hated that."

"That was one of the writers' terms," says McMahon. "I didn't make that up. I gave myself a shitty haircut, and all the sudden I was a punk rocker. It was like the first day of camp, and I was already bored. I just wanted to trim it a little bit. The first swipe I took at it was down to the skin. So I had to try and even it out, and it just kept getting worse, so I finally went up to Willie and said, 'Can you do anything with this?' There wasn't much he could do. It was kind of a Mohawk with long hair in the back. And it was not pretty. My daughter didn't recognize me. My wife had been cutting my hair for ten years already, and she said, 'What the hell?' But it was my head. I could deal with it. I didn't care. It wasn't gonna affect my *playing*. And that's when the punk rocker and all that shit came out. I was the so-called rebel who didn't care. And I really didn't. I just cared about winning games and staying out of jail. Which I did pretty good."

Jim McMahon was born on August 21, 1959, in Jersey City, New Jersey, but he spent most of his childhood out west. At age three, he moved with his family to Fresno, California, and then to San Jose. He had such a hard time sitting still, he was later diagnosed as hyperactive. At age six, he severed his retina when he tried to untie something with a fork and accidentally plunged it into his right eye. The vision in his eye improved gradually over the years, but it remained sensitive to light—the real reason, he says, he wore sunglasses whenever possible, even inside.

McMahon was smart and perceptive and didn't feel challenged by what they were teaching at school. From the beginning, he could be cruel to his classmates, like the pudgy Hawaiian kid in kindergarten into whose ass McMahon kept sticking thumbtacks. Later, he says, he threw rocks at a girl on crutches and slapped one of his teachers in the face, but only after the teacher slapped him first.

"I was small for my age, but I was always fighting," says McMahon. "I was always in trouble in school, when I went to school. I had a few run-ins with the cops, nothing major. Nowadays they would call me ADD. They'd give me medicine. I was just being a hyper kid. That's what kids are supposed to be. Plus, I was bored. I didn't like sitting in the classroom. The work wasn't that hard. I would do the work, and that's when I'd get in trouble. I'm finished with my work, what else can I do?"

His father, Jim, was Catholic, and his mother, Roberta,

was Mormon. Both his parents were stern and not always sure what to do with their difficult son. When he had confrontations with his teachers, his father would find out and give him a whipping. McMahon has been publicly critical of both his parents at times, but today he sounds sincere when he says, "I have thanked them many times since for how they brought me up. They were strict. I got my share of whippings. But, yeah, we got along. When I was in trouble, I deserved to be in trouble."

His neighborhood in San Jose was tough, racially mixed, and loaded with talented athletes. When McMahon was in junior high, he got thrown off his baseball team for smoking the cigarettes he had stolen from his father. The next year, in Little League, he attended a picnic held before a game against the parents, got into the cheap champagne, and ended up out in left field puking his guts out. By then he was 13.

He began playing organized football when he was ten. Although McMahon was still scrawny, his coaches saw him throw and made him a quarterback. He started at Andrew Hill High School as a sophomore, but before his junior year his family moved from San Jose to Roy, Utah, because his father got transferred. Roy High School already had two senior quarterbacks when McMahon arrived that summer, but he beat out both seniors, and his team went 11–1 before losing in the state semifinals. Roy went 8–2 and lost in the state quarterfinals his senior year.

Like so many Catholic high school football players, McMahon had once dreamed of playing at Notre Dame. He later narrowed it down to UNLV and BYU, the only schools that said he could play football and baseball. McMahon preferred UNLV, but his father pushed BYU because of its reputation for throwing the ball. The campus was also in Provo, just 80 miles down the road from Roy.

At BYU, on the field, he did almost everything right. In 1980, his junior year, McMahon threw 47 touchdown passes, an NCAA record. That season he also threw for an NCAA-record 4,571 yards. By his final college game, McMahon was the best quarterback in BYU history and arguably the best in the history of college football. He had 84 touchdown passes, 9,563 passing yards, and a staggering 71 collegiate passing and total offense records.

McMahon had a strong arm. You can't put up huge numbers like he did in college without one. But it wasn't his arm that blew people away. McMahon could see on a football field the way Larry Bird could see on a basketball court or Wayne Gretzky could see on a hockey rink or Muhammad Ali could see inside a ring. All that furious activity didn't faze him. McMahon could crouch behind center, recognize the defense, audible out of the play the coaches sent in, discover his main receiver wasn't open, keep his cool, keep looking downfield, and find his second, third, and even fourth receiver. Any quarterback can learn to run a play. McMahon knew how to play.

Off the field, well, he was Jim McMahon at BYU. Like all students, he signed a pledge promising to abide by the codes of the Mormon religion, including no smoking or drinking or premarital sex. The summer after his freshman year, he says, he got caught drinking beer on a golf course, and the school put him on "double secret probation," a line he aptly took from *Animal House*. This meant McMahon would need to be more careful while continuing to drink beer, chew tobacco, and have sex with his future wife, Nancy. On the other hand, as long as he kept throwing touchdown passes and winning games, he could be pretty sure that the BYU officials would grit their teeth and look the other way.

"There was a lot of hypocrisy there," says McMahon. "That's what turned me off about the whole thing. Even though my wife was Mormon, she grew up in northern California, not far from where I did, and she wasn't anything like what was going on there. She was getting treated poorly for going out with me. She said, 'This isn't how the religion is supposed to be.' "

In a self-righteous act of epic proportions, BYU finally kicked him out of school. But it waited until after the 1981 Holiday Bowl, which marked the end of his eligibility.

"I was conveniently asked to leave after my last game," says McMahon. "I was supposedly doing all these bad things. I said, 'Well, I've been here five years. You guys pretty much know where I am at all times. You stake out my house, you stake out her house. You guys know exactly what I've been doing. You're just barely finding out now I've done certain things?'

"Supposedly they had a list of people who had turned me in for something. Of course, they couldn't give me any names. I said, 'You know why? Because those people are all full of shit. I'll bet none of those people even know me. I never spend a weekend in this town. Yeah, I was at some parties, but they were at Weber State. Not around here.' My brother was at Weber State. As soon as a game was over at BYU, my *ass* was at Weber State. BYU wasn't a normal college. It wasn't normal college life. You're supposed to be able to get out and have some fun."

In Chicago, a city known for lacking quarterback talent, McMahon says he felt welcome from the beginning. The city's last Pro Bowl quarterback was Bill Wade, who played alongside Ditka on the 1963 championship team. Since then, the offense had been led by forgettable starting QBs named Rudy Bukich, Jack Concannon, Bobby Douglass, Gary Huff, Bob Avellini, Mike Phipps, and Vince Evans. As Chicago native Mike Downey wrote in the *Los Angeles Times,* quarterbacks in Chicago were "reviled, not revered. A quarterback might be complimented in Chicago, but never on Sunday. I know. I was raised there. Quarterbacks were held in approximately the same esteem as burglars and aldermen."

Wrote the classic Chicago columnist Mike Royko, "Part of the rich Chicago heritage is the right to invite a Bear quarterback to leap in front of a speeding 'L' train."

Maybe the single most ill-suited Chicago QB was the aforementioned Bobby Douglass, a big athletic farm boy who everyone knew should have been a tight end or halfback. But he insisted on remaining a quarterback, and since the Bears had nobody else, they acquiesced. In 1972 Douglass rushed for 968 yards, more than any other quarterback in NFL history. It was a shame he couldn't pass. Over his ten-year career, he threw for 36 touchdowns and 64 interceptions, with a passer rating of 48.5! This was mostly because Bobby Douglass threw 100 miles per hour, even when his receiver stood five yards away.

In 1981, while McMahon was finishing third in the Heisman Trophy balloting as a senior, the Bears went 6–10 with Vince Evans and Bob Avellini both impersonating professional passers. Thus, in 1982, when the Bears selected McMahon with the number-five pick in the first round, countless Chicagoans had the exact same reaction: *Thank you, God! Thank you, Ditka! We may have a real quarterback this decade!*

So no one in the city really cared when McMahon flew there from Utah after the NFL draft, got a ride from O'Hare to Halas Hall, and walked inside his new workplace wearing sunglasses and drinking a beer. That July at training camp, which most NFL teams begin with a long run to find out who is in shape, McMahon was *out* of shape because (a) he was McMahon, and (b) this being the Bears, there had been the obligatory contract dispute. McMahon says he didn't expect to *be* in camp, but when he signed his contract at the last minute, he had to run the one and a half miles like everyone else. McMahon "ran" it in 12 minutes and 37 seconds. His time was the second-slowest on the team, slightly ahead of offensive lineman Noah Jackson, who was aptly nicknamed "Buddha."

In McMahon's rookie year, Ditka started Avellini as the Bears lost their first two games. Then the NFL players' strike wiped out the next seven weeks. When the players returned, Ditka started McMahon the rest of the way. He was sacked 27 times and went 3–4 as a starter, but his 80.1 passing rating was the best in NFL history for a rookie.

In 1983 Ditka started McMahon, then went to Evans for three games, then back to McMahon. Once McMahon became the permanent starter, Chicago won five out of seven and finished at 8–8. In 1984 the job was his, and the Bears went 7–2 in the games he started. They ended up 10–6 when he was lost for the rest of the season after lacerating his kidney against the Raiders.

From the very beginning of his eight years in Chicago, McMahon impressed his teammates by showing he had the balls to stand up to Ditka. He also gained their respect by absorbing Ditka's wrath if it meant another player could escape it.

"We were notorious for running sweeps on third-down-and-long," says McMahon. "We always ran it to Walter, one side or the other, and everyone in the league knew it. So one week we put in this off-tackle play to the weak side if the defense was overloaded on third-and-long. So the situation came up. Less than two minutes in the first half, and it's third-and-long. A play comes in from the sideline, I call it, but they're overloaded, so I change to the play I'm supposed to. But Suhey doesn't get the audible, I guess, and Payton gets smacked for a loss. Ditka immediately called a time-out. I walked over to the bench knowing I did the right thing. Mike was irate, jumping all over somebody, and then he got right in my face, and he started cussing me out. I just said, 'Hey, fuck you.'

"Then I turned around and walked away. Suhey happened to be standing right behind me. He goes, 'Hey, thanks.'

"I said, 'For what?'

"He said, 'I missed the audible.'

"I said, 'Why didn't you tell him that?'

"Suhey said, 'Because he was yelling at you!' "

"That kind of stuff never bothered me," adds McMahon. "I'd tell the other players, 'Tell him it was my fault. Don't worry about it.' "

"Jimmy Mac spoke his mind," says linebacker Ron Rivera. "That was part of the appeal for some of us with him. Jimmy said things that some of us wish we could, but we couldn't say because we weren't that powerful a player. So McMahon challenged Ditka a lot simply because he felt the average guy on the team couldn't. He challenged Ditka openly at times, everything from, we don't need to run these fucking sprints, we need to get a break and take a day off. He did it out loud, he did it at meetings, and on the practice field. He stood up for us."

When told what Rivera said about him, McMahon says, laughing, "I told Mike to go fuck himself many a time. So, yeah, I'm sure a lot of guys wanted to say that."

Says tight end Tim Wrightman, "I don't think anyone *but* McMahon could have been as successful with Ditka as he was. Jim would throw an interception, and Mike would say, 'What the hell is wrong with you, you're not a fucking rookie, can't you read a damn defense?' Jim would walk right by him and flip him off. The problem was that when the other guys played, Steve Fuller and especially Mike Tomczak, they actually took to heart what Ditka said. Jim just did what he wanted to do. He had an ego to match Mike, and it worked out great."

"There were a lot of times," says McMahon's agent, Steve Zucker, "when they wouldn't talk to each other. Probably the whole '85 season, they didn't talk much. I think they loved each other, almost like father and son, but you'd think they hated each other. Ditka would say to me, Tell McMahon this. McMahon would say, Tell Ditka this. I'd be running back and forth like crazy. But, you know, they were alike. They were a lot alike. Both stubborn, both characters. But you needed them both. Ditka may not have been the greatest game coach of all time, but he was the greatest motivator of men I've ever seen."

When it came to changing Ditka's plays, something McMahon did routinely, tackle Keith Van Horne says McMahon didn't really have much of a choice.

"We were running the same offense they ran in Dallas!" he says. "I mean literally, the same terminology and everything. So it wasn't any groundbreaking offense. The other teams knew exactly what we were doing. Third downs? When we had the single back in the backfield? Here comes the trap. I was watching *ESPN Classic* once, and they had a camera in the huddle of the Cowboys when Staubach was quarterback. They're calling the same exact plays we were running 12 or 15 years later! Our offense wasn't Bill Walsh. That's what makes four years in a row leading the league in rushing even more impressive in my mind. We weren't tricking anyone. They would be calling it out—'Here comes the trap, here comes the trap.' So Ditka wasn't necessarily a great strategist. He was a motivator. That's why having McMahon was so important. He could read the defense, call an audible, and take what the defense gave us. That took our offense to another level."

Sometimes McMahon changed the play while the Bears were still in the huddle. Sometimes in the huddle he told his teammates "on the ball," and then he changed the play at the line of scrimmage. McMahon says he can't even guess what percentage of Ditka's plays he changed, but it was never an arbitrary decision.

"Had Mike ever been in my huddle," says McMahon, "he would have realized, yeah, this guy does know what the hell he's doing. I think he thought I just did stuff to piss him off. But we had eight guys stacked in the box against us every week, and we still ran the ball. We ran it better than anyone for four years. But I was always taught, why beat your head into a fence when you don't have to? I was taught I could change any play, at any time, in college. So we butted heads all the time, even when it worked. He'd still jump in my face—'What the hell you doing?' I would tell him, 'Well, we just scored again. That's my job, to get us into the end zone.' "

One time McMahon told reporters he didn't watch much game film, a remark guaranteed to outrage the football establishment. And yet, Jim Covert calls McMahon "the smartest football player" he ever played with. Jeff Fisher recalls a game against the Redskins, whose strong safety Tony Peters was known as a dangerous blitzer. But based on his tendencies, Peters would blitz only if lined up eight yards or closer from the line of scrimmage.

"So that was Jim's visual cue, his indicator," says Fisher. "Well, Jim gets in the game and calls the blitz audible, and Peters blitzes, and Jim throws to Emery Moorehead for a touchdown in the red zone. They watched the tape the next day and one of the coaches said, 'Jim, Peters was at 12 yards. We told you that eight yards or closer was the indicator that he was gonna come. Why did you audible?' Jim said, 'He didn't

look at me. He was looking down. I knew he was coming.'
That was the kind of quarterback Jim was at the time. But you
didn't see that based on his personality, and it wasn't because
of film study. It was instinctive."

Asked to describe what McMahon brought to the table as
an NFL quarterback, the man he battled with for eight years
needs no time to think.

"Jim was a tremendous competitor," says Ditka. "He had
a great understanding of the game. He had a great ability
to read a defense. He knew where the pressure would come
from, who would be blitzing. He was pretty good at audibling.
He audibled sometimes when he shouldn't. We lost a football
game up in Minnesota because he audibled. He threw an interception that got run back for a touchdown. I went ballistic.
I told him, 'There's a time and place for everything. If you're
in a bad situation, you don't make a worse situation by calling
a play you don't know if it's the right play.' That was the mad-
dest I ever got at him."

Along with Calvin Thomas and Walter Payton, McMahon
was one of the Bears' leading comedians. Thomas did spot-on
imitations of Ditka. Payton's specialty was well-placed fire-
crackers that scared the shit out of people, but before anyone
got mad, they realized it was Walter. McMahon liked to wear
ridiculous stuff to practice. He wore ancient leather helmets,
old-fashioned black high-top gym shoes, sunglasses with eye-
balls painted on the outside.

"Hey, look," says McMahon, "we were a better team when
we had fun. And that stuff had nothing to do with how you
play. It's not gonna affect *my* play. Just because I'm wearing
goofy glasses or a helmet with no face mask? It doesn't mean
I don't know what the hell I'm doing."

Says cornerback Leslie Frazier, "He broke the monotony
of the NFL season. You know how you're in the whirlpool

after a game or a practice, and you have an injury, and you're not going to get in there in the nude, so you got your shorts on? Well, Jim would jump in there with you, in the nude, and do a lot of crazy stuff and make you get out! He was just a crazy guy, man. A fun guy, but just did some crazy stuff."

During McMahon's rookie year, before Chicago's first road trip, he says Ditka told the players they could get by without sport coats but had to wear a shirt with a collar.

"I didn't own many dress shirts, if any," remembers McMahon. "But I did own a priest's collar, so I wore that. I had a jacket over it, but nothing underneath it. It was just like a vest kind of thing with no back to it? So when I took my jacket off and stood up, I was backless. The next meeting, Ditka told us to make sure we wore shirts with collars *and* backs and no religious items or some shit like that."

McMahon was extremely close with his offensive linemen, whom he famously head-butted after the Bears scored a touchdown. It started with him and Becker, his buddy and longtime roommate on the road. Then McMahon began butting helmets with any offensive lineman in the vicinity after a score. The Chicago fans ate it up, but the coaches became concerned—the offensive linemen were large and they didn't want McMahon hurting his neck—but rather than talk to McMahon, who they knew would say "go away," they went to the offensive linemen and asked them to stop. The linemen said no.

"McMahon thought he *was* an offensive lineman," says Becker. "He thought he was tough for some reason. That was his alter ego. But somewhere along the line in his college days, Jim had also learned the value of a good offensive line. He knew his success was greatly dependent on the five guys in front of him."

McMahon and his offensive linemen went out to dinner

every Thursday, different guys paying the bill, at different restaurants around the city. Becker says that at first it had only been the offensive linemen. Then the next thing they knew, says Becker, "McMahon wants to get in. He needs an excuse to go out. And of course, if he picks up the bill, no problem. But then it got away from what it was supposed to be. Too many guys started coming, guys who had nothing to do with the offensive line, friends of friends. The offensive linemen stopped going. But the original concept was great."

In 1985, as the Bears kept winning and his legend grew, McMahon was being compared to Bobby Layne, Don Meredith, Kenny Stabler, quarterbacks who read the playbook, if they read it at all, by the hypothetical light of the jukebox, quarterbacks who went out and drank as hard as they competed.

"Jimmy Mac was a throwback," says Rivera. "He was a rough-and-tumble guy. And sometimes he may have had one or two too many. For three or four years in a row, he never made it to the last practice before we broke training camp from Platteville back to Chicago. So the last time, the offensive line decided that Jimmy Mac was gonna be there. And everyone knew we were breaking camp the next day, so everybody went out and had a few cocktails, stayed up way later than we were supposed to. And the next day I would say 35, 45 percent of the team was hung over, and probably some of the coaches.

"So the offensive line decided Mac was going to make this practice no matter what. A group of them got an ice bucket, they drove back to the dorm, and McMahon never locked his door, it was always open, so the linemen snuck in and doused him with ice water, wrapped him up in his sheet, and threw him in the back of one of the equipment carts and drove him to practice to make sure he was there."

McMahon didn't advertise it, but he had another side rarely viewed by the public, though familiar to his teammates. As Dave Anderson once wrote in the *New York Times*, "This 26-year-old quarterback seems to live two lives: one as a quiet suburban Chicago husband and father of two small children, and another as the Bears' loud leader. In their own way, his offensive linemen seem to love him as much as his wife, Nancy, does."

His closest friends on the team say the same thing—McMahon was in love with his wife and good to his kids. But when he was out with the boys, and not his family, was there a tangible price for his activities? The question was sometimes raised around the NFL, and especially in Chicago as his career was hindered by injuries. The reality of it is that nobody would have cared if he was the type of player the Bears historically had at quarterback. But in one remarkable stretch from late 1984 through 1988, the Bears went 35–3 in regular-season games with him as their starter. In another span between 1984 and 1987, Chicago won 21 straight regular-season games that McMahon started. He also missed 29 possible starts in that time. Throughout his career, he played in more than 9 games just 5 out of 15 seasons.

McMahon, his head coach, and a number of his teammates were asked why he wasn't on the field more often. They were candid in their assessments.

Jeff Fisher: "Jim was a very good athlete. Jim could make all the throws. Jim *didn't* work an awful lot on taking care of himself, getting a good night's sleep, laying off the beers the night before a game."

Emery Moorehead: "Early in his career, he probably didn't take good care of himself. He was in better shape after getting injured a lot and finally realizing there's a reason to hit the weight room and protect your body and your joints. But the guy also weighed 190 pounds, and he was getting tackled by much bigger guys, and the object of the whole game is to get to the quarterback and knock him out of the game. At 190 pounds, it didn't take a lot, especially if he wasn't lifting and protecting his shoulders and elbows and knees and all the joints and building up around them. He didn't realize that until his sixth, seventh, eighth year in the league."

Leslie Frazier: "I loved playing with him, because he was such a tough-minded guy and such a winner. The downside, he was hurt so much. We never could solidify that quarterback position. His lifestyle seemed contradictory to a guy who was going to have a long career. He was going to have fun. He was going to hang out at night. I think he could have played in a lot more games if he had taken better care of himself in the off-season. It weighed on the team, and where it showed up the most was in the playoffs. You can have a good football team and a great defense, and that will carry you through the regular season. But when you get to the playoffs, that quarterback position becomes paramount to your success, because the games are so close and sometimes you're in elements that are so different than what you experienced in October or November. To not have your main guy in those situations, well, your defense can only carry you so far."

Dan Hampton: "Jim was a good guy. But at some point Jim thought maybe he didn't have to work as hard as the rest of us to stay in shape to be able to play—*for each other.* Jim seemed to shirk the usual training that should have been obvious. He was hurt every year. By '87, I was sick of the fact that we couldn't count on him. If you got a good player, you drafted him in the first round, you expected him to play. And, yeah, bad luck is bad luck. But the other part of it is, if a guy gets hurt all the time, you start to wonder. So everybody got real frustrated with the whole thing. By '87, I wasn't hiding my displeasure, and I called him out in a meeting. It started a rift on the team, but it was what it was. I'm playing, getting my knees drained twice a week, 100 ccs twice a week, McMichael is getting his shit drained, [offensive tackle Mark] Bortz can't straighten his arm out, he can't sleep because he's got so many pinched nerves. We're all hurt. But McMahon was like, well, I don't want to play because I don't want to damage my chance at having a 15-year career. That's his prerogative, but it didn't work for us."

Mike Ditka: "I think what they're saying is true. That's probably something Jim would agree with. He could have taken better care of himself. He could have been there more."

Tim Wrightman: "I think Jim got a bad rap from the media on that whole thing, but then again, I don't think he cared about the media. I think Jim was the ultimate Peter Pan. He was just a big kid with a lot of enthusiasm, and it transferred over into his play. Guys loved playing for him, and they knew he would sacrifice his body. A player like that will get hurt in the NFL."

Jim Covert: "Part of it with Jim was just bad luck. I mean, a guy hits him in '84 and lacerates his kidney. We could have won the Super Bowl in '84. We were a good team, and with Jim in there, we could have won it. In 1987 Charles Martin [defensive end for the Packers] picks up Jim after the play and slams him onto his shoulder. He was never the same after that from a physical perspective. I am a big Jim McMahon fan, and I have a tremendous amount of respect for him as a player. He's the reason why we were so successful. I just wish he would've stayed healthy, and I think everybody does. It would have been a different Bears team."

Dave Duerson: "Jimmy Mac was a linebacker playing the quarterback position. He would win at all costs. If we needed a yard to get a first down, Mac was going to get that yard. He wouldn't run out of bounds, he wouldn't slide. He laid it on the line, and that's why all his teammates believed in him."

Jim McMahon: "My going out had nothing to do with it. That had nothing to do with anything. I worked my ass off to get to where I got to. I had 15 surgeries while I played. I lived in fucking rehab. It wasn't like I never worked out. Maybe if I worked out less, I would have been better off. I see some of these skinny guys, they never get hurt. I was not a big quarterback. When I came out of college, I probably weighed 170. I played most of my career probably between 190 and 200. I worked as hard as I could work. Anybody who says I didn't doesn't know what the hell they're talking about."

CHAPTER 5

||||||||||||||||||||||||||||||||||||||||||||||||||||||||||||||||||||||||||||||||||

DITKA'S REVENGE GIVES BIRTH TO FRIDGE

On September 29, 1985, one week after McMahon's miracle at Minnesota, the Bears returned to Soldier Field and dismantled the Washington Redskins 45–10. In the process they shut up defensive end Dexter Manley, who spent the week before boasting that the Redskins would "knock Walter Payton out of the game." Ditka's response was simply, "Who would listen to Dexter Manley?"

Payton gained six yards on seven carries, one of the worst days of his career, and the Bears trailed 10–0 early in the second quarter. Then Willie Gault took a kickoff at his own 1-yard line and returned it for a 99-yard touchdown. Not only did this give pause to some of Gault's critics—*On second thought, does it matter if he's soft if he can run back kickoffs 99 yards?*—but it triggered a franchise-record 31 points in the second quarter.

Over their first four games, the Bears had now rung up 38, 20, 33, and 45 points, making them the NFL scoring leaders, and the writers were using terms like "point machine" and "high-powered" to characterize the offense. In Chicago this had happened, uh, never. Meanwhile, Payton took McMahon's emergence and his own reduced role in the offense (at least for now) with his trademark humility.

"Every time we win, it's one game closer to the Super Bowl," said Payton.

The Bears left the month of September at 4–0, their best start since their last NFL championship in 1963. The Redskins, the defending NFC East Division champs, returned to the capital with a 1–3 record and their worst beating since 1961.

At Tampa Bay the next Sunday, the offense struggled again in the first quarter, gaining only 26 yards before winding up with 433 in a 27–19 victory. At one point the Bucs led 12–0, meaning the Bears had come from behind in four out of their five wins. This could be seen as a strength (look at their fighting spirit) or as a flaw (look at how badly they play early in games, even against an 0–5 Tampa Bay team). Thus the Chicago fans, an uncertain group to begin with, could not be exactly sure how elated to feel about their 5–0 Bears.

What no one said publicly after the Tampa Bay game was nevertheless the truth: the Bears had come out flat and uninspired because they'd been looking ahead to their revenge game the next week in San Francisco. But Ditka made everything clear before leaving the locker room in Tampa Bay.

"Stop smiling. Get ready for war," he told the players.

That week the players, the fans, and the media all relived the 23–0 defeat in the 1984 NFC championship. The 49ers had gone on to win the Super Bowl, but not before telling the Bears as they walked off the field, and also through the Bay Area press, "Next time, bring your offense." And of course, with the title game already a blowout, Bill Walsh had inserted his 264-pound offensive lineman Guy McIntyre into the backfield as a blocker near the goal line.

"That 49ers game was circled for us," says defensive end Tyrone Keys. "In some ways, that game was what '85 was all about."

"The intensity probably *was* different that week," says

Ditka. "I always told our players, to get to the next level, you have to beat teams at that level. I also remembered when they put Guy McIntyre in the backfield. That was part of the reason I put William Perry in the backfield the next season. I knew when the game was ending we were going to run the clock out with Perry in there. I didn't give a damn if people were going to say, you're sending a message. Yeah, I sent a message. That I forgive. I just don't forget."

Tom Thayer says Ditka referred to Walsh as the "gray-haired wizard" that week. Jay Hilgenberg says Ditka and Walsh both had large egos and Ditka was probably jealous of all the praise and publicity Walsh received after winning his second Super Bowl in '84. Brian Harlan, the Bears' assistant PR man, has a different perspective.

"Mike was a smart man, and he could be very calculating," says Harlan. "The Guy McIntyre thing, I don't know if Mike really thought Walsh was trying to stick it to him. But he decided to use it that way. That was the perfect example of Mike finding something and telling his players, 'They don't respect us.' "

Jim Covert, for one, bought into what Ditka was selling.

"The Niners had taunted us at the end of the game," Covert recalls. "It was Randy Cross and a couple other guys. They said, 'Come back next time and bring an offense.' I went out there in '85 with a big chip on my shoulder. I told the offensive linemen, 'Stay hungry. These guys disrespected us. We need to whip their ass.' "

On the practice field that Thursday in Lake Forest, Hampton says, the Fridge was called out of defensive drills and trottled over to where the offense was working on running plays.

"I thought, *What the hell is up with this? Is somebody hurt and they need him to act like a guard or something?"* says Hampton. "Then we all got together for the team stuff, and they handed him the football. And it all came back to me. That was the genius of Ditka. He didn't forget. He didn't forget that the Guy McIntyre move was basically the 49ers giving us the heave-ho and then the finger. And Ditka was going to return the favor. It was one of those touchstone moments that season, like, okay, guys, here we go."

At this point Perry was hardly playing on *defense,* what with Ryan disliking all rookies and especially an overweight one taken by the Bears in the first round against Ryan's wishes. In a few weeks, Ditka would order Ryan to play Perry more on defense, but for now it would suffice for the offense to spring the Fridge on the 49ers.

Since all Ditka wanted to do was use him to run out the clock, the Bears would have to be winning late in the game, and that would take some doing. Although the 49ers were only 3–2, they still had Joe Montana, Dwight Clark, and Ronnie Lott, and they had added a rookie receiver named Jerry Rice. Yet Ditka hardly seemed scared while telling reporters that week, "This will be one of the hardest-hitting games you'll see in a long time. It might make you forget about the Raiders game last year. I don't think they like us. I know we don't like them."

On Sunday morning in San Francisco, the players entered the visitors' clubhouse to find that their coaches had posted nine-month-old local newspaper stories from the Niners' humiliating win over Chicago. This time around, however, the Bears had McMahon, the NFL's second-ranked passer, starting at quarterback instead of Fuller.

On the Bears' first possession, he needed only six plays to drive them 73 yards for a touchdown. McMahon already had

115 passing yards in the first quarter as Chicago sprinted to a 16–0 lead. San Francisco fought back to make it 16–10 at halftime. The stage appeared to be set for the Bears to be denied their chance at payback, but then Payton and the line led two long, clock-eating drives to seal the outcome. Payton ended up with 132 yards, his season high so far, two touchdowns, and one lethal stiff arm to Ronnie Lott's head. When Butler, the rookie kicker, made all four of his field goal attempts, he instantly became one of Chicago's darlings. On defense, where the Bears were still picking up momentum, they had entered the game ranked just number 12 in the NFL. But at Candlestick they sacked Montana seven times and limited him to 160 yards passing.

The Bears led 26–10 late in the fourth quarter, and then came the final indignity for San Francisco: William Perry, the 325-pound defensive tackle, trotted into the huddle, lined up at fullback, and carried the ball on the final two plays of the game. Perry gained only two yards each carry. The CBS announcers didn't mention, and didn't appear to notice, that he was even on the field until after the first time he handled the ball. It all seemed very low-key, but the Refrigerator phenomenon was just beginning. For the moment, it was enough that the 49ers were whipped and one-upped on their own field by Mike Ditka.

"That was sure fun to watch," says Fencik. "Was putting William Perry in pure payback? It sure looked like it to me."

"The Fridge thing became a circus after that," says McMahon. "And the only reason it happened was that Ditka was trying to get back at Bill Walsh. We were beating them up, and he put Fridge in just to spite Bill. It was actually comical to see him carrying the ball and hitting people. A guy that big moving that fast, the sounds it made, the sounds the other guys made when he hit them—it became a pretty good weapon for us. But once the thing got started, Buddy Ryan used to say, keep him on offense. We don't need him over here. Eventually Ditka made Buddy start him on defense. They were paying him a lot of money, and there was only so much he could do for us on offense. The only bad thing with the Fridge was when he grabbed the ball from me, he almost ripped my arm off. I told him, 'I'll put it right here, you don't have to take my whole arm with you.' "

Chicago's victory reverberated across the entire league. The Bears were not just 6–0, they had gone on the road and manhandled the defending Super Bowl champions. Gary Pomerantz wrote in the *Washington Post,* "Somebody better call the sheriff, real quick. The Chicago Bears are breaking apart every team, every expectation and every bit of law and pecking order in the National Football League."

But the NFL season is long and filled with unwanted surprises. The Bears received one that evening when Ditka was arrested back in Chicago for speeding, improper lane usage, and driving under the influence of alcohol. Fortunately, neither Ditka nor anyone else was injured.

Many people thought the episode began on the flight back to Chicago as Ditka and his players celebrated at 35,000 feet. Actually, it started that week in the Bay Area when Ditka stocked up on California wine while visiting vineyards. Ditka says he drank two bottles and possibly more on the flight back to Chicago. When the plane landed at O'Hare, there were members of the team who wanted to drive him home, but even a sober Ditka wasn't an easy guy to talk into doing things. As Ditka arrived at his car in the O'Hare parking lot, Bears center Tom Andrews was parked right next to him.

"When Ditka went to put his bag on top of his car, his bag flew completely over the car to the other side," says Andrews.

Ditka was stopped by a state trooper at 12:14 A.M., Monday, on Interstate 294, about two miles north of the airport.

"I heard they were waiting for him," says McMahon. "He did a few interviews before he left San Francisco. He said, 'I won't be able to see when I get home.' I guess a few of the cops were watching TV, so they were waiting. Everybody drives through that tollway the same way home, so we all saw it. The next morning he came in apologizing, he made a mistake that night, and this and that. I think he got cuffed because he got a little mouthy with the cop."

With the Bears undefeated and their coach's popularity ever soaring, hundreds of irate fans flooded the state police with phone calls and letters of protest. "We've been called everything in the book that you can think of," said one of the troopers. Another trooper reported that one of the angry callers told the police that Ditka was "the best thing that has ever happened to Chicago."

Illinois secretary of state Jim Edgar did what politicians do. He straddled the fence. "It's not right to heap abuse on the police," said Edgar. "I watched the game just like every other loyal Bears fan. Mike Ditka has done a great job as coach. I'm sure people were disappointed with what happened last night. I just hope an awareness on the public's part will come out of this; that no matter who you are, don't drink and drive."

The next day Ditka appeared at Halas Hall. He had tears in his eyes when he said he was sorry for embarrassing the franchise. He was later convicted of the drunken driving charge and sentenced to court supervision for one year. He also lost his license for six months. As for Ditka's players, several of them say he was hardly the only Bear who could have gotten in trouble as he drove home from the airport after the San Francisco game.

"The fact of the matter is, the police could have arguably stopped any of us on *that* night," says Dave Duerson.

Once upon a time, Mike Ditka was more of a shot-and-a-beer guy.

The grandson of Ukrainian immigrants, Ditka was born on October 18, 1939. He grew up in Aliquippa, Pennsylvania, 25 miles from Pittsburgh. His father, also named Mike, was a Marine who enlisted after the Japanese bombed Pearl Harbor. He never went overseas, but had to leave his family when assigned to basic training near San Diego. Once back in Aliquippa, he worked as a welder for Southern Railroad, and much of his life was spent "burning" inside a local steel mill that was serviced by the railroad. Like the fathers of other young boys in west Pennsylvania, he encouraged his son to try to escape the mills and go to college.

"You'd see guys coming back at night from the factories, dirty, tired, and they stopped in the beer garden, and they'd have a shot in their beer," Ditka once told the *New York Times*. "It was a ritual. Then they'd come home and take a bath, and get the grime off and leave a ring around the tub, then eat and probably go back to the beer garden."

Ditka and his family lived in a government-subsidized housing project, but he says it wasn't the vertical kind. It was a small single house in a row of six. Although money wasn't abundant, he says, it wasn't a struggle during his early childhood. His mother, Charlotte, gave him a complete football uniform when he turned four. Ditka also played baseball, and his father later said there was no middle ground: either his son hit a home run or he struck out swinging and broke his bat in a rage.

While his father exaggerated, it was common knowledge in Aliquippa that by high school Ditka's temper bordered on legendary. There are published reports of Ditka walking into another team's huddle and screaming at the players that he was going to kill them for breaking the leg of his teammate. Once, during a high school basketball game, he broke his own wrist when he smashed his hand into a wall after missing an easy shot.

Ditka says he has no idea where his childhood anger came from, but he knows where he got his drive. "I got that from my father," he says. "From watching how hard he worked for our family."

But in his 2005 memoir of the 1985 season, *In Life, First You Kick Ass,* he expressed some hostility toward his father. "He was tough with my mom," wrote Ditka. "And he was tough with me. He got on me hard, but he didn't go after the other kids. I was the oldest and I had two brothers and a sister. I was talking to my sister the other day, and I said, 'Dad never touched you, did he?' And she said, 'One time when I was a sophomore or junior in high school I said something to him, and he slapped me.' I said, 'I never thought he slapped anyone but me.'

"I blamed him for a lot," Ditka continued. "I didn't like him, basically, until I went off to college and lived away from home."

As a sophomore at Alaquippa High School, he was only five-foot-seven and 135 pounds. He put on weight as a junior and played linebacker and offensive end on a team that won its league championship. Ditka played football, basketball, and baseball at the University of Pittsburgh, but football was the best fit for his temperament. During an era when ends still played both ways in college, he lined up on defense against much bigger offensive tackles. On offense he played tight end, and he was also Pitt's punter, which pretty much ruled out any roughing-the-punter ideas.

By 1960, his senior year, he was an iron man who played 55 minutes a game, an All-American, and sixth in the Heisman Trophy voting. His three-year numbers at Pitt were a seemingly modest 45 catches for 730 yards and 7 touchdowns and 44 punts for a 39.7-yard average. But with Mike Ditka the *how* was often more meaningful than the *how much*. His college coach Paul Ashman described him as "tough as nails." His teammates nicknamed him "the Hammer."

In 1961 the American Football League was in its second season, and the Houston Oilers chose Ditka with their first pick. He had also impressed the Bears, and they went ahead and made him their own number one. Halas called Ditka himself and offered him $12,000 for one season with a $6,000 bonus. When Ditka asked his father what he thought, his father told him, "That's a lot of money. You work a long time to get that kind of money." Ditka decided to take the one-year deal with the Bears for $18,000, and the next day the Oilers offered two years for a total of $50,000. But, Ditka says, he had given his word, and had always wanted to play in the NFL anyway.

In 1961 he caught 56 passes and beat out Fran Tarkenton for Rookie of the Year. In 1963 his iconic 63-yard run against the Steelers helped the Bears win a crucial game on their way to the NFL championship. The Bears trailed 17–14 in the fourth quarter when Ditka caught a short pass from Bill Wade in the flat. Ditka raced around his first two would-be tacklers and then ran *through* three others. What was more, he seemed to be *looking* for people to run over.

"That run against Pittsburgh was unbelievable," says Gary Fencik, who grew up in the Windy City. "It came right after JFK was killed, and everyone was asking why the NFL was even playing. But nobody ever forgot it in Chicago."

Nobody had a choice. Simply known in Chicago as The Play, it showed up year after year on all the TV sports shows.

In 1964, with a separated left shoulder, Ditka caught 75 passes, then an NFL record for tight ends. But once again, with Ditka, the attitude always impressed more than the numbers. Once, the Bears were playing the Rams at the Los Angeles Coliseum. When a fan ran onto the field with a banner, Ditka stepped out of the huddle and dropped him with a forearm.

In his six seasons with the Bears, he went to five Pro Bowls while waging epic battles with Green Bay's equally crazed middle linebacker Ray Nitschke. Mike Ditka became a civic legend, the blood-and-guts tight end who helped lead the Bears to the 1963 NFL championship. Then, in 1967, during a contract dispute, Ditka threatened to jump to the AFL's Oilers, adding his fateful comment, "George Halas throws nickels around like manhole covers."

The Old Man traded Ditka to Philadelphia, where his life and career both spiraled downward. He had a wife and children by then, but they still lived in Chicago. Ditka became depressed, and his drinking intensified. He was kicked out of a game—an exhibition game—for fighting. He was suspended for criticizing his coach, Joe Kuharich, who in truth could not coach his way out of a paper bag. But the other disgruntled players on the Eagles, unlike Ditka, didn't express their feelings about Kuharich with several newspapermen standing around.

He spent two desultory seasons in Philadelphia and was about to retire when he received a surprising phone call from

Dallas coach Tom Landry. Landry wanted to see if Ditka had anything left. When Ditka told him he did, Landry traded for him in 1969. In his first few months with the Cowboys, Ditka made headlines when he was involved in a car wreck after a night on the town in the preseason. Ditka slammed into the side of another car while driving his own at 50 miles per hour. Although his steering wheel embedded his two front teeth into his gums, Ditka played in an exhibition game that Saturday.

In 1972 he caught a touchdown pass as the Cowboys thrashed Miami 24–3 in Super Bowl VI. By 1973 Ditka was done as a player, but Landry changed his life a second time by asking him to join the Cowboys' staff to work with receivers.

In Dallas, Ditka broke racquets when he lost in racquetball to his fellow coaches. He once famously went wild and tore up a deck of cards when he lost in gin rummy. He threw clipboards and cursed out players on the sidelines. During one game against Pittsburgh, he picked up a ball that had rolled out of bounds and threw it back onto the field. The only problem was, Ditka "accidentally" hit one of the Steelers in the back of the head with it.

Still, as an assistant in Dallas from 1973 to 1981, his proximity to Landry had a semi-calming effect. Ditka didn't quit drinking, but over those years he gradually cut down. In addition to working with the receivers, Ditka made his mark as a special teams coach whose players worked hard. Furthermore, he connected with some of the Cowboys' young and volatile players who were reticent around the distant Landry.

"The coach I had the best relationship with my first year was Mike Ditka," Thomas "Hollywood" Henderson told Peter Golenbock for his 1997 oral history of the Cowboys. "Ditka was a very, very intense man. All he wanted you to do was do your job and do it right. He would tell me to go down the field and do this or that, and I did it, and he liked the way I got things done."

By 1981 Ditka wanted to move up the ranks, and he knew the only place he had any chance at all of becoming a head coach was back in Chicago for Halas. With the current head coach, Neill Armstrong, struggling to keep the job, Ditka sent Halas a simple handwritten letter. "I know you have had some bad times and I just want to renew our friendship," wrote Ditka. "I want you to know if you ever make a change in the coaching end of the organization, I just wish you would give me some consideration."

As he later explained in his 1986 autobiography, *Ditka,* "I didn't hear back from him until I got the phone call after the season telling me to come into Chicago. We did the deal right at his kitchen table. He liked that I went to bat for myself. My contract for $100,000 was by far the smallest in the league, but that's OK. That wasn't my worry. My problem was whether I could get the job done. I wanted to prove to Mr. Halas that he made the right decision."

When asked today what he thinks George Halas saw in him, Ditka says, "I would assume he saw a little bit of himself in me. Besides the X's and O's of football, there has to be a thing called passion. A thing called desire. I loved the Bears. He understood that. When I left there, it wasn't on the best of terms, and the thought of coming back and doing something with him would be pretty special. I told him that in my letter. I think he realized that I was a Bear."

Halas also recognized that Ditka would be absolutely nothing like his predecessor, Armstrong.

"Neill was a true gentleman," says Fencik, who played four seasons for him. "But he was probably not enough of a disciplinarian, and some of the players took advantage of him. In '81 we had a guy named Rickey Watts at wide receiver. We were playing at Detroit toward the end of the season, and late in the first half he walked off the field. When we came back into the locker room at halftime, Rickey was on the telephone. So now we're all wondering, *What are they gonna do?* because this is ridiculous. The buzz after the game was, Rickey is gonna be gone. He'll be out of here tomorrow. And Neill didn't. He gave a speech about all of us sticking together. I liked Neill a lot, but the team was out of control. The Bears' slogan that year was 'Whatever It Takes.' Someone taped over the 'It Takes.' And that pretty much told you about that season."

As the 1981 season ended, few people in Chicago thought Armstrong should get a new contract. One of the few who did and had any clout was the team's general manager, Jim Finks. But Halas resisted Finks, and soon it was widely rumored that Chicago's next head coach would be Buddy Ryan, the defensive coordinator who (like Ditka) had been campaigning for the job behind the scenes.

In early January 1982, at a news conference held at the Bears' office downtown, Halas said that Armstrong was fired and Ryan would be retained. But when Halas didn't announce who the new head coach would be, Ditka's name kept surfacing in the press. This was when some people charged that Halas had lost his mind and should not be running the Bears at age 86.

"Ditka had not been a head coach," remembers Fencik. "He was not a coordinator. He was a special teams coach. I'm not saying there was any big debate among the players about who would be the next head coach. We didn't know. But I don't think Ditka was on anybody's list."

The respected *Sun-Times* columnist John Schulian didn't even pretend to be diplomatic. Beneath the headline "Hiring

Ditka Would Be Madness," Schulian wrote, "Again and again you are confronted with visions of him throwing clipboards and cursing officials when he should be sending in the next play on offense or calling the next defense. He is, after all, a creature of brute force, the quintessential Midway Monster, and such is not the stuff head coaches are made of."

Halas may have been aging and losing his battle with cancer, but Halas still knew more than Schulian ever could about the stuff head coaches are made of. On January 20, 1982, Halas sat next to the 42-year-old Ditka at another news conference held downtown. The speculation was true. Mike Ditka was back.

It would not be easy for him, though. Ditka went to work each day with a general manager, Finks, who didn't hire him and a defensive coordinator, Ryan, who thought *he* should be head coach and made no effort to hide it around the players.

Ditka had no choice but to go about his business, and that business was restoring the physical toughness the Bears had once been known for. In May 1982, at the team's first mini-camp in Scottsdale, Arizona, *"Ditka wore us out,"* Jeff Fisher says emphatically. "To a man, we were sore for a month after that."

"It was like we were on a track team instead of a football team," recalls Leslie Frazier. "We ran and ran and ran and ran."

"Some of the guys who had been there under Neill Armstrong weren't used to that kind of thing," says fullback Calvin Thomas, who signed with the Bears that spring as an undrafted free agent from the University of Illinois. "They were veteran players, but they were kind of whining and complaining about all the conditioning we had to do."

Ditka wasted no time getting his team's attention. In his

first speech to the players at mini-camp, he says, he told them, "I got good news and bad news. The good news is, we're gonna win the Super Bowl. The bad news is, a lot of you guys won't be here."

"It was, either you're on the bus or you're under it," says Fencik. "He was my third head coach with the Bears, and it was the first time someone had clearly articulated the goals of the organization. Then he started remaking our roster. Only about a third of the guys who heard that speech were still there in 1985. That's why, when Mike came in, you could say he was crazy. But he was crazy with a tremendous sense of urgency."

Says Hampton, "He had been to a Super Bowl as a player and as an assistant coach in Dallas. He had won a Super Bowl. Nobody on the Bears had even gone to a Super Bowl. Nobody knew shit about it. I remember thinking, *I've never won any-thing in my life, maybe I'm not a winner. But maybe this is the guy who will show us how.*"

When the '82 Bears reconvened, in Lake Forest that July, Paul Zimmerman of *Sports Illustrated* described Ditka's first full training camp. "Ditka's first morning workout featured full pads and a live, 30-play scrimmage, 11 against 11, with more of the same in the afternoon," Zimmerman wrote. "He ended his first practice with 10 40-yard sprints. The next day there were ten 70s, then eight 110s."

And that was just the running. Fencik told Zimmerman that the last time he'd done so much hitting was in high school.

"Back then, in the NFL, training camp was a five-week af-fair," says Keith Van Horne. "It was brutal. You were in full pads twice a day. It was 100 degrees, or 95 and 90 degrees humidity. Ditka set a tone, no question. This was when he first started, so he was all fire and brimstone."

Kurt Becker, a rookie that summer, had just gotten through playing for the legendarily strict Bo Schembechler at Michigan, where players showing up late for meetings was unheard of. "Then you get to the NFL and it's like, what's going on around here?" he says. "When training camp started, some guys were showing up late, and I'm thinking, *Wow.* But Ditka responded accordingly. He started bouncing guys immediately. That sent the message that maybe this guy is serious about what he's talking about."

Even as Ditka began getting rid of the slackers in his first season, there were still important questions about his ability to manage a game. On September 12, 1982, in his head coaching debut at any level, Ditka gratified his critics when the Bears lost 17–10 to the Lions and his players could not get into their offensive formations. After his second straight loss, a humiliating 10–0 defeat to New Orleans, Ditka called his players cowards for not hitting anyone. The NFL then shut down as the players went out on strike. When the season resumed eight weeks later, Ditka seemed slightly less manic. He also started McMahon the rest of the way, and the Bears ended up 3–6, with McMahon winning the NFL's Offensive Rookie of the Year.

By 1983, the media was noting that Ditka ran Payton too often and too predictably even though the Bears finally had a quarterback who could pass. Ditka was also criticized when he started yanking McMahon in the second half of games and replacing him with the undistinguished Vince Evans. Then Ditka benched McMahon and started Evans for three games. Then Ditka went back to McMahon. Depending on how you viewed his handling of quarterbacks, he was either a new head coach learning from his mistakes or the guy couldn't make up his mind.

Meanwhile, the florid displays of anger continued. When his players made mistakes, Ditka not only berated them on the sidelines but sometimes looked like he wanted to strangle them. After a brutal overtime loss at Baltimore in week five, Ditka rushed into the visitors' locker room fuming.

"That was my rookie year," says Jim Covert. "Something happened with the snap count, and I missed my assignment, and my guy got to Vince Evans. Ditka pulled me out of the game. Ditka called me every name in the book, and then we ended up losing in OT, and then he got me again in the tunnel. Then we went in the locker room, and everybody was quiet when he came in. We had this equipment trunk we called 'Big Bertha.' Ditka hauled off and punched this trunk while he was yelling. Ditka is grimacing, and he goes, 'Vince, why don't you lead us all in the Lord's Prayer? Doc, I need to see you.' "

Jeff Fisher says, "Then he walked out. You could tell how competitive he was, how much he despised losing. He came in the next day, and his hand was in a cast. He broke his hand."

Before the next game, against Denver, Ditka gathered his team in the locker room at Soldier Field and held up his injured right hand. "Okay, men," he said, "I want you to go out there and win this one for Lefty." After the players saw that their high-strung coach at least had a sense of humor, they defeated the Broncos, 31–14.

By the end of that transformative 1983 season—when the team's remarkable draft brought in Covert, Dent, Duerson, Thayer, Gault, Richardson, and Bortz—the Bears had taken another step forward under Ditka. They finished 8–8 and missed the playoffs, but they won five of their last six games to close out the season. The players in the front office were changing as well. By season's end, Finks had resigned and become president of the Cubs, Halas had died of cancer on October 31, and his grandson Mike McCaskey had been named team president. Shortly before his death, Halas gave Ditka a bottle of Dom Perignon champagne with one final instruction from the Old Man: "Mike, don't open until you win the Super Bowl."

In 1984, Ditka's third season, the Bears went 10–6, won their first playoff game against the Redskins, and lost to San Francisco in the NFC championship. Soon afterward, Ditka received a three-year contract extension. But if he now had some job security, he remained as volatile, complex, and contradictory as ever.

None of the players are sure how and when Ditka acquired the nickname "Sybil." But several players say it was around 1984, and that it was probably dreamt up by McMahon. *Why* Ditka got nicknamed Sybil is open to various interpretations.

Van Horne: "Because he's got about 20 personalities! Well, not 20. But every morning you'd have a team meeting. Ditka would come in and talk to the team as a whole. He'd come in and be in the greatest mood, smiling and laughing and cracking a joke, and then it would be like a switch went off, and he would just turn into this raving lunatic, about *something.* It could be that we were playing Green Bay that week or something some reporter said about him in the press. We'd all just stare at each other like, what just happened?"

Fencik: "He was an ex-player with the reputation of being a big partier. He was a big disciplinarian. He was emotional. He had so many different facets. You didn't always know which one was going to come out."

Becker: "Mike would metamorphosize into different personalities depending on how practice went. And as he

transformed into whatever he was, it was usually some negative force that made him change—practice wasn't going
well, mistakes were being made—and he would change into
an alter ego. And once he got into it, you were blinded.
Anger and emotion just took him over."

Cabral: "But the ranting and raving was not an everyday
thing. That was mostly during games. During the week he
would tell you what he thought, but he was pretty quiet. The
ranting and raving, man, he was so competitive, that was a
game-day thing."

In 1985, in Kevin Butler's first NFL game, the Bears trailed
Tampa Bay 28–17 just before halftime. Butler had come out
of Georgia touted for his strong leg, and on the final play of
the half Ditka sent him out to try a 64-yard field goal. If Butler could nail it, he would surpass the NFL-record 63-yarder
made by Tom Dempsey in 1970.

"My heart is beating," remembers Butler. "I'm thinking,
Here's my chance, first game my rookie year. The kick was long
enough, but it was to the left, and I don't think it ever got over
about ten yards high. Everybody starts for the locker room,
and someone comes right up next to me, and it's Ditka. He
says, 'That was your one chance. You'll never get another
chance again.' I was thinking, *Wow, I never had a coach say that
to me.* But that was how Ditka coached. He liked to put a period on each statement."

In another game against the Bucs, later in Butler's career,
Ditka sent him out to kick the game-winning field goal. Earlier in the game, Butler had kicked the ball out of bounds on
a kickoff.

"Right before I went on the field, he told me I was the
worst fucking kicker he'd ever seen and to just try and put my
goddamn foot on the ball," recalls Butler. "And I'm just shak-

ing my head because I knew him by then. And I'm thinking, *I'm gonna kick it, and we're gonna win, and I'm coming right back here and letting you know I made it!* And he would enjoy that moment. Because he knew he had gotten your goat and made you focus. Once you understood him, Ditka was really fun to have as a coach."

On the morning after games, Ditka ran the film projector, and nobody was exempt from his withering comments. This included punter Maury Buford, who was particularly adept at pinning the other teams deep at their end of the field. In 1985 Buford and Butler played crucial roles on Chicago's strong special teams, which endeared them both to Ditka, since he'd been a punter in college and a special teams coach under Landry in Dallas. Of course, this didn't keep Ditka from annihilating Buford when he screwed up.

"I had an extremely bad game in 1985 against the Jets," says Buford. "We were in films the following Monday, and Ditka turned the film off and turned the lights on. He never could pronounce my name anyway. He still to this day doesn't know how to pronounce my name. He said, 'Murray, Maury, Marty, whatever the fuck your name is, you better get your shit together, son, or I'll have so many goddamn punters in here tomorrow, it will make your head spin.'

"A lot of guys didn't like Ditka. He could care less if you liked him or not. But the players respected him. He expected as much from himself as he expected from you. He was in there working his ass off in the weight room at five-thirty, six every morning. He would be working out before we had our first meetings."

Even though McMahon was mostly impervious to him, Ditka was probably roughest on quarterbacks. In 1984 he released Bob Avellini, his former starting QB and a ten-year veteran who had spent his entire career in Chicago. Such things happen in the NFL. But typically not the first week of October.

"I can't play him here," Ditka told the local reporters when he waived Avellini. "The fans would boo him unmercifully."

Not even the most naive Bear fan believed Ditka's explanation. This is what Ron Rivera says really happened: "McMahon was hurt that game, so Avellini had to play. Ditka called a play. Avellini got under center, read the defense, audibled, turned to throw, and the ball got intercepted for a touchdown. Avellini came to the sideline, and he and Ditka got into this heated conversation. Ditka said, 'You're through. You're done. You'll never play for me again.' He cut Avellini the next week."

In 1985 Mike Tomczak signed with the Bears as an undrafted quarterback out of Ohio State and then rarely saw action behind McMahon and Fuller. As his playing time later increased, he sought counsel from a sports psychologist who helped him try to cope with Ditka's eruptions.

Says Tomczak: "I met someone who said, 'That Ditka is an asshole. I can't believe how he rants and raves on the sidelines.'

"I said, 'Well, he's the coach.'

"He said, 'How do you deal with it?'

"So I shared some things with him, and he said we should sit down and talk. It helped me to understand that it wasn't directed only at me, it was just an outward emotion that Ditka would direct at quarterbacks, or anyone in general. Ditka was fair with me, and he gave me every opportunity to succeed. But there were times he was abrupt in pulling me out of games."

"For a guy who never played the position, he thought he

understood every nuance," continues Tomczak, who would later play for the Packers, Browns, and Steelers. "I didn't think he was as bright as some other offensive people I've been around in my career. What Ditka was really good at was getting people to play with a chip on their shoulder. There was one game I wanted to take a swing at him. It was a home game, and he was riding me from the time I got to the sidelines. I just wanted to go after him, but Keith Van Horne stepped in between us. And actually Keith was the guy who always wanted to jack Ditka."

Not always, but on occasion. Van Horne was a first-round pick in 1981 from USC. Once the six-foot-seven, 280-pounder moved in permanently at right tackle, the Bears were on their way to building the NFL's most physical offensive line. Van Horne was a rock-and-roller from California who became close friends with McMahon as well as with Keith Richards and Rod Stewart. He married Eleanor Mondale, Vice President Walter Mondale's daughter, but they later divorced. In 1985 Van Horne should have joined his fellow linemen Covert and Hilgenberg at the Pro Bowl, but he was passed over.

Van Horne says he respects what Ditka did to resurrect the Bears, but he also says, "He and I did not get along. Ditka didn't like me, and I found he could be a hypocrite."

In a game against Green Bay, it was third-down-and-three when Van Horne was called offsides by the officials. Van Horne was sure he wasn't, but that didn't matter. It was now third-and-eight, and the Bears wound up punting.

"As I'm coming off the field, Ditka said, 'You motherfucker, I'm going to kick your ass!' " remembers Van Horne.

"I said, 'Then bring it on, motherfucker!' I started walking toward him. Jay Hilgenberg grabbed Ditka, and Dick Stanfel, our offensive line coach, grabbed me. We were heading for each other. It was going to happen. I was ready. I had my helmet in my hands. I would have clocked him.

"The next day in the team meeting, he basically just rips me one in front of the whole team. He told the guy playing behind me, 'You're starting next week.' Then we broke off, and the offensive line went off and watched the game film. We watched that play probably eight times. Stanfel said, 'You weren't offsides.'

"I said, 'I know.'

"Stanfel was old-school, kind of a company guy, and he said, 'I think you need to apologize to Mike. I don't care what happens, you never call your coach a motherfucker.'

"I said, 'He should apologize to me.'

"He said, 'No, you need to go to him.'

"So I went into Ditka's office. I said, 'I'm sorry about the blowup yesterday. It was the heat of the game, and it was a bad call.'

"He said, 'I appreciate you saying that. The league office called me and said they reviewed the tape and it was a bad call. But don't tell anyone I said that.'

"So after Ditka knew it was a bad call, he still ripped me a new asshole in front of the whole team. That was my experience with him, and that was where the hypocrisy came in."

And yet, whatever questions were raised about Ditka's methods and his mood swings, the 1985 Chicago Bears played hard. They played with confidence. They played with intelligence. In any sport, at any level, these are the signs of a well-coached team.

"I never relaxed when I played for him," says Tom Thayer. "I don't think I took a deep breath until I retired. You should look at the tapes of when he played in Chicago. He's a Hall of Famer because people respected the way he played. Ditka was a model of toughness for us."

"Ditka was search and destroy and dominate. Not win, dominate," says rookie defensive back Ken Taylor. "He was as big as life, and I was terrified. He'd walk over and watch the defensive backs and chew his gum. He was the fastest gum chewer I've ever seen. I wouldn't breathe until he walked away."

"For me, he was the perfect head coach to play for," says Jay Hilgenberg. "I grew up in a football family. My uncle played 16 years in the NFL. Guys like Ditka were the guys who I watched growing up. And I just had a whole lot of respect for him."

"He was the right guy at the right time in Chicago," says Covert. "He changed the culture there. Before, it was a culture of separation—defense, offense, the cliques. Basically, the defense thought the offense wasn't worth a shit. Some of that still existed, but Mike came in there and drafted the players he wanted and proved that the Bears could win."

Jeff Fisher, himself an NFL head coach now, says simply, "Guys in the NFL like to talk about their coaches. There was a lot more respect for Mike than what was let on."

CHAPTER 6

||||||||||||||||||||||||||||||||||||||||||||||||||||||||||||||||||||||||||||||||

PAYTON SAVES THE DAY

On August 11, 1984, the Bears had played the Packers in the preseason, which the two teams hadn't
done since 1975. It was a bad idea then, and just
as bad an idea nine years later. Green Bay and Chicago both
played in the NFC Central, the Black and Blue Division, and
they despised each other. Wasn't it enough that they'd face
each other twice when the games really counted?

Adding gasoline to the fire, the exhibition game in 1984
was played in Milwaukee at County Stadium, the baseball park
for the Brewers, and in the makeshift configuration for a preseason football game, the two teams' benches were placed on
the same sideline. Green Bay's rookie head coach was Forrest
Gregg, who called a time-out shortly before halftime, which
Ditka deemed to be unnecessary.

"Mike Ditka and Forrest Gregg were both coaching the
teams they used to play for, so it was like their era all over
again," says fullback Calvin Thomas. "So you always knew when
the Bears and Packers played, then there was going to be some
shit, there was going to be some shots after the whistle. In 1984
I distinctly remember Mike and Forrest on the same sideline,
yelling at each other and shooting each other the bird."

Dan Hampton says Ditka stood on one 47-yard line and

Gregg stood on the other 47 as they shouted a stream of ob-
scenities at each other. According to John Mullin, who covered the '84 Bears for the *Chicago Tribune,* at one point Ditka
called Gregg "a sorry son of a bitch!" To which Gregg quaintly
replied, "Suck my cock, Ditka."

"I played in college in the SEC, and I'd been in some
heated rivalries, but I'd never seen anything like the Bears
and Packers," says Kevin Butler. "There were illegal, violent
hits after the whistle was blown. I'd be warming up for the
game, and I'd have their defensive backs coming up to me and
saying they were going to break my fucking legs. They would
tell me, 'Hey, Butler, we're coming at your legs when you kick
a field goal.' So I would go back and put these one-inch metal
tips on the bottom of my spikes."

The psychotic tone was set by Ditka and Gregg, who would
both end up in the Hall of Fame for their playing careers.
Ditka played tight end for Halas in the 1960s, while Gregg
played offensive tackle for Vince Lombardi. In those days,
Halas believed the Packers were sending spies to watch the
Bears' practice, and the Bears were never allowed to mention
the words "Green Bay" the week of a Packer game.

"But remember, the best franchise I've ever seen in the
history of the NFL was the Packers under Lombardi," says
Ditka. "I played against those guys. They're friends of mine.
Paul Hornung and Jim Taylor. Bart Starr. That was a great,
great team and a great, great coach. And there was respect
back then. When I played against Ray Nitschke, he knocked
the hell out of me and I knocked the hell out of him. But
then it got kind of cheesy and cheap a couple of years in the
eighties, cheap shots, and trying to intimidate through words.
That's bullshit."

Buddy Ryan never played for the Bears, or for anyone
else in the NFL, but he never required a reason to despise

another football team. In 1980, two years prior to Ditka becoming head coach, the cantankerous Ryan kept the rivalry warm as Chicago's defensive coordinator. Linebacker Brian Cabral played for the Packers that season before signing with the Bears the following year.

"Bart Starr was our coach," says Cabral. "We got killed, 61–7, at Soldier Field. Buddy Ryan just kept coming and coming and blitzing late in the game. I remember going back to Green Bay and Bart Starr was humiliated. He said, 'If that ever happens again, we're gonna come back here after the game and scrimmage.' As someone who played for both teams, it was obvious how much hatred there was."

The first time the two teams met was in 1921, 64 years earlier, when the Bears still played their games at Wrigley Field. As 7,000 fans watched the Bears defeat the Packers 20–0, Chicago's John "Tarzan" Taylor broke the nose of Green Bay's Howard Buck with a sucker punch. At least, the Packers called it a sucker punch. The Bears said Buck was ready and Taylor just drilled him.

With all their harsh history—and only 200 miles between small-town Green Bay and big-city Chicago—the Bears and Packers became the NFL's most malevolent rivals. They were not the league's oldest rivals, however; they were second-oldest behind the Bears and the Cardinals. Still, by 1985 Chicago had played Green Bay 130 times. And with the belligerent Gregg now having replaced the more reserved Starr, Ditka had the perfect foil to pit his players against.

"To me, it was like Forrest Gregg was a Buddy Ryan who Ditka could actually go to battle against," says Tom Thayer. "Ditka could bring his offense, his defense, and special teams. It wasn't going to be Buddy's guys practicing against Mike's guys. This was the Bears against the Packers. Ditka's full team against Forrest Gregg's full team."

In 1985 the first game against the Packers was played at Soldier Field on October 21. Eight days earlier in San Francisco, Ditka had used the Fridge to carry the ball on two plays near midfield, running out the clock while also saying Screw you to Bill Walsh's 49ers. Now on *Monday Night Football,* against *another* coach Ditka disliked, Perry would not just run but also block, and Perry would do it down near the goal line.

The Bears trailed 7–0 early in the second quarter when they drove to Green Bay's two-yard line. Ditka called time-out, and Perry trotted out to join the offense, which told the excited crowd of 65,095 that something unusual was in the works. Perry lined up at fullback, a few yards in front of Payton and to his right. McMahon handed off to Payton, running behind Perry, as linebacker George Cumby stepped forward to make the tackle. Cumby weighed about 224 pounds, Perry about 325. Cumby got totally schooled as Perry's block bent him backward and Payton ran through a large hole into the end zone.

With the score tied 7–7, the Bears were soon back near the goal line, and Ditka called again for Perry to enter the game. But this time McMahon handed Perry the ball, and he barged into the end zone from the one-yard line. In the words of *Chicago Sun-Times* columnist Ray Sons, it was "the best use of fat since the invention of bacon."

Basking in the *Monday Night Football* spotlight, Ditka wasn't through yet with his new toy. With the crowd at Soldier Field egging him on—"Perry, Perry, Perry!"—Ditka brought the Fridge in again at fullback with a little more than a minute remaining in the first half. Fridge blocked for Payton again, he buried Cumby again, and Payton easily scored his second touchdown.

By the time Chicago had won, 23–7, there had been several scuffles between an assortment of players. As for the two guys in charge? Ditka was still passing and Gregg still blitzing with 20 seconds left in the fourth quarter.

Monday Night Football's Joe Namath and O. J. Simpson decided it was mostly Ditka's fault. They each criticized Ditka during the broadcast, and then Simpson had more to say to the media afterward. "We know Ditka's personality is, 'Hey, let's pick a fight. Let's pick a fight against Bill Walsh. Let's pick a fight against Forrest Gregg,' " said Simpson.

Meanwhile, Gregg told the press that using Perry on offense was a gimmick that would probably wear out quickly because "somebody will break his leg."

"When the opposition tells me how to coach my football team, then my record would probably be 3–4 also," Ditka shot back. "Anybody who says we were trying to rub it in, as a matter of fact, they're stupid. If the announcers felt that way or the coaches do, it doesn't make any sense. We put the kid [Perry] in the backfield because he was going to lead us into the end zone. Maybe we ought to forfeit the game."

The Packers would get their shot at retribution only 12 days later, when the Bears played them again, but this time at unfriendly Lambeau Field. In the meantime, the Bears were 7–0, and the Fridge phenomenon was blowing up big-time in the wake of his *Monday Night Football* conquest.

"There were rumors before that game that Fridge might run the ball again because of what had happened at San Francisco," says cornerback Leslie Frazier. "So people all over the country were tuning in to see what would happen. Man, the Fridge became a national star. The endorsement deals began to come. He just took off."

Says rookie linebacker Jim Morrissey, "Before that, in my opinion, he was a pretty darn good defensive lineman. But that *Monday Night* game made him a household name, and the darling of the town. Chicago loved him."

"Fridge was just having fun," says tight end Emery Moore-head. "He was just making fun of the whole thing. He had his own little cheerleading team, the Refrigerettes, a bunch of overweight women. He started doing commercials. And then he bought a tooth to put in for his commercials. And he had Ditka's blessing. This was Ditka's way of digging at Buddy Ryan. It was Ditka telling Buddy, 'I made the Fridge, I made him a national hero,' while Buddy still wouldn't even use him on defense. So Ditka puts Fridge on offense, and Buddy has to watch him have all this success and get all this publicity. I think Ditka enjoyed that a lot. He was telling Buddy, 'I'm in charge of this team, and I can make this guy a hero if I want to.' "

Perry's best friend on the team was his fellow defensive lineman Tyrone Keys. The week before the Green Bay game, Keys had lined up a postgame radio engagement at one of Chicago's sports bars. Keys asked if he could bring along the Fridge, the show's producer said yes, and Keys agreed to split his $1,000 payday with his young teammate.

"Then Fridge carried the ball against the Packers, and when we got there that night the sports bar was packed," says Keys. "The line was down the street. And Fridge tells me, as we're about to go in, 'I can't go in there right now. My agent just called and told me I can't go with you. My fee has gone up to five thousand.' So they had to come up with the money to pay him more because he was definitely not going in there. The tide had turned. It was never the same for him from that moment."

It was seven games into the season, and the Fridge wasn't even starting on defense yet. Buddy Ryan still thought he was a waste of space. But why would corporate America care about that? McDonald's, Coca-Cola, Pontiac, White Hen, Kraft Foods, NutraSweet, Drexel Burnham Lambert, paper towels,

long underwear, bacon, hair care products, commercial re-
frigeration for trucks and trailers—the Fridge would endorse
them all. None of his teammates know how much he earned,
but several believe he became a millionaire a few times over.
One newspaper guessed that Perry made $4 million off the
field—just as a rookie—to go with the estimated $340,000 an-
nual salary he received from the Bears.

Jim Steiner was Perry's agent. His very happy agent. He
doesn't have exact numbers, but according to Steiner, "the
Fridge made millions. Everything was over six figures for national ads, and then his price kept increasing. McDonald's
was the first big sponsor to get in, and then Pontiac and
Coca-Cola and the others. It started to happen literally overnight. Once he ran over George Cumby and then he scored
a touchdown, the phones in our office were ringing off the
hook. For a time, it was as hot as it can be."

But why? Why this particular player, at this particular moment, creating this kind of national sensation?

"It wasn't because he was a good defensive lineman," says
Steiner. "It was because of his size and the way Ditka used
him. That was totally novel and totally new. When you combine that with his personality—he had this great naive stage
presence about him—and then on top of that the Bears' success, it just exploded."

Says split end Ken Margerum, "The nickname had a lot to
do with it. His body type had a lot to do with it. His smile without one tooth had a lot to do with it. The stars all aligned for
him. It was a phenomenon you don't really see happen that
often in sports. Still, to this day, people remember 'Refrigerator' Perry."

He was hardly the only Bear getting attention and supple-
menting his income from the stingy Chicago front office. As
Bob Verdi wrote in the *Chicago Tribune* on October 31, "Hardly

an hour passes at the team's Lake Forest training headquarters without somebody out there somewhere dialing to hire one of them for something, from a fashion show to a television show. To please just show your face. Car dealers, official and unofficial lunches, *Time* magazine, they all want a piece of the NFL's newest darlings, the born-again Monsters of the Midway."

By then, the Bears had improved to 8–0 with their second win over the Vikings—a 27–9 thrashing at Soldier Field—and there was already some talk of an undefeated season. The only time this had happened in the NFL, the 1972 Miami Dolphins had gone 17–0. Now some people said the 1985 Bears had their own shot at immortality.

Thus in addition to Perry, McMahon, Ditka, and Payton all cashing in, backup quarterback Steve Fuller had his own radio show, and so did third-string quarterback Mike Tomczak. Virtually every player had something going on commercially, even the offensive linemen, who dressed up like John Belushi and Dan Akroyd in their "Black and Blues Brothers" poster.

"When the offensive line gets a poster, that's unheard of," says offensive tackle Keith Van Horne. "And that explains right there the media mania that was happening. It was quite a circus, but you have to keep yourself focused. And I think that might have hurt us a few weeks later, when we played at Miami."

Still, it was the Fridge who had emerged as the single biggest star on what was widely assumed to be the best team in football. But while blue-chip corporations, the local and national media, the city of Chicago, and anybody who needed to lose a few pounds adored him, professional resentment was simmering among some of his teammates. The Fridge was a pretty good player his rookie year, and undeniably athletic for his girth, but he was making serious money almost purely for his persona. Today that's commonplace. Any player with pizzazz can put big extra bucks in his pocket. But in the NFL of 1985, there was still the old-fashioned notion that players should be rewarded commensurate with their production *on the field.*

"When the hype hit that season, nobody knew how to take it," says safety Dave Duerson. "You look at all the endorsements that athletes are doing now—a lot of that basically started with the '85 Bears. So that whole year, everything was new to everyone. But it was particularly strange that a rookie who was not a major contributor to our team at that particular time was becoming a phenom."

"The whole year, for me, the William Perry running the ball thing was a joke," says rookie defensive back Ken Taylor. "We had a guy who was faster, had more talent, big as a house, aggressive. Calvin Thomas. He was 235, fast. Fridge was 300 or more, but it doesn't matter because Calvin could run faster than him and put the same type of blow on a guy once he gets going. So to have Fridge do that, what is this, Hollywood? It worked out because that team was larger than life and everyone remembers that team, but I didn't think that was right at all. You got a guy who's extremely skilled, who's been doing it his whole life, in Calvin Thomas, and you give the ball to Fridge?"

According to guard Kurt Becker, "I don't think the linemen really cared one way or another, except when he ran up the back of one of us. But I do think the running backs may have felt somewhat slighted, like, 'Why is he back here? That's what we're supposed to do.' Calvin Thomas was a great fullback. They had Matt Suhey back there, Walter Payton. They had talent back there. I don't know if it started out as a gimmick or what, but it turned into something bigger."

Walter Payton may have been a saint, but he was a human one. There were rumors around the league that Payton wasn't pleased about the new media star in the Chicago Bears backfield. One of Payton's best friends on the team was Calvin Thomas.

"I'm only talking now from the perspective of the running back crew," says Thomas. "Initially it was okay, it was fine and dandy. This is Mike Ditka getting back at San Francisco. But as the season went on, as the running back crew, you began to wonder, how often is this going to happen? And after a while, you knew how often it would happen. Anytime we got into a goal-line situation, you ain't gonna be playing because a defensive lineman is gonna be coming in to play your position. We all kind of found that rather disrespectful, because we were the running back crew who got the team down there, but then there's this other guy who knows nothing about your position, who wasn't drafted in your position, but this is just some type of toy or gimmick that the head coach has decided to do. And that happened all year long, even in the Super Bowl. After a while, you start to resent it.

"So, yes, it bothered Walter. It bothered the running back crew, not just Walter. It was like a slap in the face, really. Ditka got caught up in the whole gimmick thing. Ditka was doing his own thing at the time, doing commercials, and he did some stuff with William Perry. Ditka would get on our guys about doing promotional things for themselves. He complained about guys doing this commercial or that commercial, and Ditka was doing the same thing."

If anyone other than Thomas had grounds to brood, it was the future Hall of Famer Dan Hampton. The first week of November, before the upcoming second game against the

Packers, he was shifted from tackle to end so that Perry could move into the starting lineup at tackle. This was a Ditka decision against Buddy Ryan's wishes.

"There were so many subplots," says Hampton. "Was I a little bit jealous about the fact that I'd been two-time Defensive Lineman of the Year and nobody knew who I was and everyone knew who Fridge was? Sure, a little bit. But Fridge was a great guy. If he was an asshole, we'd all have probably resented him. But we didn't because he's a good guy. Fridge was like the lottery winner. It wasn't like he connived and cheated."

Ditka says he never saw coming what happened with Perry that season. He scoffs at the idea that his own commercial success was tied to Perry's. True to his character, he makes no apologies either.

"We finally got him on the field," says Ditka. "And actually, the reason he played offense was because he wasn't playing defense. And then we finally got him on the field playing defense. But we had fun with him on offense. We designed these plays to take advantage of his talents. He did everything: he ran with the ball, he passed the ball for a touchdown, he caught the ball for a touchdown. Most 330-pounders can't do that. He had the agility of a 220-pounder.

"I really don't know why Buddy was so resistant to using him on defense. It's hard for me to say why. I never understood that. Buddy is an old-style coach, and he was really loyal to a lot of his old players. He was reluctant to change. Finally I told him it was time, he plays, period. Here's what we're gonna do. You're gonna move Hampton out, Hampton will play end, and we'll play Perry and McMichael inside, period. It wasn't complicated. We were a better team that way. Dan could play inside or outside. Dan was as good as there was."

If the '85 Bears were combative, they were also pragmatic.

So they tried to put aside their internal issues and focus on their next opponent, the still-angry Green Bay Packers, who were lying in wait for them at Lambeau Field. As the game approached that Sunday, the trash-talking started in earnest.

"We call them the Green Bay Quackers," said Dennis McKinnon. "Crybabies about every little thing that doesn't go their way."

"I wouldn't give you two cents for the whole Green Bay Packer team," said Hampton.

"Have his shock treatments taken effect yet?" said Green Bay offensive tackle Greg Koch, who had played in college at Arkansas with Hampton. "When you're 8–0, everybody gets to talk. I see that Ditka has gone from almost getting fired to the wise old sage of football."

"They don't like us and we don't like them," said Ditka. "That's the way football is supposed to be played. I didn't know it was supposed to be buddy-buddy. I know they don't like us. They don't even like me and I'm a nice guy."

"Yes, sir," said Gregg. "I sure do think Mike is a nice guy. I'm a nice guy too."

Kickoff was set for noon. When Packer fans arrived in the parking lot that Sunday morning, they found a refrigerator that they could smash with a sledgehammer for one dollar, the proceeds all going to United Cerebral Palsy. When the Bears arrived in their dressing room that Sunday morning, they found a large bag of horse shit. The note from a local radio station said, "Here's what you guys are full of."

There was no more whimsy on that cold November 3 at Lambeau. During the first few minutes, it was apparent that this game would be played at a more primal level than any Bear game all season. On the second play, Green Bay safety Ken Stills leveled McMahon on a late hit. On the ninth play,

Green Bay cornerback Mark Lee drove Payton out of bounds and then kept riding him over Chicago's bench, a reckless move that didn't faze Payton but got Lee kicked out of the game. There were six personal fouls called in the first half, the most glaring after Stills ran halfway across the field and blew up Suhey *after* the whistle.

"That had to be a bounty," says cornerback Ken Taylor, getting his first pro start in place of injured Mike Richardson. "It's one thing to be at the bottom of a pile and someone tries to break your rib or step on your finger, versus Suhey standing out there in the open. That was my first NFL start, and my teammates were telling me, 'Don't stand around the pile. Keep moving, keep your eyes open, whatever you do, don't stand around the pile. You'll get knocked out.' "

"When Mark Lee took Walter Payton over the bench, I don't think he was trying to hurt him," says Fencik. "But that Ken Stills cheap shot on Suhey really pissed everyone off. I couldn't believe the running start he took. And that was right in front of our bench. After that, it was, man, we're gonna stomp these guys."

But the 8–0 Bears nearly lost to the 3–5 Packers. McMahon's right shoulder was hurting—though he and the Bears had downplayed it publicly—and he had his worst game all season. He was sacked four times and connected on only 9 of 20 passes for a paltry 91 yards. On several plays, he missed a wide-open McKinnon.

McMahon couldn't possibly miss the super-sized Perry when Ditka used him again to torment the Packers—this time in a whole new way—in the second quarter. Chicago had the ball at the Green Bay four when Perry lined up in the backfield and then went into motion toward the left flat. Victimized, again, was linebacker George Cumby.

"The first time we played Green Bay," says Emery Moore-head, "the Fridge had flattened Cumby on the goal line. This time the Fridge faked like he was going to block him, and being a nimble athlete, he slipped out into the flat and caught a touchdown pass. Cumby, of course, was supposed to be covering him."

Perry's four-yard touchdown reception was another major media moment for him, right between his guest spot on *The Today Show* the previous week and his appearance with David Letterman coming that Monday. But beneath all the nonstop hype, the Green Bay game would end up being a humbling experience for the Fridge. In his first NFL start at defensive tackle, he was benched in the fourth quarter when the Packers kept moving the ball successfully on the ground. Ryan replaced him with Mike Hartenstine, the starter who lost his job when Perry moved in, and Hartenstine did a better job of stopping the run. In case anyone missed the point, Ryan later said that Perry had graded the lowest of all the defensive linemen.

Chicago led 7–3 at the end of a violent and sloppy first half. Both offenses kept stalling, and the Bears trailed 10–9 in the fourth quarter. With the Green Bay fans exulting at the prospect of ruining their rival's perfect record, Chicago began its next drive near midfield. Payton carried the ball on three straight downs. On the third, an off-tackle play with 10:31 remaining, he scored the game-winning touchdown with a 27-yard run that reduced Lambeau Field to a library. Payton ended up with 28 carries for 192 yards, the third-best rushing performance of his career, the 68th time he had reached the 100-yard mark, and the 13th time he had done it in his 20 games against the Packers.

The 1985 Bears had done it again as well, finding a way to grind out a 16–10 victory that pushed them to 9–0 for the first time in franchise history. But the *style* of the game reminded real Bear fans of the old days. The Chicago defense was savage. The Chicago offense was dreadful, except for the player called Sweetness, who flat-out saved his team on that nasty Sunday in Green Bay.

On July 25, 1954, Walter Payton was born in Columbia, Mississippi, about 80 miles from New Orleans. His father, Edward, worked as a custodian at a parachute factory. At night his mother, Alyne, worked in the same factory her husband did. During the day she took care of Walter, his older brother Eddie, and his older sister Pam. Money was always tight, and all three Payton kids were always on the lookout for odd jobs.

Walter didn't start playing organized football until his junior year of high school. As a freshman and sophomore, he was a long jumper on the track team and a drummer in the school band. Walter's decision to go out only for track disappointed the locals because Jefferson High School was small and needed every good athlete it could find. Furthermore, people figured Walter had talent since his brother Eddie was the team's star running back.

Wrote Don Yaeger in the book *Never Die Easy,* which Yaeger coauthored with Payton in the final months of Payton's life, "The belief around Columbia was that Walter never wanted to compete with his older brother on the Jefferson playing fields. For his part, Walter said he was more into the band until he realized that girls paid running backs more attention than drummers."

In 1970 Walter was a junior when Eddie graduated. The Jefferson football coach asked Walter to join the team, and Walter said he would if he could stay in the band.

But after one great season at Jefferson, the nearby all-white

Columbia High School was ordered to integrate, and Payton and some of his teammates transferred there. As a senior, he made All-State, but Payton had limited options. College football was so racially backward that if he wanted to play at a major program, he would need to enroll in the Big Ten or the Pacific 8. The other top conferences still mostly ignored even the best black athletes. This included the Southeastern Conference, the closest to his Mississippi home.

It's hard to believe today, but when Walter Payton graduated from high school, only Kansas, Alcorn State, and Jackson State offered him scholarships. Payton chose Jackson State, a historically black school where his older brother Eddie already played. In four years at Jackson State, Walter scored 65 touchdowns and a collegiate-record 464 points, and he averaged 6.1 yards per carry. He also punted, kicked field goals and extra points, and threw four touchdown passes. In 1974, his senior year, Payton probably should have won the Heisman Trophy, which went to Archie Griffin at Ohio State. But Jackson State was too small and too black, and Payton finished fourth.

Not only was he perhaps the best college football player in the country, he also may have been in the best shape. Before his senior year, Payton found a sandbank near the Pearl River outside Columbia. He laid out a training course of 65 yards, which felt like twice as long because he was running in sand. Early in his NFL career, before he became more comfortable in Chicago, Payton continued to train there in the off-season.

"I'll run it five times, sometimes ten, depending on how many other people are there and how it is," he told *Sports Illustrated*. "Running alone is the toughest. You get to the point where you have to keep pushing yourself. You stop, throw up, and push yourself again. There's no one else around to feel sorry for you."

In 1975 he was selected by the Bears in the first round of the draft, the fourth college player taken overall. By then, he already had his nickname, Sweetness, given to him by his teammates in the Senior Bowl all-star game. It was reportedly for his sweet moves in the open field, and Payton was in fact light on his feet. But when he knew contact was coming, Payton liked to explode *into* the tackler. He also had a vicious stiff arm. Thus, in the NFL, he became the anti–Franco Harris. Rather than run out of bounds to save his body, Payton punished someone.

"I'm not gonna run out of bounds before I hit somebody first," he later wrote in *Never Die Easy*. "I wanted to make them feel me a little. I took great pride in that. A lot of guys are afraid of injury. Personally, I liked contact. I enjoyed it. My whole thing was, I'll give it to them before they give it to me. Every play, I wanted to go full blast."

Payton was five-ten, small by NFL standards, and his old-school leather spikes were only size 8½. But at 204 pounds, Payton was chiseled, with remarkable strength in his shoulders, hips, and thighs. He was never a hard-core weight-lifting guy, which made it truly amazing to his teammates when Payton would bench 390 and leg-press 700. Then sometimes he'd blow their minds by going out to practice and walking the width of the field *on his hands*.

"I saw other people walk on their hands, but never like him," says Jim Covert.

"Walter just couldn't sit still for very long. At practice he'd never stop moving. He always had a football in his hands. He was always throwing, catching, punting. He'd throw as many passes in practice as the quarterbacks. You could make arguments for the other running backs like Jim Brown or Emmitt Smith. But they weren't as good a receiver as Walter was. They didn't block as well as he did. When you put all that together, he was the best football player that ever lived. And then there was his toughness, just his straight-up toughness. He was tougher than lots of guys, and he proved it for 13 years."

In 1975 his pro career began slowly when he gained zero yards in eight carries in a 35–7 loss to Baltimore. After the game, he cried about his performance. Four weeks later, Payton was angry when his coach, Jack Pardee, made him miss the Pittsburgh game with a sore and swollen sprained ankle. It was, remarkably, the only game Payton sat out in his 13 NFL seasons. And although he forgave Pardee, he never forgot it.

"I never counted it as a game missed due to injury, because I was ready to go. Just like every other week," he said.

In 1975, his rookie year, Payton gained only 679 yards. His career took off in 1976 when he ran for 1,390 yards and finished second behind O. J. Simpson for the NFL rushing title. His third year was one of the best in league history. In 14 regular-season games—not 16 as there would soon be—he ran for 1,852 yards and averaged 5.5 yards per carry. In one epic performance against Minnesota, he rushed for a record 275 yards. He was named Most Valuable Player, and the Bears made the playoffs for the first time in 14 years. But here was perhaps that season's most *telling* statistic: Payton carried the ball more times himself (339) than the entire Chicago Bear team threw it (305).

From 1978 to 1981, Chicago went 7–9, 10–6, 7–9, and 6–10. Over the same four seasons, Payton gained 1,395 yards, 1,610 yards, 1,460 yards, and 1,222 yards. In other words, he was a stud on a lousy team.

"Half of the yards he gained in his career were probably behind an average offensive line," says guard Kurt Becker. "When Walter finally had a whole offense around him, and with guards who could pull and tackles who could block, he was unbelievable. But he didn't have that for a while, and he took a beating."

Says cornerback Leslie Frazier, "There were games when I would think, *There's no way he'll be able to play next week, because he's taking such a pounding.* He carried the ball about 20, 30 times a game, and everybody *knew* the ball was going to him. The defense isn't afraid of your wide receivers, they're not afraid of your tight end, they're not afraid of your quarterback. So everyone's geared to stop you—and try and take you out—because they know if they take you out, you're the whole offense."

By 1981, wrote Scott Simon in *Home and Away,* his beautiful memoir of being a Chicago sports fan, "a lament, and even a loneliness had begun to attach itself to Walter Payton. Journalists began to place him in that exceptional company of Chicago greats—Ernie Banks, Fergie Jenkins, Gale Sayers and Dick Butkus—who were considered the best of their times, and yet had no championship to show for it.

"In the early '80s," Simon continued, "opposing players began to shake Payton's hand after peeling themselves off his knees in a tackle. He accepted their hands as a gentleman, but cursed what they signified—that for all of Walter's endowments and deeds, opposing teams had nothing to fear from his Bears."

In 1982 Mike Ditka and Jim McMahon arrived on the scene. And while Ditka would often resist his headstrong quarterback, it was apparent times would be changing in Chicago.

"My first start my rookie year, it was just after the strike," remembers McMahon. "It was third down, we got the damn sweep on, and they got nine guys on the right side of the ball, waiting there for Walter. So I changed to an off-tackle play, a simple play that we'd practiced thousands of times, but it wasn't in the game plan for that particular week. It was third-and-eight, and I gave it to Suhey for a nine-yard gain and a first down. Walter told me in the huddle, 'Just keep doing what you're doing, you're making us better. We've never done this around here before.'

"That stuck with me. I was like, *Shit, these guys have been in the pros for how many years and they don't know how to change plays? It's crazy.* But Walter understood. He didn't like running into a brick wall either. You know, Walter never said a word in the huddle. Never said, 'Give me the ball,' like you hear a lot of guys these days. He was just professional. Even when I changed plays that were for him, it didn't matter. He wanted to win."

In 1983 Ditka still put the ball in Payton's hands, but he started devising new ways to get it there. Payton caught 53 passes that season, after catching just 27 in his entire college career. On October 7, 1984, Payton gained six yards on a pitchout at Soldier Field against the New Orleans Saints. This increased his career rushing total to 12,317 yards—five more yards than the great Jim Brown, making Payton the leading runner in NFL history.

Brown called Payton after the game to congratulate him, a phone call broadcast live by a Chicago radio station. By then, Brown had made it clear to NFL fans that if anyone broke his rushing record, he wanted it to be Payton and not Franco Harris. As Brown later wrote in his 1989 autobiography, *Out of Bounds,* "I've always favored the hardnosed backs. The guys who were purest of heart."

In Brown's estimation, Walter Payton had "the ultimate heart."

Brown referred to Franco Harris as "one of those guys running out of bounds. He was infamous for it."

Brown wrote in his book that he didn't like to block and

wasn't good at it when he did. Harris was never much of a blocker either. The same went for Emmitt Smith, the Cowboy halfback who later surpassed Payton's all-time rushing mark.

Ditka says about Payton, "He was one of the best blocking backs ever."

When asked for one adjective to describe Payton, wide receiver Ken Margerum says "unconventional." This is interesting, since that's not one of the words typically used when the conversation comes around to Walter. But Margerum, who now coaches receivers at San Jose State, is an analytical sort.

"He held the ball with one hand, but he wasn't a fumbler," Margerum says. "That was because he had such strong arms and hands. Most guys couldn't get away with doing that. Today he would be benched. He wouldn't even be playing if he held the ball that way. His workouts were unorthodox as well. A lot of it was bar dips, push-ups, pull-ups, sit-ups, and running hills. I don't know if you could get away with that either nowadays, with all the so-called brilliancy of the weight-room gurus. I think Walter's way was a lost art."

Guard Tom Thayer remembers a practice when the Bears kept working on their inside running game. On a play called "Slant 45," Thayer says, Payton got drilled by the ferocious Todd Bell.

"Walter wasn't ready for it," says Thayer. "And I mean Todd Bell comes up and lays him out. Todd Bell just *bones* him, and bam, right on his back, Walter Payton went down. He popped back to his feet and said, 'Run the play again.' We ran the play again, and there was a collision you could have sold tickets to. Nowadays, you have a strong safety light up a starting tailback, and it's either fisticuffs or the safety gets in trouble with the coaches. Walter just took it, popped up, and said, 'Let's do it again.' "

Early in his career, Payton sometimes stood up reporters or gave them flat and cautious interviews. One local headline asked, "Payton Withdrawn or Just Rude?" "Walter could be moody," says Brian Harlan, Chicago's assistant public relations director. "You could tell when he was approachable and when he wasn't. I think he had the regular ups and downs most people had. Sometimes he could be the greatest guy in the world, and sometimes he gave you a look like, *Stay out of my way.*"

As Payton became more relaxed in the big city, he was increasingly admired by the people who covered him. With his teammates, he became a notorious practical joker. Payton's specialty was fireworks, which Jim Covert discovered his rookie year.

"Training camp was still in Lake Forest then," recalls Covert. "There was no air conditioning in our rooms and it was brutal. So the rookies would sleep down in 'the Dungeon,' the rookies' locker room, at night because it was cooler. Payton would chuck a lighted M-80 down there, and he would think it was the funniest thing in the world. His other big one was, he would call your house and want to talk to your wife and pass himself off as a girl. He would first talk to you, and say, 'Hey, remember me, we were together up at Platteville.' You would say who is this and hang up, and then he would call back and ask for your wife."

Payton would shake a guy's hand, even a big guy's hand, and the next thing that guy knew, he was almost down on his knees because Payton's iron grip had driven him there. Toward the end of a practice, he would run inside a few minutes early and then lock out the whole team in the dead of winter. Above all, Payton played a lot of grab-ass.

"When he stepped into the shower," says linebacker Brian

Cabral, "and you were washing your face or your hair and you didn't know he was there, he was going to see how big a welt he could leave on your butt with his hand. If you played him in pool, his whole thing was to see how much he could cheat. He was always looking for ways that he could get you."

"Yeah," says defensive end Tyrone Keys, laughing, "you really had to watch for him in the showers. He had those rugged hands, and he'd come up and smack guys on the behind so loud, you'd turn around and be ready to fight and it would be Walter. You'd just look at him and keep going because nobody wanted to fight Walter Payton."

Once, when Keys was with Payton at training camp, they saw another black guy walking along. Payton had his BB gun with him. Keys says Payton told him, "Watch me shoot right through this guy's Afro." Payton shot at the guy, but Keys says he made sure to aim high. "Payton was just a character," he adds. "He and McMahon had no fear of anything."

If virtually everyone on the '85 Bears has a Payton-as-prankster story, Dave Duerson thinks he may have the best one. It happened after the 1985 season as Duerson made the first of his four consecutive trips to the Pro Bowl.

"We were in Hawaii, and unbeknownst to us, Walter had this thing that he did with quote-unquote rookie Pro Bowlers," remembers Duerson. "So we're over at the stadium, and it's media day, and we got our shorts on, and we get on the field, and it's this beautiful 85-degree day on the island of Oahu, and there's this wonderful island breeze—and I'm sweating bullets. But the heat is coming up from my nuts. Walter had put liquid heat, unscented liquid heat, on each of the first-year guys' jocks, both in the NFC *and* AFC. The equipment guys were all in on it with him. He got there early in the morning and put this all in our jocks. So we come running off the field, almost in unison, because our balls are literally heating up."

But more than his playfulness, even more than his toughness, what his teammates still talk about is Payton's kindness.

"I played with a bunch of really good players," says Dan Hampton. "Who was the nicest one of the bunch? Walter. To my mom, to my sister, to the bread guy in the grocery store, to the guy pumping the gas. He was also a ferocious competitor who had the misfortune of playing for a decade with virtually no real good players around him. Finally at the end came along some guys who could play. It was great. The old adage is, they love you when you're young and they love you when you're old, but in the middle nobody loves you. Nobody felt that way with Walter. They loved him the whole 13 years. He transcended the game."

In Chicago people wept when Payton died on November 1, 1999. Dozens of fans called into TV and radio talk shows and couldn't get through their comments without breaking down. At his public funeral service, held at Soldier Field, many fans wore Payton's number 34 uniform and carried banners with his photograph on them. The service was attended by many of his former teammates and coaches, his family and friends, the governor, the mayor, and thousands who didn't know him but wanted to honor him. Mike Singletary said if Walter could see all the tears, he would say, "Hold everything—I'm on hallowed ground. I'm running hills. I'm running on clouds. I'm running on stars. I'm on the moon."

In February of that year, Payton had announced that he had a rare and incurable kidney disease. That day Payton said he needed a transplant, and he admitted when asked that he was scared.

"Hell, yeah, I'm scared. Wouldn't you be?" Payton said.

By that May, he was close enough to the top of the donor

list that he needed a thorough physical to determine if he was healthy enough for a transplant. His physical revealed that he had a malignant tumor in his liver. Payton was shocked to find out he had cancer, which meant he was not fit enough to have a transplant. At the same time, without a transplant, he could not get strong enough to withstand chemotherapy.

Near the end of his life, Payton had lost about 60 pounds, and the whites of his eyes had yellowed because of his failing kidney. He died at his home in Barrington, Illinois, surrounded by his family and close friends. Walter Payton was 45.

"It's still hard to believe that he was the first guy in our group to pass away," says Emery Moorehead. "That was a huge shocker, because he was in the best shape of all of us. He was the best-conditioned athlete we had."

"Nobody worked harder, nobody was more disciplined about his body," says Mike Ditka. "That's the tragedy of Walter. He was the strongest guy we had, pound for pound, and then at the end to see what that disease could do to him."

In 1985 Thomas Sanders had been a rookie running back. A ninth-round pick from Texas A&M, he was the 246th player chosen. In other words, he was a guy whom many superstars would probably ignore. After Sanders found out he made the Bears, he says Payton walked up and shook his hand. Then Payton shook the hand of every other rookie who made the final roster.

"Right before he passed away," remembers Sanders, "my wife and I were on our way home from church, and we were passing the exit to his house. My wife said, 'Why don't you go and see him?' And I had seen him before, but I hadn't seen him since he had gotten real bad. I didn't want to go. My wife said, 'If you were any kind of friend, you would go and see him.'

"We went there, and they were all coming out of the

house—his wife, his mom, some other people I didn't know. I asked them where Walter was, and they said he would be out in a second. So I'm standing there talking, and here he comes, walking out of the house. Of course, he was moving slow, but he was walking, and that's when I noticed that his feet were all wrapped up and they were swollen. I didn't know what was going on. I knew he was very sick, but I didn't know why his feet were swollen. He sat down in the car, and he said, 'It's good to see you. We have to get together and go to dinner or something.' And the last thing he said to me was, 'Take care of your family.' That was the last thing he said. And I said to myself, this man is dying and he's telling me to take care of my family. He's not even concerned about himself.

"That will always stick with me. I don't know if you ever met him, but just sitting and talking to him, he was a real and genuine person. There wasn't any phoniness in him. Did he have times when he wasn't up to par as far as wanting to do everything that people wanted him to do? Of course, because he's human. Sometimes you don't want to be bothered. But all around, he was a person who wanted to help. And it didn't matter who you were. If you needed some help, Walter was there."

CHAPTER 7

|||||||||||||||||||||||||||||||||||||||||||||||||||||||||||||||||||||||||||||||

MONSTER HITS AND BOUNTIES

A s the 9–0 Bears prepared for their home game against Detroit on November 10, Fridgemania continued gaining momentum. About half the calls coming into the Bears' PR department for personal appearances by the players were now specifically requesting Perry. There were New York publishers offering book deals and magazine pieces on him in *Newsweek, People,* and *Omni.* Earlier in the season, the rookie defensive tackle could command $500 in return for signing autographs for one hour. Now a full-blown sensation, he was asking for and receiving $5,000 an hour.

On November 11, the Fridge flew to Manhattan to appear on *Late Night with David Letterman.* As he watched from a monitor in the green room at 30 Rock, he was preceded on the set by Emmanuel Lewis, the 14-year-old star of the sitcom *Webster.*

"He's a good kid," said Perry. "Man, last time I was that small was when I was born."

The New York audience cheered when Perry came out. Letterman, a lifelong sports fan, seemed charmed. First he asked Perry if he would *throw* a pass next, and Perry told him, yes, that could be in the making. Then Letterman wanted to know if it was true that when Perry was in college he once drank 48 beers after Clemson beat North Carolina. Fridge said it was true, adding with perfect timing, "It was a big game." After the show was over and Perry had signed autographs for the NBC staff, Letterman proved he knew more about the Chicago Bears than the typical talk-show host. He walked around 30 Rock in a Walter Payton jersey.

Payton was hot then, too, but in a different way than Perry was. Payton was making *his* mark on the field. He had four straight games of 100 yards or more, including his 192 the previous Sunday against the hated Packers. As everyone started noting that Payton and the running game were in a nice groove, it was impossible to ignore that McMahon and the passing game had fallen off. In the last five games, McMahon had thrown only four touchdown passes. In the ugly 16–10 victory at Green Bay, he had been 9 for 20 for 91 yards.

Still, the Bears were 9–0 for the first time ever, so their fans weren't too concerned that the offense was grinding it out instead of lighting it up. The fans became concerned, however, when they found out McMahon was struggling because he was injured. The week before the Detroit game, the Bears revealed that McMahon had sprained his right shoulder during the first quarter at Green Bay. What the team didn't disclose was that his shoulder had hurt him ever since the 49ers game in week six. Now it was inflamed and throbbing, and at one point, McMahon says, surgery was considered.

Though the Bears didn't list him on their injury report, McMahon missed that whole week of practice, and all the old scary questions were raised in the city: Will McMahon play this Sunday against Detroit? If he's out, will he be back in time for the playoffs? Is this season just another cruel mirage?

McMahon didn't play that week, but for now the Bears were still safe. The Lions were so bad at stopping the run, they were ranked last in the NFL. That Sunday at Soldier Field was also cold, wet, and windy, unsuited for passing much anyway. So the Bears kept the ball on the ground for their first 21 plays, virtually unheard of but effective. They ran the ball 55 times over the course of the game, while Fuller threw 13 passes. Payton rushed for 107 yards, and fullback Matt Suhey gained 102. Buddy Ryan's 46 defense, impressive the last four weeks but now turning into something spectacular, recorded four sacks, two fumble recoveries, and two interceptions while allowing Detroit a paltry 106 yards of total offense.

The Bears rolled over the Lions, 24–3, pushing their record to 10–0, but there was danger ahead. The Cowboys were next on the schedule, the Dolphins two weeks later, and the games would be on the road at Dallas and Miami. And although shoulder surgery was no longer being discussed, for the moment McMahon was out indefinitely.

Getting fired up for the Cowboys wasn't an issue. The Bears had a number of reasons to want to destroy them. Chicago had last beaten Dallas in 1971, then lost the next six encounters—meaning nobody on these Bears had ever defeated the Cowboys. Ditka had coached only once against his mentor, Tom Landry, in 1984 at Soldier Field. In an unguarded moment after the Bears lost 23–14, Ditka blamed himself and admitted how much the game had meant to him.

"I got uptight. I choked. I really wanted to win that one," said Ditka.

More recently, in August 1985, the Bears and the Cowboys had played in the preseason. Dallas won, 15–13, but the real story was all the fights the players got into. Most of the scuffles involved the Bears' offensive linemen and the Cowboys' defensive linemen. In one of the feature bouts, Keith Van Horne got into a boxing match with Ed "Too Tall" Jones.

In the game's most dramatic skirmish, Randy White hit Mark Bortz over the head with a helmet—which White had just ripped off the head of Van Horne.

"Randy was kind of nuts," says Van Horne. "Randy looked at me at one point, and he goes, 'I'm gonna break your balls!' And he's, like, gesturing with his hands, like he's gonna snap 'em in half."

After six of the Bears were fined $300 apiece—and White was thrown out of the game and fined $1,000—Dan Hampton said of the regular-season rematch at Texas Stadium: "It's going to be World War Three in November." Lest anyone didn't get it the first time, Hampton later added, "They better have that little cart gassed up that they use to carry people off."

So, indeed, the Bears had sufficient incentive. There were the six straight losses to the Cowboys. There was all that bad blood from the preseason. And then there was always that annoying nickname.

"They were America's Team. But that was *self*-accreditation," says Gary Fencik. "If you asked any other players in the league, I can't imagine they'd say, 'Yeah, that's how we look at it, they're America's Team.' That whole thing was a bit much. However, I will say this: They were America's cheerleaders."

Football players by nature are sarcastic. Violent and sarcastic. While the violence would have to wait until that Sunday, the sarcasm reached new heights as the game approached.

"There were a lot of comments that week at practice," says linebacker Cliff Thrift. " 'Don't forget, you're going up against America's Team.' But clearly we thought we were the better team. So the America's Team thing wasn't even a slap in the face. We thought it was a joke."

"We considered ourselves America's Team," recalls rookie

kicker Kevin Butler. "And going into that game, we were going out there to try and take that slogan away from them. I remember the defense sitting around and talking about how many quarterbacks they were going to knock out that day."

On top of it all there was Ditka, who couldn't stop talking all week about his great respect for Tom Landry and the Cowboys, where he had played and assistant-coached for 13 years.

"Ditka revered that team," says cornerback Leslie Frazier, "but that kind of motivated the guys on our defense. Buddy Ryan said, 'Who cares about the Cowboys? We're gonna kick the shit out of the Cowboys.' So we had one of our coaches showing respect for the Cowboys and another coach totally disrespecting them and what they stood for."

In 1985 the Cowboys were somewhere between their glory years and their bottom. During the 1970s, they had played in five of the decade's ten Super Bowls, beating the Dolphins in 1971 and the Broncos in 1977. By the late 1980s, they were a broken dynasty, plummeting all the way down to 1–15 in 1989.

On November 17, 1985, as the 10–0 Bears took the field at Texas Stadium, the Cowboys were 7–3 and leading the NFC East, arguably the best division in football. On paper it seemed to be a pivotal game between an emerging powerhouse and an established one. In Dallas the fans had been scrambling for their tickets, which were reportedly tougher to get than even a game against the rival Redskins. On CBS, the game would be shown to 68 percent of the country, compared to 30 percent of the country for the typical regular-season NFL game. And it turned out CBS made the right decision: Chicago against Dallas was the highest-rated game on the network in ten years.

Even though the game itself was a drubbing.

By halftime, the Bears led 24–0, and it appeared as if Dallas had already quit. The final was 44–0, the worst defeat in the 26-year history of the Cowboys and the first time in 15 years they were shut out. Thrift, who grew up in Oklahoma but was born in Dallas, says he had rounded up a large number of tickets and then handed them out to his relatives. But after the game, he says, "they were all pissed off at me because we humiliated their Cowboys on national TV. And then it made the cover of *Sports Illustrated*. Front cover of *Sports Illustrated*—Bears 44, Cowboys nothing. Then they were *really* complaining and pissed off at me. I was like, well, get your damn tickets somewhere else then. Gol dang."

The Dallas offense took a terrible physical beating, especially Danny White and Gary Hogeboom, the embattled quarterbacks who were sacked six times. White was knocked out of the game in the second quarter by a blitzing Otis Wilson. White came back to start the third quarter and was knocked out by Wilson again. The second time White was carried off on a stretcher. Before the debacle was over, the Cowboys punted ten times, never advanced past the Bears' 38-yard line, and had two of their four interceptions run back for touchdowns by Richard Dent and Mike Richardson.

Still filling in for McMahon, Fuller connected on only 9 of 24 passes, but those nine completions were good for 164 yards. Payton gained 132 yards. The Refrigerator played fullback and ran for a yard. Butler kicked three field goals, one from 44 yards and one from 46, continuing his sizzling rookie season. Punter Maury Buford kept pinning the Cowboys down near their goal line, not a fun place to be against the Chicago defense.

The 1985 Bears were now 11–0, the first team to clinch their division, and the only unbeaten team in the NFL. And yet after the Bears had looked so incredibly strong against the Cowboys, the players looked at Ditka and saw a man with mixed feelings.

"He was coaching against his mentor, who he absolutely respected," says linebacker Ron Rivera. "And even after we won, Ditka seemed a little sad about it. He wanted to beat Tom Landry, but not that badly."

Ditka did not make it public, but he says he was angry that day at Buddy Ryan, who came into the game badmouthing the Cowboys. Then, once the game was played—and the outcome long decided—Ditka couldn't believe it when Ryan kept pouring it on.

"What was it, 44–0 or something?" says Ditka. "And we're still blitzing at the end of the game? That makes a lot of sense. I had to tell the guy, 'Quit blitzing, what the hell you gonna accomplish? You knocked out two quarterbacks.'

"I mean, it's crazy. And that game was embarrassing to me because there's no man in football I had more respect for than Coach Landry. It was just our time. We were a better team than them, period. Let it go at that. Did we rub it in? The score would indicate we rubbed something in. I told him [Landry] after the game I was sorry that it went the way it went. He said, 'You have to do what you have to do. You have a heck of a football team.' But still, that didn't change the way I felt. I'm sure somebody else would tell you, that was the Cowboys, America's Team, it was good to stick their noses in it. I didn't feel that way."

After taking apart the Cowboys on national television, some of the players say the 1985 Bears became America's Team. Their contrarian quarterback has a different view.

"They'd been America's Team for what, 20 years or whatever?" says McMahon. "But they were pretty much done in '82 when the 49ers beat them in the championship game. They didn't do much after that for a while, not really until the nineties. But even after we beat them, we weren't really America's Team. We were the anti-heroes."

Of course, anti-heroes are seductive, especially when they romp 44–0. It was also against the Cowboys when Dave Duerson and Otis Wilson started barking to each other after a sack. It started on the sidelines as the Cowboy fans were heckling Chicago's defensive players who were seated on the bench. Duerson inexplicably barked at the fans. Wilson looked at Duerson and started barking. Then they both began barking when they went back on the field. Afterward a reporter asked Duerson where the barking had come from. Duerson said, "We're just a bunch of junkyard dogs." The nickname stuck.

Leslie Frazier says the shellacking in Dallas cemented the Bears' reputation as the most entertaining team in the NFL. "You're playing the Dallas Cowboys and you're dismantling those guys and you're doing it with personality," says Frazier. "So the fans arc saying, 'Man, these guys are having *fun*. And they're kicking butt at the same time.' So the respect for the Bears, especially our defense, really went to another level after that game."

Nobody could deny that the defense was on a rampage. Over the last two weeks, Detroit had scored three points and Dallas none. The following week, the Bears posted their second straight shutout, thumping the Falcons at home, 36–0. This meant, in the past three games, the Bears had outscored their opponents 104–3.

But that was only one of the gaudy statistics. As the *New York Times* pointed out after Chicago routed Atlanta to improve to 12–0, there were other "amazing facts about the Bears: 1. The defense has allowed just three touchdowns in the last seven games and none in the last 13 quarters. 2. When they beat the New England Patriots early in the season, 20–7, the Patriots had the ball on the Bears side of the field for all of 21 seconds. 3. Seven players have intercepted three or more passes, and four have five or more sacks. 4. With three safeties, they are one short of tying the National Football League record for most in a season. 5. Through 12 weeks of play, the defense leads the league in—take a deep breath—fewest points allowed (127), fewest touchdowns allowed (15), fewest yards allowed (256.9 per game), fewest rushing yards allowed (82.3 per game), most sacks (50), most interceptions (30), and most interceptions returned for touchdowns (4)."

The Bears had accomplished all this without Todd Bell and Al Harris, who had both been hailed by Buddy Ryan as key elements in the success of the 1984 defense. Throughout their protracted holdouts, Ryan had lobbied Chicago's front office to sign them, but the last time general manager Jerry Vanisi had talked to either player or his agent was on October 15, the trading deadline. Now it was late November, the Bears were 12–0, and Bell and Harris were the only unsigned players left in the NFL. Furthermore, their replacements, Duerson and Marshall, were emerging as young stars.

Bell and Harris had no leverage, and management knew it. The point of no return came on November 23. There were now 30 days left in the regular season, and under NFL rules, Bell and Harris could no longer play for anybody in the league that year. With their decision to hold out irreversible, they joined only a handful of NFL players who had ever missed a whole season because they demanded more money.

"It's a darn shame," said Bears president Michael McCaskey.

"I would think there's a chance they will play next year,"

said Vanisi. "We'll negotiate next February and offer them a contract."

Bell didn't talk to the press when his phone began ringing, but Harris told reporters, "I don't think I'm done with football. So many circumstances could change. I don't know what might happen."

Given the '85 Bears' remarkable season, Dan Hampton calls the season-long holdout "the worst mistake of their professional lives."

"Todd Bell had a terrific year in '84 and made the Pro Bowl," says Hampton. "Al Harris had been around for five years, and although he never completely nailed down a starting job, I guess he thought he should be paid like a starter. Todd Bell thought he should be paid like one of the best safeties in the business, even though he had only done it for one year. They felt like they had to stand on principle. But physically, mentally, emotionally, it hurt them. But nobody told them to sit out. That was their choice."

As the NFL season rolled on without Bell and Harris, the accolades kept coming in for the team's extraordinary defense. The same week the *New York Times* raved about Ryan's unit ("For the 12–0 Bears, Defense Mauls with Imagination"), *Sports Illustrated* ("The Brawny and Brainy Bears") and *Newsweek* ("The Bears: Honey of a Team") also ran admiring feature stories. It was around this time when all the talk began that the 1985 Bears might have the best defense in NFL history. It was also when the talk of bounties started.

Bounties had been around the NFL forever. They were financial incentives, usually offered by coaches, to knock players out of games with ferocious hits. Some bounties were general—knock out anyone in the other uniform and pick up some extra bucks—and some bounties were directed at

specific players. Most frequently, they were placed on starting quarterbacks, since a second-string quarterback was
second-string for a reason.

In 1989, as head coach of the Philadelphia Eagles, Ryan
would be accused of putting bounties on Dallas quarterback
Troy Aikman and place kicker Luis Zendejas. The charge
was initially made in a postgame press conference, held by
an angry Cowboys head coach, Jimmy Johnson. Ryan dismissed the claim as ridiculous, but the Dallas fans and media
weren't convinced. Hadn't the '85 Bears been accused of
bounties, and wasn't their bellicose defensive leader Buddy
Ryan?

The '85 Bears became associated with bounties after
they beat the Cowboys 44–0, the game in which Otis Wilson
knocked out Danny White twice. The next day cornerback
Mike Richardson made a remark to reporters about players
buying lunches for anyone who knocked out a quarterback.
Richardson later said he was only joking, but his comments
got back to the league office in New York, where Commissioner Pete Rozelle wrote a letter to the Bears warning against
such tactics. This issue would surface again just five games
later, when Wilber Marshall leveled Detroit quarterback Joe
Ferguson in the regular-season finale. According to several
Bear players, Ferguson was unconscious before even hitting
the ground.

So . . . did the 1985 Bears put bounties on other players?

Not every Bear is eager to discuss it.

"There were discussions behind closed doors that I can't
comment on. How's that for an answer?" says safety Jeff Fisher.

"I don't want to be the player who goes there," says linebacker Clift Thrift.

But then Thrift goes there, sort of, anyway. "Buddy Ryan

would say little subtle things like, 'The best way to defend this guy is to put him out of the game.' Nobody has to be a rocket scientist to figure that out."

But . . . was cash ever involved? Or maybe free lunches, like Richardson said?

"If there was a bounty set, I wasn't aware of them until Mike Richardson made that remark," says the team's PR director, Ken Valdiserri. "Whether anything ever exchanged hands, I don't know. I know that a letter came from the NFL, and then an internal meeting resulted from that. The players were told to just cool their jets if this stuff was going on, that this was against the NFL rules if we were really going down that path. The players were expected to stay within the rules and not be exchanging anything other than high-fives or pats on the ass when someone made a significant hit."

Cornerback Leslie Frazier says Ryan read the letter from Rozelle to the defensive players during a meeting. As for offering bounties to the players, Frazier says he never heard Ryan do it. "But, yes," Frazier says, "Buddy would promote knocking out other people's quarterbacks. He would tell us, if a quarterback tried to scramble, 'Take him out at the knees. Don't be tackling him high. We're going to find out how good their second quarterback is.' That was the mind-set, and Buddy really pushed that."

Says linebacker Brian Cabral, "We never had a bounty, but that was the name of the game. Let's get the quarterback. Let's knock him out. Buddy's favorite phrase was, 'Let's open up a new can of quarterbacks.' "

There were different ways to knock out a quarterback. Rookie linebacker Jim Morrissey says if any of the Bears made an interception, "Buddy always said—and this is illegal today—that he better see ten other guys going after the quarterback. He wanted their quarterback down if there was an interception."

"Buddy talked about that religiously," says Fencik. "Back then, an interception was one of those times when you could legitimately go after the quarterback. But as far as bounties go, that was mostly just BS. I don't know that anybody ever collected a bounty. We would just talk about it. Number one, it had to be a clean hit. And it had to be a knockout. But you didn't need the bounty. You just wanted the glory."

Dave Duerson, Kevin Butler, and Dan Hampton all say the '85 Bears *did* put bounties on opposing players. But they say the players did it, not the coaches.

"We had our little banks for the hit of the day and stuff like that," says Duerson. "We weren't trying to kill anybody. We just wanted them on the sidelines for 60 minutes. We were like, play next week, and play your ass off. But not this week."

Says Butler, "It was a team thing. It wasn't just the defense. We'd be sitting around before we'd go out for the opening kickoff, and the guys on our special teams would be saying, 'I got a hundred for a recovered kickoff fumble.' Then somebody else would say, 'I'll make it two hundred.' Then you'd start hearing a defensive player say, 'I got a hundred for a quarterback knocked out.' We'd be up to the third quarterback during the game, trying to knock the third quarterback out.

"Today the NFL doesn't like quarterbacks getting knocked out of games," adds Butler. "They've proven that over the years by changing the rules. They want to protect the quarterback. But if you go back and look at NFL films, it was a more violent game when we played. Nobody said, 'Let's go out there and hurt this guy so he's never playing again.' But if your defense knows that we've got a better chance to win with that second quarterback in? Well, when we're blitzing—and that's what we did that season—they're gonna try to knock that guy out cold."

"Buddy Ryan had nothing to do with the bounties," says Hampton. "We [the players] would all take turns putting bounties on guys. We'd watch a receiver be a chicken-shit and sneak up and crack some linebacker in the back, and we'd say, 'I got a hundred for anybody that knocks that guy out.' We're not saying, put him in the hospital, we're saying, hit him so hard it knocks him out. Then everyone started going, ooh, the Bears are so violent. Well, hello, pro football is violent. So, yeah, we had bounties on guys. If I'm engaged with a guard and a tackle turns and spears me while I'm not looking, yeah, you're darn right we're putting a bounty on him. One time [Pittsburgh Steeler receiver] Louis Lipps tried to come back and crack-back-block on Otis Wilson. Otis turned and gave him a textbook forearm shiver to the face and just knocked him out. Then we heard that everyone in the league was going to come after Otis. So we started telling guys, 'Yeah? You come after him, you're next.' To me, it was just a great era in pro football. We knew what we were."

In his best-selling autobiography, *Out of Bounds,* the great running back Jim Brown devoted significant time to the subject of hitting, the violent nature of the NFL, and whether at that high level there were still players who could be intimidated.

His emphatic answer was yes.

"There were some nonviolent players, and their reputations preceded them," wrote Brown. "If a guy was a hitter, he was called just that—a Hitter. 'That guy's a hitter, he'll break your neck. He'll stick his head and his shoulders right in there.'

" 'That guy is a non-hitter. He's gonna try and find a better way.' "

Brown, who was never easily impressed, seemed nothing less than awed by the '85 Bears defense. "The Bears beat people up," wrote Brown. "Most defenses in the NFL have maybe five hitters. I can honestly say the Bears had 11 hitters, and I've never seen a team that had 11 hitters on defense. The pressure they exerted was severe. Forget about quarterbacks having time to pass—runners couldn't even get started. The Bears were shoving their blockers into the backfield."

Linebacker Brian Cabral says he thinks the '85 Bears defense may have been the most frightening in NFL history. "Because it *is* intimidating when quarterbacks get knocked down time after time," says Cabral. "It *is* intimidating when you got people swarming. Yeah, we had great athletes, but there was also a taste for blood. It was like a race to get to the ball. Buddy's whole mentality was, sic 'em."

To be perfectly candid, says Mike Tomczak, he was intimidated that season at practice. As the third-string quarterback behind McMahon and Fuller, it was his job to run the scout team each week. "You're taking a five-step drop and already there are people right in your face," says Tomczak. "So I would take shots at practice. They weren't trying to hurt me, but they wanted me to know they were around me. A lot of quarterbacks were rattled against our defense. Danny White was rattled. Jim Zorn at Green Bay. Phil Simms to a degree, and Dieter Brock, both in the playoffs. Tony Eason in the Super Bowl."

Says defensive end Tyrone Keys, "People were afraid because a lot of guys got knocked out by us that season. I saw Singletary knock out Sammy Winder. Sammy was sound asleep. I saw Joe Ferguson sound asleep. I saw Archie Manning after his career ended, and he said the reason he quit football was because of what the Chicago Bears did to him. He got sacked 12 times in a game [in 1984], and if he got sacked 12 times, you can imagine how many times he got hit."

The art of intimidation was not confined to the defensive side of the ball. With Jim Covert at left tackle, Mark Bortz at left guard, Jay Hilgenberg at center, Kurt Becker or Tom Thayer at right guard, and Keith Van Horne at right tackle, Chicago's offensive line was big, lean, and aggressive. Thayer and Becker were known in particular for being nasty. Both had no qualms about using the cut-blocking technique, chopping down on the outside of a defensive player's knees.

"We cut a lot," says Thayer. "But the defensive linemen and linebackers all wore thigh pads and knee pads then. Nowadays none of these guys wear thigh pads. If I was still in the NFL today, I would have every single defensive player hating me because I would cut you every chance I got. I would take my helmet and shoulder pads and drive it through your thighs so you'd be more worried about me than you would be about making tackles. Fred Smerlas wrote a book one time, and he called me the dirtiest player in the NFL because of cut-blocking. So it's a very intimidating block."

"There were ways for the offensive linemen to impose their will," says Becker. "If you had a one-on-one block, you could drive your opponent to the ground. You could work over a defensive tackle with your teammate. One guy holds him up, and the other guy comes in and cleans him up. One of the ways to attack guys was the cut-block. The NFL keeps changing the rules about the cut-block, but it was a legal tool of the offensive line. And it was a very effective tool. So we used it. We would cut your ass and say, 'That's the way it's gonna be all day long.' "

On the defensive side of the ball, none of the other Bears could ever quite figure out Fencik, the civilized Yale man who turned savage on Sundays. Fencik says for the most part he didn't go out of his way to intimidate his opponents. But if the opportunity arose, he would send a physical message to wide receivers coming across the middle, and this was back in the day when there was no five-yard bump rule.

"So you could hit a guy anytime, anywhere, even if he didn't have the ball. You could just clock him," says Fencik. "So you would take your shots early on a guy and then see how tough he was when he came across the middle for that tough catch in the fourth quarter when his team really needed it."

In his classic NFL book *About Three Bricks Shy of a Load,* Roy Blount Jr. recounted the season he spent with the 1973 Pittsburgh Steelers. In a chapter titled "Contact," Blount wrote, "Will Walls, the legendary scout, tended to see good hitting as an aspect of certain people's nature. If he ever once saw a prospect shrink from an impact, he wrote that prospect off. 'Once a flincher, always a flincher,' he said."

Blount wrote that Walls also told him, "You know when they say about a player, 'He hangs around bars all the time and gets in a lot of fights.' Well, he likes contact."

The Steelers had their share of bar fighters, Blount concluded. The main bar fighters on the 1985 Bears were Hampton and McMichael. And they didn't mix it up at just *any* drinking establishment.

"They would get into fights at biker bars," says Leslie Frazier. "And Buddy Ryan promoted it. He wanted his linemen to go out and be fighting in bars. Steve and Dan were inseparable during that time. They did a lot of crazy stuff together."

"What was that movie with Mac Davis and Nick Nolte?" asks Hampton. "*North Dallas Forty?* McMichael and I kind of thought of ourselves like that. Drinking, carousing, tough guys. Every team, the badasses on a good team are your defensive linemen. Randy White in Dallas, John Matuszak for the Raiders. When *you* think of the Steelers, you think of Franco Harris and Terry Bradshaw, but the first guys *I* think about are Joe Green and Dwight White. Those are the badasses! Well, that's who we wanted to be. Chasing blondes, going out, it was a band of brothers thing. We'd do all kind of crazy stuff. Like go into biker bars and try to defy them so they'd start a fight with us. But by the end of the night we'd be slapping them on the back and we'd be drinking with them. There were a lot of babes in the hot tub, that type of thing. It was just a great time to be The Guys."

When Hampton stepped on the field, he says, he rarely thought about intimidating the men who blocked him. Hampton just lined up and played his relentless game.

"I had heard about all that stupidity since eighth grade," he says. 'The first play of the game, you line up and you jack their jaw.' What if the fucking guy goes 80 yards for a touchdown? You think Buddy Ryan is gonna be impressed because you tried to whack somebody in the head while the running back went up the middle? Did some people do that? Maybe. I didn't. What's the most intimidating play in football? The defense knocking the shit out of the quarterback. You know, I got the pleasure of getting to know Dick Butkus. Most intimidating man in the world of pro football. Everyone was afraid of him. And the Bears used to have Doug Atkins and Ed O'Bradovich. They were on the '63 championship team. Everyone in the league was afraid of the Monsters of the Midway. That's why they were *called* the Monsters of the Midway. 'Cause they were badasses. I used to tell McMichael, 'That could be us! That's what we want right there, what those guys were!' That was a conscious decision, so that was

how we *played.* We played the game tough. We wanted everybody fearing for their lives. We wanted everyone saying, 'We
gotta go through Chicago.' Just like the Pittsburgh Steelers
had everybody scared in the seventies. We were that team
in 1985."

CHAPTER 8

||||||||||||||||||||||||||||||||||||||||||||||||||||||||||||||||||||||||||||||||

BEARS HAVE (TOO MUCH) FUN IN MIAMI

The Miami Dolphins were next, in a hugely hyped game at the Orange Bowl on *Monday Night Football.* As Mike Singletary recalled in his 1986 book *Calling the Shots,* "It never ended. The week before our December 2 Monday night game against Miami, reporters fell from the sky like a seven-inch snow. We were completely covered. They waited for us in our lockers and called our homes; the practice field was staked out like the Democratic National Convention. Everyone wanted answers from a team that hadn't given up a touchdown in its last 13 quarters, was 12–0, and was on its way to immortality."

The only unbeaten team in the NFL, the Bears had already clinched the NFC Central Division and home-field advantage throughout the NFC playoffs. They had outscored their last two opponents (Atlanta and Dallas) by an astonishing 90–0. In comparison, the Dolphins were 8–4 and unsure of a play-off spot in the AFC East, where there was a three-way fight with the Patriots and Jets.

So why wasn't Mark Duper more impressed?

"We'll beat the Bears," said the short, tough Miami receiver. "I promise you, we'll beat them." A few days later Duper told reporters, "We are going to kick the Bears' butts. The Bears are in for the treat of their lives."

Las Vegas liked the Bears, but only by three and a half points. At first glance, this was surprising, but the oddsmakers were aware of certain statistics the public frequently wasn't, and this knowledge influenced the spread. For example, the Bears were 0–8 in *Monday Night Football* road games. Miami was 15–3 in *Monday Night Football* home games. The Dolphins had won 17 of their last 18 overall home games. They were 8–0, all-time, when they were underdogs at the loud, sweaty Orange Bowl. Thus they were still underdogs against Chicago, but only by three and a half.

Furthermore, *everyone* knew this game was deeply personal for Miami. Don Shula's 1972 Dolphins were the only NFL team to go undefeated, finishing 14–0 in the regular season and 17–0 overall. Since then the league had added two regular-season games, which meant if the '85 Bears could run the table, they would be the winningest team in NFL history at 19–0. Thus even the rock-jawed Shula admitted how much he wanted to keep the '85 Bears from surpassing the '72 Dolphins.

"It's important to us," said Shula. "We'd like to see that stay in the record books for a while."

The matchup between quarterbacks favored Miami in a big way. While the Bears still had Fuller starting instead of an injured McMahon, the Dolphins had Dan Marino, who in 1984 had produced one of the most spectacular NFL seasons ever. Marino broke six single-season passing records, including most touchdown passes (48) and passing yards (5,084). While winning the league's Most Valuable Player award, Marino led the Dolphins to Super Bowl XIX, where they lost 38–16 to the same 49ers who had crushed the Bears 23–0 in the NFC title game.

The week before the Bears arrived in Miami, the city

seemed nearly as giddy as it had been in the buildup to the Super Bowl. Dolphin owner Joe Robbie said he had never seen Miami "this upside down" in the 20 years since the team had been created. Before the Bears left for the game, Chicago was upside down too. As Singletary wrote in *Calling the Shots*, "Most of us were fielding 15 to 20 personal appearance requests a day. Ten guys—Ditka, Walter, Fencik, Hampton, Gault, McMahon, Fuller, Wrightman, Tomczak, and Van Horne—had radio shows. Ditka had three TV ads running, Walter was doing a spot for Diet Coke, the Black-n-Blues Brothers were working on a poster of the offensive line for the local Chevy dealers. Fridge? Well, he was beyond belief. Mega-stardom."

In addition to those potential distractions, the frigid conditions throughout the Midwest were conspiring against the Bears, one of the league's few cold-weather teams without their own indoor practice facility. Instead, the Bears prepared for their big Monday night game at Miami on the frozen grass practice fields in Lake Forest.

"It was really cold in Chicago for a couple weeks, and we didn't have any really good practices," recalls Jay Hilgenberg. "There was some talk among the players about maybe going down a few days early and getting acclimated to the Miami weather. But I don't think it was even considered."

"That genius Mike McCaskey didn't think we needed an indoor workout facility," says Dan Hampton. "So we would go outside and virtually just stand on the snow and ice for two hours a day and freeze instead of have a good practice."

December 2, 1985, fell on the Monday night after Thanksgiving. It was 13 degrees in Chicago and 75 in Miami, with 82 percent humidity, as the 9:00 P.M. kickoff approached in the warm, sticky tropics. It probably didn't help the players' stamina either that after they ate their team dinner Sunday night at the hotel, a bunch of the Bears ignored curfew and partied all the way through to Monday morning.

"Every time we had a game in Florida, some Bears fans were going too—and the Sunday night before that Miami game, I think I saw just about all of them out somewhere," Steve McMichael recalled in his 2004 book *Tales from the Chicago Bears Sideline.* "I think we started out at Hooters and it just degenerated from there. We were thinking, 'We've got plenty of time to recover. It's not a 12 o'clock game, we don't play till late.' "

"Oh my God! Absolutely!" says Kevin Butler when asked if any Bears went out partying in South Beach that Sunday night. "Personally I was with some friends on a cigarette boat at about two in the morning going up and down the coast. We were enjoying the weather probably more than the opportunity at hand, but going undefeated just wasn't the goal of our team. We had already clinched our division. McMahon wasn't playing. I just don't think we were caught up in that record as much as Miami was. And on South Beach, no doubt about it, everybody wanted to be around us."

On Monday night at the Orange Bowl, a few hours before the pregame warm-up, the screwing around continued as several of the Bears acted like tourists who had never been to Florida.

"Our whole offensive line was there early," says Hilgenberg. "It was such a warm night, and we all went outside in shorts and T-shirts, and McMahon came out with us, and we're all out there running routes and playing catch and messing around for about 20, 30 minutes. We came in just soaked with sweat, and Ditka got so pissed at us. He said, 'What are you doing wearing yourself out like that before a game?' "

All in all, says Hampton, "we were full of ourselves. We had a lot of hubris."

"Truthfully," says Fencik, "they wanted it more than we did. After beating the last two teams by 90–0, we weren't ready mentally for that game."

Meanwhile, waiting for the less-than-focused Bears was a proud NFL franchise determined to remain the only unbeaten team ever. To help mark the occasion, several of the '72 Dolphins were lined up on the Miami sideline that Monday night.

"I remember before the game they were standing there watching us, and I was like *wow*," says rookie safety Ken Taylor. "I was like, *Is that Larry Csonka? Is that Jim Kiick and Paul Warfield?* They all had their arms folded, and it was like they were trying to put the voodoo on us. They're standing with their legs kind of spread apart like Superman or something, and they got their big arms folded like they are measuring us up. It was all just kind of weird."

The night was young. It would soon get even weirder.

The Orange Bowl crowd started rocking before the kickoff, and Frank Gifford had to speak up to introduce what would become the highest-rated game in the 16 years of *Monday Night Football*. "We are live from the Orange Bowl at Miami Florida!" said Gifford. "There's a sellout crowd, of course, a wild air of anticipation! The undefeated Chicago Bears are in town to meet the Miami Dolphins! It should be a wild one!"

After ABC aired a few commercials, Gifford resumed his exuberant introduction. "I'm Frank Gifford, and we are glad you are with us tonight! We think we have what could be a classic! The undefeated Chicago Bears, they are 12–0, looking to go 13–0 against Miami! They are looking ahead, even beyond, to perhaps a 19–0 season! No football team has ever done that! The Dolphins in '72 went to 17!"

Joe Namath then dialed it back a little bit. "This is still a game of emotion. And if either team has an emotional edge tonight, it's the Miami Dolphins. They need this game to keep their playoff hopes realistic. Now, the Bears are a sensational team, but they haven't faced the likes of Dan Marino, Mark Clayton, and Mark Duper yet."

Then O. J. Simpson cranked it back up again. "When you talk about Chicago, you're talking about a happy team! These guys enjoy each other, they enjoy their coaches, they can't wait for game day, and normally that spells victory no matter what game you're playing!"

The Bears were happy, all right. So happy that Ditka and Ryan tried beating the shit out of each other at halftime.

But first, the first half.

The Bears received the ball, and their offense looked awful. First-and-ten, a short sideline pass to Dennis McKinnon—Fuller sailed it two feet over his head. Second-and-ten, Matt Suhey went off-tackle and barely fought his way back to the line of scrimmage. Third-and-ten, on a post pattern to McKinnon, Fuller made a decent throw but McKinnon dropped it. In case it wasn't yet clear this might be one of those nights, reliable Maury Buford shanked a 34-yard punt, and Miami's first possession began at its own 44.

The Chicago defense strutted onto the field having given up only three points in its previous three games. Its coordinator, Buddy Ryan, was routinely being hailed as a genius. There was talk that the Bears might have the most dominant defense of all time.

By halftime, Miami led 31–10.

By then, Jim Covert was thinking about his short conversation with Ryan a few days before the game. Ryan knew Covert had been Marino's roommate in college when they played together at Pittsburgh. Says Covert, "Buddy came up to me and said, 'We're going to blitz your asshole buddy this week and knock him on his ass.' I said, 'If you do, he'll kill you.'

"And he did, didn't he? They tried to come after him, and they couldn't get him on his ass, could they? Because if you look back at '85, the amazing thing about our defense was that you would see receivers running wide-ass open down the middle of the field, but the quarterback was on his ass. So it didn't matter if a guy was open. They brought so much pressure with that 46, and they confused so many people because they didn't know who to block or who was going to blitz, and so the quarterback was on his ass. So they tried to do that with Marino, but you can't do that with him because he got rid of the football so fast."

Buddy Ryan kept blitzing anyway, and Dan Marino kept making him pay. Ryan expected Marino to sit back there in the pocket, the way he normally did. But Shula was two steps ahead of Ryan that night. Marino kept dropping straight back into the pocket and then quickly rolling *outside* the pressure. Shula also kept bringing Nat Moore into the game, lining him up in the slot as a third receiver, and Ryan kept covering him with linebacker Wilber Marshall. Had Ryan adjusted out of the 46 and into the nickel package, it would have given the Bears an extra defensive back to cover Moore.

"Buddy was at fault that game," says Hampton. "Trying to cover Nat Moore with Wilber Marshall? That's 240 pounds on 180 pounds. It was a mismatch."

Keith Van Horne calls it "pride. I think Buddy's pride got in the way, and we paid for it."

Miami shredded Chicago in the first half, scoring on all five of its possessions. Marino already had completions of 52, 42, and 33 yards, 194 total yards passing, and two touchdown passes to Moore. Even on third-and-long—a dangerous circumstance for quarterbacks against the '85 Bears—Marino converted on third-and-18, third-and-19, and third-and-13. Marino looked fabulous. The defense looked lost.

Meanwhile, Ditka and Ryan were screaming at each other. It started after Miami blocked a punt at Chicago's six-yard line and the Bears allowed their fourth touchdown of the first half. Ditka yelled at Ryan in frustration, and Ryan yelled back.

Hampton says, "Ditka was right. He was basically saying, Hey, Buddy, quit being an asshole and put the nickel back in there on Nat Moore. Wilber can't do it. Buddy was saying, Screw you. Buddy thought Wilber Marshall could jump over buildings, but he was getting his ass wore out by Nat Moore. So Ditka was right and Buddy was wrong. But Buddy was too headstrong to admit it."

As the Bears went inside at halftime losing 31–10, Ditka and Ryan began to argue in the visitors' locker room. Then, in a new low even for their bizarre relationship, the two coaches had to be restrained by their players.

Everyone agrees there was an altercation, but different players have different memories of how physical it became. Brian Cabral remembers "just some pushing and shoving, which ended quickly once the players jumped in."

Leslie Frazier remembers that "they ended up coming to blows, and the players ended up pulling them apart. But it was an ugly scene when you got the head coach and defensive coordinator ready to be Muhammad Ali and Joe Frazier at the halftime of a game."

Maury Buford remembers that "they were physically going after each. The players had to jump in and break them up. I think a lot of teams, it really would have affected the psyche. But we just kind of laughed. I looked over there at McMahon, and we were like, *Damn, this is a crazy son of a bitch around here. Coaches fighting each other.*"

Not all of the players laughed off the halftime incident. Dave Duerson says, "It showcased the selfishness of both of them. It was as if they forgot about the players, the guys who are putting it out there out on the field. In that particular instance, both of them let us down with their own selfishness and arrogance."

Describing it as a "cat fight," Duerson says he was surprised they took it that far. But he adds that the season-long tension between Ryan and Ditka was especially apparent the week before the Bears left for Miami.

"For the three years that I had worked with Buddy, Mike had never come into our defensive meetings," says Duerson. "That week he popped his head in, and Buddy threw an eraser at him and screamed at him, 'These are my guys, these are my guys!' Ditka never came all the way in. He just poked his head in. When Buddy threw the eraser, Ditka left and shut the door.

"Then Ditka did a number of things during the Monday night game. He was pulling defensive starters out of the game and putting in subs. Ditka wanted to prove to Buddy this was his team, and he could pull starters off the field and put in reserves without even asking Buddy one iota. Then he and Buddy got into the fight at halftime. It was just a disruptive game all the way around for us."

When Ditka is asked what transpired that chaotic Monday night at the Orange Bowl, he says in his blunt fashion, "We got outcoached. They put Nat Moore in the slot as their hot receiver, and we covered him with a linebacker some of the time, and we covered him with a safety some of the time, and he chewed us up. When they went to a three-receiver set, we should have gone to a nickel defense immediately, but we didn't. Well, we got our ass whipped. So people can tell you anything they want. Just look at the film. So just write it down. We were outcoached by one of the greatest coaches in the league. So I don't feel too bad about that either. But in football you got to be flexible if you're a coach. You can't be *rigid*. You gotta be willing to change if things aren't working."

As for the halftime episode between him and Ryan, Ditka remembers it as "a lot of hollering and pushing. There was no fight, no punches thrown. But it was pretty ugly. It wasn't good for the team and wasn't good to be seen by the players, but that's what happened. Arguing about the defense, that's all—put the goddamn nickel back in there and play the defense and let's go. Well, you know, Buddy is Buddy and I am me. So whoever was right or wrong, I don't know. But it was a hell of an argument anyway."

It wasn't only Ryan who got outcoached by Shula that Monday night. Miami had the league's worst rushing defense, but Ditka decided the Bears should come out passing. Furthermore, Payton was in the midst of a hot streak with seven straight games of more than 100 yards, tying the all-time NFL record. But he didn't carry the ball against the Dolphins until the Bears trailed 10–7 late in the first quarter.

"We got outcoached offensively and defensively," says McMahon. "We got down early in the game, and I think Mike just kind of panicked. We kept throwing the ball and we're not a catchup, throw-the-ball football team. I think if we would have been patient and kept running, who knows how far Payton could have run for that night?"

Says Hampton, "We have the number-one running game in football, and Miami has the worst run defense. So what does genius Ditka do? We throw the ball. Meanwhile, Marino threw the ball like a rocket that night. How many times does every idiot armchair quarterback say, 'You've got a good quarterback? Then we're gonna run the ball and keep it away from you.' Well, *duh*! But Ditka is gonna outsmart them. They're expecting us to run so we are going to throw—with our backup quarterback Fuller."

Plain and simple, Ditka had gotten too cute. And even he later questioned his own play-calling that game. "I think we could have run the ball all day. I haven't seen them stop us running yet," Ditka said.

The strange doings didn't end in the second half. Fuller most of the night was throwing wild-high, but midway through the third quarter he threw his first TD pass of the season, and the Bears narrowed the lead to 38–24. That was still the score early in the fourth quarter when Fuller sprained his ankle and McMahon entered the game for the first time in a month.

"Jim didn't think he was going to play," says Jeff Fisher. "So he had some Heinekens on the beach on that Monday afternoon. He was knocking Heinekens down, and then Fuller got hurt and he had to go in."

McMahon says he doesn't recall how he spent that Monday afternoon, but he confirms that he didn't think he would play against Miami. Having missed the last three games with an injured right shoulder, the last time he had played was on November 3 against the Packers. The week the Bears faced Miami, McMahon says, he was finally throwing freely and could have started that night if Ditka wanted him to. But since he had missed one practice with a sprained ankle, he says Ditka told him he couldn't play.

According to McMahon, "I said, 'Look, I'm ready to go if you need me.' Ditka said, 'No, you're not playing.' He actually said, 'We're not going to have another Minnesota.' I will never forget that. I went, 'What? Why wouldn't you want another Minnesota?' "

Immediately McMahon had the Bears on the move, but his fourth-down interception in the end zone seemed to seal Chicago's fate with 6:12 to go. The next time the Bears got the ball, still behind 38–24, McMahon started giving the ball to Payton, who had largely been ignored earlier in the game when it really mattered. Now Payton had a chance to get his eighth consecutive 100-yard game, which would break the NFL record shared by O. J. Simpson and Earl Campbell.

Payton wound up rushing for 121 yards on 23 carries. In his *Chicago Tribune* column the following day, Bernie Lincicome pointedly questioned Ditka's priorities, writing that Payton's record "was the reason the Bears gave up trying to beat the Miami Dolphins. Ditka traded a chance for a perfect season in order to pad Payton's legend."

The columnist didn't know it, but the decision had been McMahon's.

"By the end of the game," says Van Horne, "McMahon was just telling us, 'They're sending in plays to throw the ball down the field.' And the game was pretty much decided by then. So McMahon said, 'To hell with that. We're gonna get Walter his 100 yards.' "

"We're 14 points down, and Ditka sends in a pass play," says McMahon. "So I got in the huddle, and I said, 'Look, boys, we're down 14 points. We are already in the playoffs. Let's get this man the yards he deserves.' Not one guy in the huddle had a problem with that. But Mike knew I didn't call the play when we lined up, so he starts yelling and screaming. I give the ball to Walter. They were only rushing three at this point, and he busts up for good yardage. Mike burns our last time-out and starts cussing me up and down. I said, 'Hey,

Mike, you know, they're dropping eight. Walter only needs about 15 more yards for his record.' Ditka said, '*What?*' I said, 'His record.'

"It finally kicked, in and then he said, 'Yeah, we'll get him his record. But first we're going to do this play.' So I just said, 'Okay.' Ditka gave me another pass. I went in the game, and I said, 'Boys, the shit is going to hit the fan, but we're going to run the ball again.' As soon as we lined up, I looked over, and he knew I didn't call it, and he threw his clipboard and his headset. I gave it to Walter again, and then it was pretty much done."

In the aftermath of their 38–24 loss on *Monday Night Football,* the Bears seemed much less alarmed than their fans and the media would prove to be.

"Hey, we're human," said Otis Wilson.

"This is not a catastrophe," said Singletary.

"Nobody's perfect, and we proved it," said Ditka. "Now it's what you do with it. Do you bounce back? We'll be back. They deserved to win, and we didn't. I hope they go as far as we're going to go and we play them again."

Back in Chicago, however, the hand-wringing started in earnest. In dissecting the team's first loss, everybody was asking: Was it simply poor strategy and bad execution? Or is it something deeper and thus harder to rein in? Are the '85 Bears overrated? Overconfident? Overexposed? What if they do make it to the team's first Super Bowl? Will they fall apart again if they have a rematch with Marino and Shula? Will they even advance that far, or will they turn into the '84 Cubs, who choked on it during the playoffs against Steve Garvey's Padres? Good thing they've already *clinched* a playoff spot, huh? Otherwise, maybe they'd bow to the pressure *before* then and never even get *into* the postseason, like the freaking '69

Cubs when they blew that huge lead in August to the freaking Amazing Mets. Hey, how long has it been now since *any* of our major sport teams won a championship? The Bulls last did it, uh, never? The Cubs last won it all in 1908? The White Sox in 1917? The Bears in 1963? Now it's already 1985 and . . . !!!

In other words, this was Chicago, and after the Miami game, people were rattled.

Today the '85 Bears themselves have varied perspectives on that peculiar night in the Orange Bowl where they lost their chance at perfection.

Tim Wrightman: "Looking back on it, yeah, it does piss me off. I think we would have liked to be the last undefeated team in the NFL."

Keith Van Horne: "It would certainly be nice to hold that place in NFL history. But the Dolphins were all fired up, and still to this day, every time some undefeated team loses, they are all popping champagne. They still do it, and that gets a little obnoxious. But you know what? They've got the right to do it."

Thomas Sanders: "I think it was probably a blessing in disguise, because we got our butts handed to us out there. I mean, they just manhandled us. And you saw guys circling the wagons, saying this wasn't going to happen to us again. Had we not lost that game, I don't think we would've gone to the Super Bowl."

Jim Covert: "What would have been worse, going 16-and-0 and losing in the playoffs? That's a hell of a lot worse. I'd rather lose and realize that you still have a lot of work to do yet. My only regret is, I wish we could have played them in the Super Bowl. That would have been a hell of a football game. If we were to beat them, that would have shown them what we were all about. That wasn't meant to happen, I guess."

On the flight back from Miami to freezing Chicago, Duerson says the Bears held a players-only meeting called by Payton. "The theme of it was, screw Mike Ditka, screw Buddy Ryan, screw Mike McCaskey. We were winning this for ourselves and for the fans. That was the message," says Duerson.

But on the same flight to Chicago, Willie Gault also had something he wanted to say, and his message had nothing to do with football.

On Tuesday, Gault reminded certain players, they had a music video to shoot.

CHAPTER 9

||||||||||||||||||||||||||||||||||||||||||||||||||||||||||||||||||||||||||||||||

SHUFFLING TO THE PLAYOFFS

After suffering a loss like the one to the Dolphins, some NFL teams might lower their profile. Their confidence might shrink. They might gaze into the metaphysical mirror.

The Bears returned to Chicago and filmed the video of the "Super Bowl Shuffle."

Dick Meyer had dreamed up the original concept, his widow said later, while he was in his dressing room. The president of Chicago-based Red Label Records, Meyer purchased the rights to "The Kingfish Shuffle," a comedy rap based on the Kingfish character from the TV show *Amos 'n' Andy*. Then Meyer blended the beat with new, brash, and wildly premature lyrics that referred to the Super Bowl even though it was still the *regular season*. Those lyrics, by the way, can easily be found on the Internet, but they can't be found in this book because Meyer's representatives refused to allow us to quote them.

Of course, Meyer needed the Bears to perform the song. So he enlisted Gault, whom he knew previously, to recruit his teammates. A key part of the pitch: a substantial part of the proceeds would go to charity.

"Willie wrapped it up like, hey, we're just doing this little video thing for the needy people in Chicago," says punter Maury Buford. "A lot of us didn't even know they were going to call it 'The Super Bowl Shuffle.'"

"I don't remember," says Fencik, laughing, "but I *hope* I didn't know it would be called 'The Super Bowl Shuffle.' How on earth could I have possibly agreed to that? It just made no sense for me, being from Chicago. Let's put a big jinx on us! We're the Chicago Bears, and we've never won a Super Bowl! Let's make a video!"

The presumptuous project unfolded in stages. It started with only the song. But it wasn't the first song by an NFL team. In 1984 the 49ers had released their recording of "We Are the 49ers." Then they won the Super Bowl. But you don't hear much about that tune anymore, do you?

The Bears recorded their song in November on the Friday after they pulverized the Cowboys. Ten players rapped the lyrics: Richard Dent, Gary Fencik, Steve Fuller, Willie Gault, Jim McMahon, Walter Payton, William Perry, Mike Richardson, Mike Singletary, and Otis Wilson. The song was quickly released as a record and a cassette and sold 500,000 copies in two weeks. Chicago radio stations played it ceaselessly. Everybody was stunned by its sudden success. By then, it had been decided to make a music video too, but not everyone knew that yet.

"Willie Gault said we were doing a video," says Fencik. "We were like, 'Fuck you, Willie. I didn't say I was doing a video. I said I was doing a record.'"

Ten players no longer sufficed. Additional ones were needed to be backup singers and pretend musicians. Some of the potential newcomers had already been told that the video would be filmed on December 3. Some found out the night before as the defeated Bears flew home in the wee hours from Miami.

"Willie Gault approached me on the airplane," remembers Jay Hilgenberg. "He said, 'Hey, what are you doing tomorrow?' He told me about this video. I said, 'Willie, we just got embarrassed on national TV. You're gonna sing and dance about the Bears in the Super Bowl?' "

Says Dan Hampton, "Great tune, catchy beat, I give it a B+. I just didn't want no part of it. We were close enough now to smell it, and everybody's gonna start acting like Hollywood actors? No!"

Leslie Frazier says "Hollywood Willie" is what some of the Bears called Gault. And aside from the sheer audacity of the Shuffle, some players felt wary because he was the front man. Gault wanted to act. He wanted to model. He had already danced in a Sister Sledge video, which was how he had hooked up with Meyer in the first place. Some players questioned whether Gault was actually dedicated to football. It didn't help his standing that Dennis McKinnon, the other starting wide receiver, was seen as one of the team's grittiest players. Whereas Gault was thought to be incredibly fast but lacking toughness, in a league where that quality was appreciated.

The video was filmed at the Park West nightclub on the city's North Side. Most players showed up when they were expected, at 2:00 P.M., but some were running up to three hours late. Various reasons were given, but the consensus was that the tardy players had been snoozing after the Bears had flown half the night getting home from Miami. Thus some guys felt rested, some felt tired, and everyone was pissed off about getting their asses handed to them by the Dolphins. But once the video session finally got rolling, Singletary calls it "the best thing that could have happened. It brought us all together. We went in there feeling like crap, and at the studio we were laughing and having fun and we were a team again. We were loving each other and ready to go."

The Bears wore their navy-and-orange uniforms without the helmets and pads. In addition to the "featured artists," the new players there were Maury Buford, Leslie Frazier, Shaun Gayle, Dennis Gentry, Stefan Humphries, Tyrone Keys, Jim Morrissey, Keith Ortego, Reggie Phillips, Dan Rains, Thomas Sanders, Ken Taylor, Calvin Thomas, and Mike Tomczak. The solos were to be performed by the 10 original rappers, but two of them didn't attend.

"Walter and I didn't go," remembers McMahon. "We promised to do the record. The video came up later. I ended up doing my part at the racquetball court at Halas Hall. Walter did his later too. Then they stuck us into the video." Meyer's widow had a different recollection. She says, "Payton didn't show up because he thought he might have a concussion."

Fuller, to use the term loosely, was also one of the "rappers." But he showed up on crutches after hurting his ankle against the Dolphins. No Solid Gold dancer to begin with, Fuller edged out Fencik for the Shufflin' Crew member with the whitest moves.

Says Butler, who had declined to participate, "I was a kicker. I knew I was one kick away from being fired, and I didn't think singing and dancing about a Super Bowl would be in my interest. Steve Fuller took care of bad dancing anyway. They didn't need two of us in there."

The video took off running, and the record kept moving too. By January 15, 1986, reported Betty Franklin in *Forbes*, "The Bears' single had gone gold (more than 1 million copies shipped), and a $19.95 video of the session had reached triple platinum (150,000 shipped)." The record ended up selling an estimated two million copies and received a Grammy nomination for best rhythm-and-blues performance by a duo or group (it lost to Prince and the Revolution's "Kiss"). Within months, no fewer than 10 other sports teams had recorded their own videos, most of them rap. But only the "Super Bowl Shuffle" appeared on MTV's regular rotation list.

Too bad it became so messy. The helping-the-needy angle had tempered the criticism from those who found the whole enterprise insufferably cocky. But in a city that knew something about corruption, now there were questions about where the money went to. Did the players receive what they were promised? More important, did the needy? The controversy spread to the pages of *Sports Illustrated,* where Bruce Newman wrote, "Some of the Bears accused Gault of getting them involved in a slick hustle, and worse, of lining his own pockets at their expense."

Many years later, Gault told the *Chicago Tribune,* "Some people thought I got more money, which I should have because I was the producer. Anytime you produce something, you do get more money. But I got exactly what all the other guys got."

And yet, according to Fencik, one way or another, the players got "ripped."

"Then the guy [Meyer] had the balls to come back and ask us to do 'The Super Bowl Shuffle Two,' " he says. "I thought Otis was going to throw the guy in the trash can. Singletary threw his *gold record* in the trash can. He threw it away and walked out."

In January 1986, the Illinois attorney general's office began to investigate. There were no improprieties found, and a disbursement plan was eventually worked out. More than $300,000 was given to charity.

Some of the players saw "The Super Bowl Shuffle" as an innocent lark that got tangled up in events beyond their control. Veteran guard Kurt Becker saw it as a sign that even if the song's lyrics came true, the 1985 Bears might not be equipped to handle prosperity.

" 'The Super Bowl Shuffle' was kind of a secretive thing," says Becker. "Not everyone was asked to be in it. A lot of us didn't know what was going on. And those exploits were the things that were starting to really deteriorate the chemistry of our team. As our notoriety built, the outside influences made us take our eye off the prize."

Even after the unattractive loss to Miami, the Bears were still 12–1 and still had home-field advantage throughout the NFC playoffs. And yet, in a city where even the most die-hard fans were fatalistic, it was impossible for them not to wonder: Will the Bears bounce back from defeat or have they already peaked? Are they fixated on playing football or being famous? With three meaningless games left in the regular season, will they cruise or build momentum for the playoffs?

Their first game after Miami was deflating. Playing at Soldier Field on December 8, Chicago seemed lethargic in a 17–10 win over the lowly 3–10 Colts. There were even scattered boos as the Bears came off the field tied 3–3 at halftime. Ditka blasted the team at intermission, and Ryan said afterward his players were selfish, thinking too much about whether they would be named to the Pro Bowl and not enough about the team. McMahon started for the first time in five weeks and played the entire game, but he didn't look any sharper than his teammates with only 11 completions for 145 yards. Fortunately, Payton had rushed for his league-record ninth-straight 100-yard game.

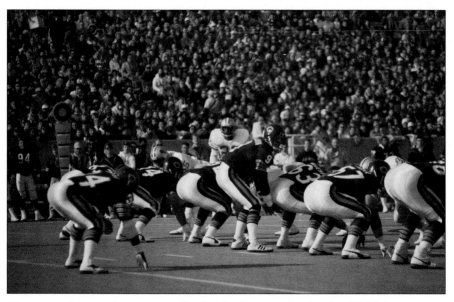

On a team known for years for having bad quarterbacks, Jim McMahon (9) finally gave the Bears a legitimate passer. Of course, it helped to have Walter Payton (34) in the backfield, making other teams respect the Bears' running game.

With tightly wound Mike Ditka roaming Chicago's sideline, the mood could switch from calm to volatile in an instant.

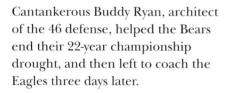

Cantankerous Buddy Ryan, architect of the 46 defense, helped the Bears end their 22-year championship drought, and then left to coach the Eagles three days later.

The famous 46 defense was innovative, deceptive, and, above all, aggressive. There was even talk that the defense put bounties on opposing quarterbacks.

Fast-rising Wilber Marshall (58) and already terrific Mike Singletary (50) gave the '85 Bears two of the hardest-hitting linebackers in the league.

Early in the season, it was Payton, McMahon, and the rest of the '85 offense that bailed out the team while the '85 defense was still finding its way.

McMahon was best-known for his instincts and fearlessness, but he was more athletic than he received credit for.

Keith Van Horne was perceived as a laid-back Californian—until the offensive tackle stepped on the field, where he was willing to tangle with anyone.

Veteran safety Gary Fencik graduated from Yale, made Chicago women swoon, and on Sundays knocked opposing receivers senseless.

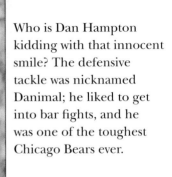

Who is Dan Hampton kidding with that innocent smile? The defensive tackle was nicknamed Danimal; he liked to get into bar fights, and he was one of the toughest Chicago Bears ever.

Although very different personalities, Payton and McMahon were both deeply admired by their teammates—even their defensive teammates, who sometimes had little use for the players on offense.

Kevin Butler kicked in cold and blustery Soldier Field, and yet still managed to set an NFL record for rookies with 144 points scored.

Butler and McMahon had at least two things in common: they were both characters and they were both winners.

McMahon earned his teammates' respect by standing up to Ditka, including the many times when Ditka got angry after McMahon changed a play.

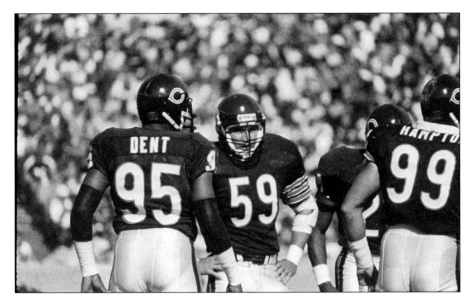

Ron Rivera (59) was hardly as renowned as Richard Dent (95) and Dan
Hampton (99), but the backup middle linebacker (behind Singletary)
was a smart player who later became the defensive coordinator for the
Chargers.

Chicago Bear fans finally rejoice as it becomes apparent their team will
defeat the Rams in the NFC championship and advance to Super Bowl XX
in New Orleans.

McMahon came up huge in the '85 postseason, including this improvised run against the Rams, which turned into Chicago's first touchdown in the NFC championship.

Payton gave his teammates and the fans everything he had on every Sunday. In return, Payton was probably the most beloved figure in the history of Chicago sports.

Payton's string finally ended the following Sunday, but the Bears played harder and more efficiently against the 10–4 Jets in cold and windy New Jersey. The offense wasn't great, but it controlled the ball for an implausible 39 of 48 minutes. The defense allowed just 70 yards rushing. Butler kicked four field goals, giving him a franchise-record 28 in his impressive rookie year. As the Bears won, 19–6, it seemed to indicate that pride was enough motivation for Chicago. They had just won on the road in nasty weather against a playoff-bound team fighting to win its division.

At Detroit the following Sunday, Joe Ferguson threw a pass in the first quarter and was crushed by Wilber Marshall on one of the biggest hits of the NFL season. Though no penalty was called, replays showed that Marshall lowered his helmet just before making contact. Ferguson, knocked unconscious for several minutes, finally walked off the field under his own power. But he would not return to the game.

"Joe Ferguson was out cold even before he hit the ground," says cornerback Leslie Frazier. "If you see photos of that hit, you can see Ferguson is parallel to the ground, still in the air, and you can see that he is done before he hits the ground. He's done. It was a vicious hit on the quarterback."

Butler calls it a "kill shot" and says he thought Ferguson might have been dead. Fencik ran into Ferguson many years later, and the retired QB was friendly until Fencik made the mistake of mentioning that play.

"He got real distant," says Fencik. "He said he never watched it, and he said he didn't want to talk about it."

The Bears defeated Detroit, 37–17, to finish at 15–1, the most glorious regular season in the team's history. Still, they had led only 6–3 at halftime and 16–10 at the end of the third quarter.

"We would not have beaten a playoff team the way we played today," Ditka growled to reporters. "We didn't play well anywhere. Maybe we were doing too many 'Super Bowl Shuffles.' "

"We did that record five weeks ago," said an apparently sensitive Willie Gault. "Maybe there's too many McDonald's commercials, or too many car commercials. It hasn't affected anybody's play. That's absurd."

"Heck, we won," said McMahon, always eager to contradict his head coach. "I don't put any weight on that. It has nothing to do with our play."

Ditka's pointed postgame remarks were not just for the sake of the media. Right after his team beat the Lions, Ditka screamed at his players inside the locker room.

"I was probably starting to feel the pressure and tension," says Ditka. "When you get that close, you don't want it to slip away. And I wasn't very pleased with the way we played against Detroit."

Several of the Bears say they knew Ditka was right. Over the preceding three weeks, their enthusiasm and intensity had been erratic. Now, with the playoffs at hand, they needed to regain the focus they had entered the season with. On the other hand, the players say, it wasn't as if Ditka was turning down all the endorsements and personal appearances coming his way. In fact, he was cashing in more than most of the players except perhaps for McMahon and the Refrigerator.

"Everything was spinning around us," says Kurt Becker. "There were still some contractual problems with some players. And all the endorsement things were continuing to happen. Some players were saying, 'How come he's doing this? How come I'm not doing it?' And not only were the players doing stuff, the coaches were doing stuff. So there was dissatisfaction on a lot of different levels, and Mike wasn't happy with us."

Neither, in one respect, was the league office. As the Bears prepared for their playoff game against the New York Giants, Commissioner Pete Rozelle fined Marshall $2,000 for his enormous helmet-first hit on Ferguson. The NFL didn't care that no flag had been thrown on the play. In a letter written directly to Marshall, Rozelle charged him with "spearing and blatant unnecessary roughness." The letter also rekindled the talk of the Bears and bounties when it cited the "published reports" after the Dallas game that Chicago was trying to injure quarterbacks.

Ditka shot back at Rozelle: "He's been around this long and he doesn't know how players talk? He's got a lot to learn."

The Bears also compared Marshall's fine with the smaller fine Rozelle had levied against Packer safety Ken Stills for blowing up Chicago fullback Matt Suhey after the whistle had blown back in early November. Said team president Mike McCaskey, "The thing that upsets all of us at the Bears is to see a $2,000 fine levied against Wilber Marshall for his hit and then Ken Stills, more flagrant, more blatant, clearly outside the lines of good hard football, gets a $500 fine. It's inequitable."

This being the wild and conflicted '85 Bears, there was a second controversy that week. Everett Glenn, Richard Dent's agent, threatened to hold Dent out of the Super Bowl if the Bears made it that far. Glenn said Dent had deserved a contract extension since the preseason, but he said the Bears had refused to even discuss it.

"Anyone out there want a Pro Bowl defensive end?" Glenn said the week before the Giants game. "Call me. I'm dead serious. We've got to do something. If they go to the Super Bowl, I'm not guaranteeing that Richard will be there to play."

Two weeks earlier, Dent had been named to the Pro Bowl along with Payton, McMahon, Singletary, Hampton, Covert, Duerson, Wilson, and Hilgenberg. It was the second straight Pro Bowl for Dent, who in 1984 had led the league in sacks with 17½. Dent had followed that up in '85 by leading the league again, this time with 17 sacks. And yet in this final year of his three-year contract, he was paid $90,000, which was five or six times less than other top defensive linemen.

None of Dent's teammates really believed he would sit out the Super Bowl if they got there. They thought it was just an agent trying to get his man paid when his man was in the midst of another big season.

Still, as Frazier says, "as a player, you're pulling for Richard and you understand the timing of it to a degree. This was an opportune time to voice his displeasure because of the type of season he was having. But it was weird to be talking about a contract as you're getting ready for the playoffs."

Meanwhile, behind closed doors, says linebacker Brian Cabral, Buddy Ryan was calling Dent selfish. But not because of his contract.

"Buddy flat-out called him the most selfish player he ever saw," says Cabral. "Buddy said he didn't play the run, he only played the pass."

Which was undoubtedly true and, as good as Dent was, one of the reasons why he had so many sacks.

Having won their division, the 15–1 Bears would have the first round off while the wild-card teams slugged it out the opening weekend. Then at Soldier Field on January 5, 1986, the city of Chicago would host its first playoff game since 1963. But first the Bears left town. Since their own practice fields

were frozen—and they had no indoor practice complex—
they went to the Atlanta Falcons' training facility in Suwanee,
Georgia, to get ready for the Giants.

It was Chicago's first big challenge since playing Miami.
The Giants had just gotten done pounding San Francisco in
a 17–3 wild-card victory. They had a terrific coach in Bill Par-
cells, who for weeks had been talking about "the invincible
Bears," which clearly meant he thought his own guys could
beat them. New York also had a well-balanced offense, led by
quarterback Phil Simms and halfback Joe Morris. And it had
the number-two defense behind the league-leading Bears.
Linebacker Lawrence Taylor, maybe the best defensive player
so far that decade, was a lock for the Hall of Fame despite his
self-destructiveness off the field. One ferocious hit from Taylor and a now-healthy McMahon could instantly be finished,
along with Chicago's Super Bowl aspirations.

Fortunately, the Bears had Jim Covert assigned to block
Taylor. Nobody in the franchise doubted Covert, including
Buddy Ryan, who knew Covert was one of the league's most
dominant offensive tackles. Still, Covert says, Ryan told him
a few days before the game, "Lawrence Taylor is gonna whip
your ass."

Ditka took a different motivational tact. While repeatedly
praising Taylor during the offensive meetings, Ditka also kept
saying the Bears would run straight at him. This was vintage
Iron Mike, setting the tone for the playoffs by saying the Bears
would come out and challenge the Giants' best player. At the
same time, on the defensive side of the Bears, linebacker Ron
Rivera says, "Buddy predicted a shutout the night before in
our meeting. That was pretty bold."

As 62,076 fans shivered with cold and excitement at Soldier
Field, it was 14 degrees at kickoff and 13 below zero with the

windchill. Midway through the first quarter, with the Giants backed up near their goal line, it looked like Sean Landeta whiffed on a punt when another powerful wind came gusting in from nearby Lake Michigan. Actually, Landeta almost whiffed, the ball barely grazing his foot before bouncing into the hands of the Bears' Shaun Gayle, who ran in for a famous five-yard touchdown that no Chicago fan of a certain generation will ever let any New York fan of that same generation ever forget.

At halftime, the Bears still led 7–0, but that was all they needed the way the defense was playing. Joe Morris would end up with just 32 yards rushing, and 14 of those yards came on his first carry. By late in the game, says Dave Duerson, "We were hitting him so hard he said he got a migraine, so he would not have to play. Joe Morris did not want to run the rock anymore." Then again, you couldn't really blame Morris. He probably had a concussion after the Fridge nailed him with a monster hit in the first half.

Phil Simms didn't have much good fortune that day in Chicago either. He was sacked six times, including three and a half times by the financially disgruntled Dent.

On the other side of the ball, Jim Covert shut down Lawrence Taylor as few offensive linemen ever had. Ditka, for his part, kept his pregame word: Chicago ran straight at Taylor instead of away from him. Ditka also sent Taylor a brutal message—which Taylor never saw coming—on a first-quarter running play.

"If you choose to ignore a player the talent of Lawrence Taylor, you're going to get your ass kicked," Ditka explains. "So, yeah, we challenged Covert to handle him. And we didn't give him much help. But early in the game, we cracked back on Taylor with Dennis McKinnon, and he knocked the shit out of him. We had this all set up. I told McKinnon before the game, 'The tight end is going to stand up like he's gonna block him, you're gonna come in, and you're gonna knock the shit out of Taylor.' As it happened on the field, Taylor started screaming at me because he knew I told McKinnon to do it. I said, 'What am I gonna do, let you run around out there all day and kill us? That ain't gonna happen. We're gonna block ya.' "

The frustrated All-Pro kept yelling at Ditka, the entire Chicago sideline, even his own teammates. At one point, says tight end Tim Wrightman, "Taylor was telling his guys when they were tackling Payton to hold him up so their other guys could hit him."

With Taylor and the rest of New York's defense in check, McMahon was never sacked and barely pressured. In the first playoff game of his NFL career, McMahon threw two clutch touchdown passes to McKinnon—both against the wind in the third quarter. Payton pitched in with 93 yards, and the Bears defeated the Giants 21–0.

"It wasn't easy," Ditka said. "Nothing in life is easy, but our players were on a mission. We beat a good football team."

The Los Angeles Rams were next in the NFC championship at Soldier Field. But as Dan Hampton says, "We weren't really worried about the Rams. We thought the Giants were the best team in the league besides us. We saw the Giants game as our de facto Super Bowl."

The Thursday before the Rams game, the Bears practicing again in Suwanee, Georgia, they received another letter from the NFL office. The last one had said Wilber Marshall was fined $2,000 for spearing Detroit quarterback Joe Ferguson. This letter said Jim McMahon was fined $5,000 for his repeated violations of the NFL's uniform code—in this case wearing a headband with a commercial name on it.

During the New York game, McMahon had worn an Adidas headband under his helmet, which was, well, obvious when he took his helmet off. McMahon says he'd been wearing one since around the fourth game of the season. Although the Bears had been warning him he was breaking the NFL's rules, he kept wearing the headbands anyway. McMahon says he never gave the issue much thought until Ditka announced his $5,000 fine during a team meeting in Suwanee.

"I never got fined all season, but now it was in the playoffs, so the NFL made a big stink out of it," says McMahon.

Asked if the Bears paid the fine on his behalf, he starts laughing as he says, "No, I had to pay. Shit, the Bears aren't going to pay anything for me."

It was the second week of January 1986, and only the 12–5 Rams stood between the 16–1 Bears and their first Super Bowl. Just as the offense had focused the previous week on Lawrence Taylor, the defense now concentrated on Eric Dickerson. The All-Pro running back had just shredded Dallas by gaining a playoff-record 248 yards in a 20–0 win in the NFC semifinals. Rams quarterback Dieter Brock, on the other hand, had completed just 6 of 22 passes for 50 yards. Brock, 34 years old and *maybe* six feet tall, was in his rookie year in the NFL after 11 seasons and two MVP Awards in the Canadian Football League.

"I thought it was temporary," said Rams coach John Robinson, when asked for his assessment of Brock's 6-for-22, 50-yard dud against Dallas. "I think Dieter Brock will have an outstanding game against Chicago."

Really? Not a mediocre or average game, but outstanding?

Then again, what could Robinson say? *I can't believe we're in the NFC title game without any passing attack. I can't believe we're playing the number-one team in the league against the run, which will be headhunting Dickerson, and our only alternative is asking a guy named Dieter Brock to beat it. In fact, as long as I'm being honest here, I think it's fair to say that Dieter Brock against the 1985 Chicago Bears defense will be the biggest mismatch in the history of the playoffs.*

"We kept hearing what a great quarterback Dieter Brock had been in the Canadian Football League," says Leslie Frazier. "But I remember watching the tapes of the Rams and thinking, *Canada is a little different than the NFL.* I don't think we had any fear of Dieter Brock, which allowed us to put our focus where it needed to be—on Eric Dickerson, a great running back."

In 1984 Dickerson had gained 2,105 yards while setting the NFL's single-season rushing record. He was not as brilliant in 1985, but Dickerson was still good, rushing for 1,234 yards. Now he was coming off the biggest game of his career—248 yards against the Cowboys.

So what did Buddy Ryan elect to do? Ryan publicly called out Dickerson, announcing before the game, "We're going to make Eric Dickerson fumble three times."

"When it was just him and us," says linebacker Ron Rivera, "Buddy called out Eric Dickerson *and* Dieter Brock. He said Brock was a high school quarterback, a Canadian quarterback, didn't know how to play the NFL game, we're gonna knock him back to Canada where he belongs. Buddy told us, 'We're gonna get Eric Dickerson. He's gonna fumble three times, and he's not gonna rush for 100 yards.' I really think Buddy got into Dickerson's head."

"Buddy Ryan was dumb like a fox," says Dan Hampton. "Dickerson was a supremely gifted running back, but not the toughest guy in the world. Well, the week before, against Dallas, nobody hit him and he ran for [almost] 250 yards. Buddy's comment was a gauntlet thrown down. When your brother opens his mouth up in a bar, you gotta back him up. So Dickerson had to deal all that week with knowing what was coming. We're not gonna take it easy on him and make Buddy Ryan look like an idiot."

Even Walter Payton stepped out of character and tried to burrow inside Dickerson's psyche. "He's had an easy life on the West Coast with all the palm trees," said Payton. "If it's cold enough Sunday, he'll have to dress for it. With all of those clothes on, it might make it hard for him to move."

As if the Bears weren't already providing enough good copy, Ditka groused to reporters that the NFL had been unfair in the fines it had recently levied against Wilber Marshall ($2,000 for spearing Joe Ferguson) and Jim McMahon ($5,000 for wearing his Adidas headband). Ditka even suggested that the NFL didn't especially *like* the Bears.

"There are teams that are fair-haired and there are teams that aren't," said Ditka. "There are teams named Smith and teams named Grabowski. The Rams are Smith. The Bears are Grabowski."

Ditka was doing what Ditka was very adept at—keeping his players on edge by making it seem as if they were disrespected. In reality, the NFL loved the Bears because they were great for business. Making popular Coke and McDonald's commercials—and "The Super Bowl Shuffle," a gold record—they drew national attention to the entire league. Of the NFL's 28 teams, the Bears were easily the biggest reason why TV ratings were up by 22 percent from the previous season. When they destroyed the Cowboys, it was the highest-rated game on CBS in ten years. When they were whipped by the Dolphins, it was the highest-rated *Monday Night Football* game ever.

Today Ditka admits, "I think the NFL liked the Bears. I think Pete Rozelle liked the Bears. I think he liked the way we played. I think he was a good guy, and good for the game.

I think that was evident by the way he got the league the TV contract initially, and the game started growing."

Of course, behind closed doors, the 1985 Bears were an even better and more complicated story, a soap opera that kept running despite the endless grudges between the actors. For example, the week before the Bears–Rams playoff game, Ryan was alone with his defensive players when he took the opportunity to mock Ditka. Again.

"At our first team meeting that week, Ditka started to talk about playing the Rams," remembers safety Jeff Fisher. "It was a great speech. He said, 'We're playing this game for Chicago Bear pride. We're not playing this game for money. We're playing for pride.' Then he broke up the meeting, and we split up offense and defense. When Buddy stands up, the first thing out of his mouth is, 'Pride, my ass. I go down to the corner market to get groceries, they sure as shit aren't taking pride. They're taking money.' "

When that Sunday morning arrived, the quarterback for the Chicago Grabowskis wasn't exactly chastened by his $5,000 fine for wearing an Adidas headband against the Giants. Inside the locker room at Soldier Field, McMahon was weighing his options on how he could once again violate the NFL's uniform code.

"I knew there would be a big fine if I did it again, and I was in there trying to figure out what to put on there," says McMahon. "I almost put 'fuck you' on it, but I didn't. Then McCaskey walked over to me and said, why didn't I put his name on it or George Halas? I said, 'Why would I be going around with your name on my head?' But that gave me the idea to put Pete's name on it. I thought, *Yeah, I'll put 'Rozelle.'* "

Without an internal censor, McMahon's thoughts often turned into real behavior. He found a white headband and a marker and printed ROZELLE in large black letters. The game was on CBS, and Rozelle sat up in the press box. When McMahon removed his helmet, gleefully, during the game, Rozelle saw the headband on the press box TV.

"He got a big kick out of that," says McMahon. "He actually called me later and thanked me for the free advertising. And I didn't get any fine."

Despite what the calendar said—Sunday, January 12, 1986—and rendering moot all the talk about how the sun-loving Rams would curl up and surrender in the cold weather, it was a mild 39 degrees at kickoff. But the howling Chicago winds were measured at 25 miles per hour.

Still, the confident Bears came out passing on their first possession. And McMahon, who may have been a lot of things, but was, above all, a winner, came out throwing spirals. By the end of the first quarter, Chicago led 10–0 and McMahon had scrambled for a 16-yard touchdown. He was also 5-for-6 on his way to a 16-for-25, 164-yard passing performance in high winds. Dieter Brock, running for his life, ended up sacked three times and completed just 10 of 31 passes for 66 yards.

Ouch.

Chicago still led 10–0 in the third quarter when Ditka called for a draw play on second down at the Los Angeles 22.

"It was second-and-long, and the draw play was our play in that situation, and that's exactly what Ditka sent in," remembers McMahon. "As the play was coming in, I could hear the defensive players saying, 'Watch the draw, watch the draw.' So I thought, *Hell, I'm not even gonna call it. I'm gonna call a roll-out.* Ditka knew I didn't call the draw as soon as we lined up, and he started yelling.

"One of our backs went in motion, and either I hit that guy in the flat or I just throw the ball away. But they screwed up in the secondary, and we hit a home run. Willie Gault was running a corner route. He pushes into the middle and then cuts back to the corner. If the cornerback makes any move toward the inside, I know we got a TD because Willie is going to beat him to the corner. So I threw it for the TD. The guys on the sidelines told me after the game that Mike was screaming that whole play, '*You son of a bitch!*' Then we throw it and he was like, '*Good call!*' "

The Bears led 17–0 on McMahon's 22-yard improvisation to Gault. With about six minutes left in the game and the score still 17–0, the temperatures had dropped enough for a light snow to start dusting Soldier Field. A stadium packed with people who had spent much of their lives dealing with snow, hoping it wouldn't snow, shoveling their cars out of the goddamn snow, began to applaud. Then, with less than three minutes remaining in the last game at Soldier Field that season, Dent unloaded on Brock and the overwhelmed quarterback coughed up the football. Marshall picked it up, and as he ran 52 yards for a touchdown he was sprinkled by the silvery snowflakes.

"That was the best moment of my life," says the Chicago-born Fencik. "We're going to the Super Bowl, and I'm chasing Wilber Marshall, and the fans are cheering, and it's snowing. It was like a movie."

For Dickerson, the game was rated R for excessive violence. Attacked from various angles by the deceptive and punishing 46 defense, he seemed to lose some resolve as Bear after Bear put another helmet on him. Dickerson wound up with 17 carries for only 46 yards, or 202 less than he'd gained the week before against Dallas. By also fumbling twice—one short of Ryan's prediction but close enough—he helped Ryan look like a mastermind.

Buddy Ryan, of course, wasn't known for his humility. "If they would have run him more, he would have had three," Ryan said afterward.

Mike Ditka, of course, has never been known for agreeing with Buddy Ryan. "Dickerson didn't fumble because Buddy said he would fumble," says Ditka. "He fumbled because Mike Singletary knocked the snot out of him."

The Bears won 24–0. On offense, the Rams averaged 2.2 yards per play. Their longest drive was 27 yards. On 8 of their 16 possessions, they went three-and-out. No wonder the CBS announcer John Madden, who used to coach the Raiders, later said, "That '85 Bear defense was the most dominant thing I've ever seen. Even the Steelers; I went against those Steelers. These guys were more dominant than the Steelers."

Clearly, no one had ever done what the '85 Bears had done in the last two weeks. With their 24–0 win over the Rams in the NFC championship, after beating the Giants 21–0 in the NFC semifinals, the Bears became the first team to reach the Super Bowl without allowing any points in the playoffs. And these back-to-back postseason shutouts finally healed the wounds from the NFC championship the year before, when they lost 23–0 to the trash-talking 49ers in San Francisco.

Says center Jay Hilgenberg, "When we got beaten by the 49ers, some of us were like, 'Damn, we're never going to get to the Super Bowl. We got a good team here, but how can we ever compete against the 49ers?' A year later, we're winning that game against the Rams in Chicago. It was just an amazing time in all of our lives."

The Soldier Field celebration began in the waning minutes of the fourth quarter. As the crowd of 63,522 chanted "Super Bowl," some fans left their seats and danced in the aisles with strangers. The Bears jumped up and down along their sideline, hugging and slapping five and getting choked up. As Ditka congratulated his players one by one, even his dark eyes got misty.

Covert passed out cigars in the locker room, and Ditka

made an emotional speech invoking the memory of the late George Halas. But none of the Bears went too wild, not with one more game to win in order to win it all. No one drank or sprayed champagne either, because there wasn't any.

Not that their Irish quarterback gave a damn.

"Fuck the champagne," said McMahon. "I want a beer."

"I don't know how to act," said the beloved Walter Payton, who ran for just 32 yards but added 48 more on 7 receptions. "Eleven years of climbing the mountain. I wish this was the Super Bowl."

Beyond the joyous Chicago Bears locker room, out in the neighborhoods, the taverns, the restaurants, the living rooms, no more fear of failure! Only raw jubilation! Chicagoans who had moved to other cities called family and friends who still lived there and said, *"I can't believe it!! We're in the Super Bowl!!"*

Through all the lousy years lately, and pretty lousy years, and pretty good years, and good years but never great years, everyone was in this thing together. You were born a Bear fan because your parents were Bear fans. Then you grew up a Bear fan, and unless you had no soul, no class, no loyalty to anything at all, you remained a Bear fan until death did you part. Now the '85 Bears were 17–1, which had never happened before. And even though there was one big game left, and even though what Chicago fans had always done best was worry, it wasn't the time for that now. It was time to be excited about something you wondered if you'd ever experience—a Super Bowl with the Bears appearing in it.

"We don't mean to cause no trouble. We're just doing 'The Super Bowl Shuffle.' "

A giddy Gary Fencik recited those lyrics to the media throng shortly after the Bears shut out the Rams.

Next up, in New Orleans, the New England Patriots.

CHAPTER 10

||||||||||||||||||||||||||||||||||||||||||||||||||||||||||||||||||||||||||||||||||

GOOD TIMES IN THE BIG EASY

D id you think they'd get boring now with *everyone* watching?

With two weeks of hype before Super Bowl XX, the Bears got two days off after pounding the Rams at Soldier Field. Then, on Wednesday, January 15, they took a short flight south to Champaign to practice underneath the protective bubble at the University of Illinois. The national media arrived in droves—everyone from the *New York Times* to MTV—and the Bears wasted no time showing they weren't afraid of the Patriots, whom they had beaten 20–7 in week two of the regular season.

In that game, Chicago's offense was adequate, its defense brilliant and bruising. The Bears sacked quarterback Tony Eason six times, intercepted him three times, and traumatized him indeterminately. Running back Craig James gained five yards on seven carries. As an offensive unit, New England, incredibly, spent 21 seconds on Chicago's side of the field.

In the rematch in the Super Bowl, the Patriots would have their All-Pro guard John Hannah, who had been injured the last time. But the Bears still weren't too impressed.

"The Patriots are an improved team," said Buddy Ryan. "They'd better be if they want to make a game out of it."

When a reporter told Otis Wilson there had never been a shutout in the previous 19 Super Bowls, Wilson predicted the Bears would deliver the first. "If we stick to our game plan and the tempo we have been playing, it's possible," Wilson said.

After New England coach Raymond Berry said his team might have a psychological edge because Chicago would enter the game "overconfident," Dan Hampton replied, "I wonder how many Freudian books Raymond had to look up to find that one."

The only New England player who was really bringing it, with his mouth, was the physical young cornerback Ronnie Lippert. "I am quite sure our linebackers are going to get to McMahon and take him out," he said. "They won't go for his arm, they'll go for his head."

In more objective circles, few of the league's insiders had expected the 14–5 Patriots to be the 17–1 Bears' opponent. But they had proven their grit by making the playoffs as a wild-card team and then winning on the road against the Jets, Raiders, and Dolphins. Furthermore, the 1980 Raiders had already won a Super Bowl as a wild-card entry. Still, the odds-makers didn't see it this time around. Las Vegas established Chicago as a solid ten-point favorite.

The Bears practiced Wednesday, Thursday, Friday, and Saturday morning in Champaign, putting in most of their game plan, just in case it got real crazy in New Orleans. On Saturday afternoon, they returned to Chicago, a city enraptured by its football team. In restaurants and bars crowded despite the cold weather, a healthy percentage of patrons wore orange-and-blue jerseys. In office buildings, the optimistic employees drank from coffee cups emblazoned with C's, and the water cooler debates were focused on safety blitzes and play-action passes. For tourists who came that week for the city's grand architecture, only to be overwhelmed by dangling

Go BEARS! signs, the *Tribune* explained on its editorial page "what the Bears have done to Chicago. They have given us something to hope and cheer for in January, the time when ordinarily that bleak post-holiday depression sets in, and all we have to look forward to are subzero temperatures, blizzards and watching our cars rust. This January, cabin fever has been replaced by Bears fever."

The municipal heroes took that Sunday off. They arrived at New Orleans International Airport on the Monday night before the Super Bowl. Right away, their home for the week was festive.

"We got on the buses from the airport to our hotel, and a convertible full of girls pulled alongside us and started taking their tops off," says center Tom Andrews. "That was where it started. It was bizarre."

But it was also fitting that the most colorful team in Super Bowl history was playing in the Big Easy. As the Fridge walked around the streets of the French Quarter, he had a little parade behind him wherever he went. At funky souvenir shops, ROZELLE headbands sold for five dollars apiece. The ubiquitous "Super Bowl Shuffle," which had gone gold the previous week, blared out of every speaker on Bourbon Street. When the players walked in the front door of a restaurant, they were serenaded with "The Super Bowl Shuffle" there too.

"Super Bowl week was chaos. Total chaos," says guard Kurt Becker. "Guys were going out every night. There was a caper happening all the time. And New Orleans was totally run over by Chicago people. There wasn't a New England person to be found."

Says center Jay Hilgenberg, "It was like we were the Beatles or something. We had a blast. We were the youngest team in the league. And we were in New Orleans."

Not only that but staying downtown at the Hilton, which

was walking distance to Bourbon Street. Like any other dutiful visitors to New Orleans, the 1985 Bears got plowed on the rum-drenched Hurricanes at Pat O'Brien's. McMahon and his offensive linemen were especially comfy there, but it was only one stop on their nightly prowls.

"The people there would just mob you," recalls Keith Van Horne. "So literally McMahon would jump on my back, and I'd piggyback him through the streets, and we would go from one bar to another. There we are, running down the street with McMahon on my back and Becker is kind of lead blocking, just trying to get from one bar to another. We went out Monday, Tuesday, and Wednesday nights. But Wednesday night was my last night. I said, 'I'm locking myself in my room. That's it.' It was New Orleans. The women didn't have a problem taking their tops off or lifting them up. That was all going on. We were all asked to sign some interesting spots."

"We were putting out fires all week," says assistant public relations director Brian Harlan. "I was amazed at how the players were out all the time. The family plane [i.e., the wives and kids] came in I think on Thursday or Friday. So by that point things settled down. But the first two or three nights, guys were out pretty good."

Says linebacker Brian Cabral, "We got a lot of work done before we got to New Orleans. Ditka's whole thing was, enjoy it, enjoy this experience. He thought we played better when we relaxed."

In his delicately titled 2005 book *In Life, First You Kick Ass*, Ditka wrote that he gave the players no curfew "until Saturday, the night before the game." Now he amends that by a day or so.

"I didn't put a curfew on them until Thursday or Friday," Ditka recalls. "I said, 'Do what you want to do the first couple nights. And remember, everything you're going to do is going to be magnified.' I mean, this was 25 years ago, so it [the media scrutiny] wasn't what it is now. But I still told them, 'Hey, listen, if you can't get done what you're gonna get done by 10 or 11 at night, you probably shouldn't be doing it.' That's not too complicated. I learned that when I was a player."

Even before Ditka installed the 11:30 curfew, not every Chicago player thought he was appearing in a video called *'85 Bears Gone Wild*. And once the curfew went in, some players actually abided by it. Jim Covert, for example, says, "We didn't just go down there and hang out every night until four in the morning. We had a couple nights where we did, but not *every* night."

And at least one player says he barely even left his hotel room at night.

"I was dating an actress who was blond and very busty named Judy Landers," says tight end Tim Wrightman. "And Judy Landers came down there for the Super Bowl. We were in New Orleans that week? What?"

As the spotlight on the team intensified, Walter Payton and William Perry shared the cover of *Time* under the headline "Bad News Bears." A reporter from *Rolling Stone* hung out with McMahon, working on a cover story that would hit newsstands in March. McMahon's agent, Steve Zucker, who calls that Super Bowl week "the best week of my life," says at first *Rolling Stone* asked the Bears to facilitate the whole thing, but the Bears told the magazine no.

"So we worked out the deal with *Rolling Stone* ourselves," Zucker recalls. "They rented this little house in this terrible neighborhood, so Jim and I and Van Horne snuck out, and they did the photo shoot. That was great. He was the first athlete ever to get on the cover of *Rolling Stone.*"

David Breskin's cover story was headlined "Born to Be Wild." Breskin hooked his readers in his opening paragraph by placing McMahon at "this yuppie club in uptown New Orleans on the Thursday night before Super Bowl Sunday, and this blonde in chocolate cashmere sweater-and-slacks combo comes up and says, 'Let me tell you something, Jim. I am a middle-aged woman, and I have big tits, and you know what that means!' " To Jim McMahon, wrote Breskin, "it means you have to escape with your pals, and quick, to a corner table tucked behind the dance floor."

There were approximately 2,500 newspaper, magazine, radio, and TV representatives in New Orleans that week. By comparison, Ira Berkow wrote in the *New York Times,* "there were only about 1,000 reporters covering the Reagan-Gorbachev summit meeting in Geneva last November. That either makes the Super Bowl more monumental than even its greatest boosters believe, or it means the summit meeting was less than met the global eye."

Or maybe it meant the reporters knew two politicians could never be as compelling as Jim McMahon on center stage at the Super Bowl. The reporters didn't much care if McMahon clearly considered most of them morons. Because even more than Joe Namath, Duane Thomas, or Hollywood Henderson, McMahon filled up their notebooks like no one in Super Bowl history ever had.

At Super Bowl III, Namath had said, "The Jets will win Sunday. I guarantee it."

At Super Bowl VI, Thomas had refused to talk all week to the media, but when asked as Sunday approached if the Super Bowl was the ultimate game, Thomas had said, "If it's the ultimate game, how come they're playing it again next year?"

At Super Bowl XIII, Henderson had said, "Terry Bradshaw couldn't spell 'cat' if you spotted him the 'c' and the 'a.' "

Namath, Thomas, and Henderson were all good copy. They all fed the ravenous Super Bowl media beast. And they were all amateurs next to McMahon. The rebellious quarterback got rolling immediately on Monday night, less than an hour after the Bears arrived in New Orleans, by calling out team president Mike McCaskey.

And all because Jim McMahon had a big bruise on his ass.

Playing against the Rams in the NFC championship, McMahon had slid feet first and then been speared by defensive end Doug Reed. There was no penalty called, but there could have been. And while his injury wasn't serious, it was painful.

"I took a helmet right in the ass bone," says McMahon. "Right away it swelled the whole left side of my ass up."

McMahon had walked gingerly for the next few days. Then he had thrown but not run when the Bears had practiced in Champaign. Back at Halas Hall on Monday morning, with the Super Bowl six days away, McMahon had received an acupuncture treatment from Hiroshi Shirashi. Willie Gault had flown Hiroshi in from Tokyo to help him get nice and loose for the big game. Hiroshi was a trainer for the Japanese track and field team who had been recommended to Gault when he competed in track internationally. Since then, Gault, Walter Payton, and several other players had been treated by Hiroshi late in the '85 regular season.

"That guy was good," recalls defensive end Tyrone Keys. "He worked on my wife when she had a problem."

McMahon's acupuncture session Monday morning at Halas Hall relieved some of the pain and pressure he felt. The Bears knew about the treatment, but didn't approve. They wanted McMahon from then on to be treated exclusively by their trainer, Fred Cato.

"McCaskey was against using Hiroshi," says Zucker. "NFL teams were touchy then about their players getting second opinions. But almost every time, the doctors for the teams were more beholden to the team than to the players. They would just as soon give them a shot. The needles were on the sidelines. Jim used to get shots in his hand on the sidelines. They treated the players like meat, and they still do to some extent. But at least now it's accepted to get second opinions, and they finally got it in the collective bargaining agreement. But at the time we had to fight with teams."

McMahon felt so much better after Hiroshi's first session Monday morning that he wanted Hiroshi to work on him every day before the game. But when Hiroshi showed up Monday night for the team's charter flight to New Orleans, there was an unpleasant scene at O'Hare Airport.

"We took a big-ass 747, there was plenty of room, and McCaskey wouldn't let Hiroshi get on the plane. That pissed everybody off," says tight end Emery Moorehead.

Particularly McMahon, who says he was thinking, *Whose ass is it?*

"I saw there were all kinds of empty seats on the plane, and he [McCaskey] had all his cronies on the plane," recalls McMahon. "But this little guy who wouldn't have taken up half a seat couldn't get on? He was going to help me get ready to play. All this traditional shit—your ice and your heat and your stim and whatever—wasn't working. This thing needed to drain, and he got it working. My ass started clearing up. But the Bears didn't want someone else getting publicity for doing anything."

When the Bears landed Monday night in New Orleans, McMahon made it *very* public anyway, at the week's first news conference, held inside a ballroom at the Hilton. McMahon told the crowd of reporters he had wanted Hiroshi to accompany him to New Orleans for more treatment, but McCaskey had refused.

"If it works, who cares if they approve or disapprove," said McMahon. "If it helps me get ready to play Sunday, I'm going to do it." McMahon said if he had to, he would fly Hiroshi to New Orleans himself.

Ditka had been fine with Hiroshi getting on the team's plane in the first place.

Now, at the news conference, he stood by his quarterback, although you could sorta tell he wasn't completely versed in Eastern medicine.

"I think it's a great idea if it helps. It's all mental anyway. Some of it is physical. If it helps, it helps," Ditka said.

On Tuesday the story kept simmering. It was not every year that a big-name quarterback threw his owner under the bus at the Super Bowl. In fact, this was the first year. Then again, says rookie kicker Kevin Butler, "Jim calling out our owner didn't surprise us. Jim was the biggest player in the NFL at that time, marketing-wise. Jim said what he wanted to say."

The media hordes were grateful. They kept asking acupuncture questions, and McMahon and McCaskey kept answering. Clearly, however, McCaskey wanted Ass-gate to go away.

"It's not a big controversy," said McCaskey. "Isn't there other news?"

"It should be a big story," said McMahon. "We need it to be healthy. We're going to try and get him here one way or another. If management doesn't want to bring him, the players will bring him."

McCaskey, starting to hedge, on his way to a total flip-flop, said the Chicago Bears were not against acupuncture, and they were not against Hiroshi.

"What I am against is at the last minute allowing him on our team charter, making him, in effect, a sudden member of our training staff. I don't want any last-minute additions to our staff," said McCaskey.

Charging into the fray went the Illinois State Acupuncture Association. Initially aroused by McCaskey's refusal to let Hiroshi board the team's plane—and now recognizing a chance for some primo national attention—the association announced on Tuesday that it would fly Hiroshi to New Orleans on Wednesday morning.

"Now the question is, will the Bears allow Jim to undergo treatment or will he have to sneak off to have it done?" the association's Marti Ahern said.

By then, everyone and their mom knew the president of the Bears had lost his squabble with his quarterback. Hiroshi arrived Wednesday morning in New Orleans and then treated McMahon before Wednesday's practice. Although McMahon didn't scrimmage, he did participate in seven-on-seven drills. He seemed to be moving more freely, and in case anyone wondered why, he wore a headband saying ACUPUNCTURE. But just to make doubly sure everyone stayed on-topic, when a news helicopter circled the practice field, he pulled down his pants and shot a moon.

"Just showing them where it hurt," McMahon explained.

For all the hysteria surrounding one man's rear end, Tyrone Keys says, "that guy [Hiroshi] really helped Jim a lot. We all knew how black and blue his buttock was, and Jim swears he would never have played if not for this guy. I don't even think the guy spoke English."

Actually, he did, at least enough to deliver probably the single best line of Super Bowl XX.

"I came here to make the Bears feel better so they can win the Super Bowl," Hiroshi told reporters. "I stick pins, we win."

Becker says he spent that surreal week sharing a hotel room with McMahon, hanging out on the other bed, while "he's on his bed getting acupuncture in his ass from this little Oriental guy. So I'm like, 'Hey, Jim, what's up with that?' I think Jim created some controversy there. He went to the press about Hiroshi and told everyone what was happening with McCaskey."

Says assistant PR director Brian Harlan, "Most of the players weren't real fond of McCaskey. He had just gotten there, and the players didn't like how much credit he was taking for how the team was doing. I think the whole acupuncture deal was just a perfect conduit for McMahon to express the fact that he didn't like the guy. That gave him a perfect excuse to do it on a national stage. And McCaskey wasn't going to do anything about it. You're not going to get into a pissing match with your quarterback a few days before the Super Bowl."

The McMahon-McCaskey rift would widen from this moment forward, taking a quantum leap in the 1986 season, when McMahon's scathing comments on McCaskey were published in the entertaining *New York Times* best-seller McMahon wrote with the *Chicago Tribune*'s Bob Verdi. But the catalyst for the conflict, says PR director Ken Valdiserri, was the public Super Bowl flare-up over Hiroshi.

"That's really what set Jim off when it came to McCaskey. For whatever reason, Jim got a hard-on over that," says Valdiserri.

Meanwhile, the Fridge was doing his own thing that week, but it was a much more laid-back thing than McMahon's. Perry affably answered even the silliest questions, including the popular "How many Cokes did you drink during the filming of your Coke commercials?" A few days earlier, the Fridge had told reporters he had turned down an endorsement from "some cat company." When asked what the company had wanted him to do, the Fridge said, without hesitation, "Probably pet a cat." He also confirmed the rumors that he had recently passed on a movie with Cyndi Lauper in which Lauper would play a wrestler and he'd play her bodyguard.

"I looked at the script and said no," said the Refrigerator. "I didn't want to spend seven days on a movie. They wanted me to go to California. I'd rather go fishing."

On Thursday, McMahon was right back in the national headlines, but this time unwillingly. Buddy Diliberto, a local sportscaster on WDSU-TV, had reported on Wednesday night that McMahon called the New Orleans women "sluts."

"Jim calls me Thursday morning, and he says, 'You better come up here, we got problems,'" remembers Zucker. "All hell started breaking loose. They had women picketing the hotel. I go to Vanisi and Ditka, and they barely look at me. I said, 'Jim never said it. He didn't do it.' Nobody believed me because Jim is so outspoken. But Jim never lies to me. Never has, never will. So I told Jim, 'You gotta tell the press.' They won't believe me.'"

With the media smelling his blood, McMahon flat-out denied the accusation, calling it "ridiculous." But to go along with the women now demonstrating in front of the Hilton, the hotel also started receiving bomb threats.

Diliberto at first stuck to his story. He said he only repeated on his sportscast the statement that McMahon had made on WLS, a Chicago radio station doing its morning show that week from a restaurant in New Orleans. But when WLS sportscaster Les Grobstein said he never even interviewed McMahon, Diliberto's story quickly unraveled. Evidently what really happened was that Diliberto was told by a New Orleans radio deejay that McMahon had called the local women sluts. And Diliberto inexplicably ran with it.

Diliberto was suspended and missed the Super Bowl. His mortified bosses made him issue a personal apology to "Jim

McMahon, the NFL, Chicago radio station WLS, and to the people of New Orleans for the problems caused by these unverified statements."

"That week was great," says McMahon, "until that idiot came out on TV and said I called the women sluts. Then I just wanted to get out of the town alive. I was getting death threats the rest of the week, and we had bomb threats at the hotel the day before the game. Nobody wanted to stand by me at practice because where we practiced there was an apartment complex that overlooked the field. I said, 'Shit, am I gonna get shot?'

"I don't even know where the hell this guy came from. He said supposedly I had done a radio show at like five in the morning. I said, 'Any of you idiots [the media] first should know I don't get up for you people at five in the morning. So if you believe that, you're stupid to begin with. And even if I believed in what I supposedly said, I wouldn't have said it to a reporter.' "

As Slut-gate pushed Ass-gate off the front pages of the nation's sports sections, McMahon was back in the spotlight in the most bizarre fashion yet. Thus, with Super Bowl XX now only three days away, he was bigger news than the impending game itself.

"One night I was up there on Bourbon Street with Jack Youngblood and Jeff Van Note and some other older guys who I had been to the Pro Bowl with," remembers Dan Hampton. "They wanted to know just how unhinged McMahon was. He was mooning the helicopter, the acupuncture, calling the women sluts—all that stuff. I said, 'Oh no, he's fine. This is all an act. He's probably at the hotel right now with his playbook.' About that time, he walks in holding three Budweisers, and he's wearing a pair of those glasses with the springy eyes, those nutty-looking things, and a headband with flashing lights. We looked at him, and he looked at me, and they said, 'Yeah, right.' "

By late January 1986, slightly more than 22 years had passed since the 1963 Bears won Chicago's last world championship in a major professional sport. Now the 1985 Bears were right on the brink of ending the city's long and excruciating wait. And at that revolutionary moment, Buddy Ryan was getting ready to say good-bye.

In the two weeks before the game, Ryan's name began to surface for several head coaching positions. Most of the talk centered on the Philadelphia Eagles, who were looking to replace their interim coach Fred Bruney. When reporters came to Ryan for a comment on specific rumors involving the Eagles, he said he wouldn't address it until after the Super Bowl. But Ryan also made it clear he wanted to run his own program.

"If it happens, it happens, and I'll be happy to give it a shot," said Ryan. "But I don't want to comment on that kind of stuff. I'm not looking for a job. I'm trying to win a Super Bowl."

Ryan wanted to get away from Ditka. Their marriage was an arranged one, and they had been antagonistic ever since.

But Ditka was only one factor. Ryan was 51 and the last time he'd been a head coach was in 1959 at Gainesville High School in Texas. Now in his 18th year in the NFL—and his eighth season as the Bears' defensive coordinator—he had two years left on a contract with a provision allowing him to become a head coach elsewhere. In 1984 Ryan had interviewed with the Indianapolis Colts, but they were reportedly nervous about his maverick nature. By Super Bowl week, however, Ryan had become the top head coaching candidate in the league. His vicious-yet-disciplined defense had just led the NFL in turn-overs, points allowed, and yards allowed and was ranked number one overall. And though the '85 defense was maybe the most dominant of all time, it was hardly a one-season wonder. The '84 Bears had produced an NFL-record 72 sacks.

"Buddy had this philosophy that a head coaching job in itself ain't shit," says Hampton. "You have to pick the one you think you can win at. Because you win five games in two years, you're back in the assistant ranks, and maybe you never get another chance. So he was acutely aware of the opportunity which Philly presented. And he and Ditka were obviously in a bad situation. They had outgrown the arrangement."

As the Super Bowl got closer, there were new rumors that Ryan had already started talking to Philadelphia owner Norman Braman. But with Ryan refusing to confirm or deny them, the players on the Bears kept telling reporters they didn't know if Buddy was really leaving. The only player who knew for sure was Gary Fencik, the hard-hitting safety and so-called coach on the field who had been with Ryan for all eight years.

"We were at practice early that week," says Fencik. "Buddy pulled me aside, I didn't ask him. He just said, 'I gotta talk to you a second. I accepted the job with the Eagles.' I said, 'That's great, Buddy.' It was a moment of sadness, though. I thought, *This is it, this is over.* Then I didn't know who else he might have told, so I didn't tell anybody."

Ryan all but told Jeff Fisher, who had spent the previous five years as a cornerback and kick returner in Chicago. After breaking his ankle at the '85 training camp, Fisher spent the season on injured reserve, and Ryan had made him his unofficial assistant.

"Buddy told me Tuesday or Wednesday," Fisher recalls. "He was standing behind the defense during practice, and I was standing next to him. He said, 'I think I'm gonna get the Philly job, and I want you to come with me.' I said, 'I might not be done playing. I have a contract for next year.' He said, 'Your fiancée's name is Julie? Why don't you have her throw you a retirement party. You can't play anymore. You need to come coach.' So I knew during the week there was a good chance Buddy was leaving."

Finally, mercifully, after a frantic week that could have sabotaged a lesser team, Saturday night arrived in New Orleans. The Bears were all together at their hotel, in their final full-team meeting before the Super Bowl. Ditka made sure his speech was short and playful, making fun of McMahon's escapades and then letting the players do the talking. When the offense and defense broke up, Ryan's defenders went into another room, where Ryan gave what amounted to his farewell speech.

"We got in the meeting, and everybody sat down and got quiet," says Hampton. "Buddy went up in front, and his face was all red, and he handed out his reminders, and then he kind of choked up. He said, 'No matter what happens tomorrow, you'll always be my heroes.' And he walked out with tears coming out of his eyes."

Says cornerback Ken Taylor, "It was weird from a rookie's perspective. Every defensive meeting was all about doing your job, intimidation, killing everybody. That meeting near the end turns to love, loyalty, and emotion. If it was a bunch of women, everyone would have been sobbing and crying."

"I was sitting next to Singletary," says Fencik. "I said out loud to myself, 'I can't believe he's leaving.' I looked into Mike's eyes, and he didn't know. I said, 'Mike, you have to figure Buddy is going to take a head coaching job after this season we just had.' "

Singletary *didn't* know. He had no idea the coach who called him "short and fat" and just about everything else—but also helped him become a future Hall of Famer—had already made a decision that would have a dramatic impact on the franchise.

"It was an emotional moment for a lot of the guys," says Singletary. "I couldn't really deal with it at the time. So I just kind of put it in the back of my mind and believed what Buddy had told me himself. When I had asked him about it that week, he said, 'No, I'm not going anywhere.' I left it at that and focused on the game."

"We knew what the deal was," says Hampton. "We knew it had to happen. But that was when it hit us, when Buddy walked out. We all sat there in a stunned state of silence. Dale Haupt was our defensive line coach. In an effort to jar everybody back, he said, 'Turn out the lights, let's watch this film.' And he starts the projector. We had been watching this film for two weeks. We'd seen it 20 times. And I stood up, and I kicked the projector right off the little table. At the same time, McMichael jumped up and picked up a chair and threw it at the chalkboard, and the four legs impaled into the chalkboard and stuck there. Everybody kind of looked at each other. I said, 'All right, let's get the hell out of here.' And we all walked out the door."

Good luck with that, New England.

CHAPTER 11

||||||||||||||||||||||||||||||||||||||||||||||||||||||||||||||||||||||||||||||||||

CAKEWALK IN SUPER BOWL XX

O
n Sunday morning, January 26, 1986, the Bears took a short bus ride from the downtown Hilton to the Superdome. Mike Singletary later remembered the ride as quiet except for the sounds coming from Walter Payton's boom box. Outside the ten-year-old stadium, already hosting its third Super Bowl, scalpers asked for $500 a ticket. Inside the stadium, the stands would end up packed with 73,818 fans, a majority of them rooting for Chicago.

The Bears filed off the bus and entered their locker room, where one of their coaches had posted an article by the *Boston Globe*'s Leigh Montville. Under the headline "But Chicago Will Choke Again," the columnist predicted that "the Bears are going to blow it." Montville was very good, and one of Boston's best, but nobody was as good as Chicago's own Mike Royko, who had written that same week in the *Tribune:* "My prediction for Sunday is: Bears 41, Patriots 0. If the Patriots are lucky."

In a locker room now devoid of even nervous chatter, Mike Ditka gave his final pregame speech of the season.

"Go out and play Bears football, smart and aggressive," said Ditka. "If something bad happens, don't worry. Why? Because we're in this together as a football team and we are going to play it for each other, and we're going to win this game for 49, 50, or whatever number we have in this room. We are going to win it for each other."

It didn't start off real well. With 120 million viewers watching around the world, Payton fumbled on the second play from scrimmage. McMahon had put the Bears in the wrong formation, leaving Payton with no blocking, and he dropped the ball for only the sixth time all season. As New England recovered on the Chicago 19-yard line, NBC's Dick Enberg all but shouted, "Payton fumbles the ball, and who has it? The New England Patriots do! And this is the pattern of the underdog from New England, forcing a turnover, 16 of them in the first three playoff games! And the underdogs have come up with a big break today!"

At that very moment, as the city of Chicago's collective heart raced, logic and confidence gave way to irrational fear.

"I was right there with them," says the Chicago-born guard Tom Thayer. "I wasn't Covert from Pittsburgh or McMichael from Texas or Hampton from Arkansas. The same thing ran through my head that ran through everyone else's: *Oh my God, are we gonna lose this game?* That was just from a lifetime of growing up a Chicago fan."

In the decidedly pro-Bears Superdome, offensive tackle Keith Van Horne says, "there was like this audible sigh. Like everyone was thinking, *Oh my God, here we go again, the Chicago curse.*"

Payton ran in silence to the sidelines. The 46 defense jogged on, determined to not allow a single point after posting consecutive shutouts against the Giants and Rams. What the Patriots had done best all season was run the ball, but their coach, Raymond Berry, chose to get cute. Thus Tony Eason threw three straight incomplete passes. But when Tony

Franklin hit a 36-yard field goal, the Bears trailed 3–0 after two minutes.

"God bless my good friend Walter Payton," says defensive end Dan Hampton. "But we had every intention of shutting out the Patriots. And that field goal really, really pissed us off."

On Chicago's next possession, Ditka showed how much he trusted McMahon even though they bickered all the time. And McMahon showed why he was revered even though at times he could be a jerk. On second-and-ten from Chicago's 31-yard line, McMahon threw a perfect pass down the right sideline to Gault for a 43-yard reception. Then Butler tied it 3–3 with a 28-yard field goal.

As the New England offense returned to the field, Eason *wanted* to feel relaxed in the pocket. But the Bears say he still seemed disturbed by his first harsh encounter with the 46 defense back in September.

"Tony Eason's eyes were bugging out of his head on the very first snap," remembers safety Dave Duerson. "He was terrified, really, every snap he was on the field. We were way inside his head."

Says safety Gary Fencik, "Tony Eason was ducking. I'd never seen a quarterback who was ducking."

Eason ended up throwing only six passes, failing to complete any. He was sacked three times and fumbled once before Raymond Berry yanked him with 5:08 remaining in the first half. Even though the report from the New England bench said, "No injuries, no illness," Eason never returned to Super Bowl XX.

His replacement, Steve Grogan, hadn't played in a game in two months because of a knee injury, and now the poor guy knew he would get his ass kicked. But Grogan kept climbing back up after the Bears put him down. It didn't help that by the time he entered, Chicago led 20–3 on Butler's second field goal and short touchdown runs by Matt Suhey and McMahon. This meant New England would *need* to keep passing, meaning Grogan would do well just to avoid a concussion.

All looked well for the Bears, but it was still early, and they wanted to pour it on anyway. So the next time the Patriots punted in the second quarter, the Bears tried a gadget play involving Leslie Frazier. He was a cornerback who had never returned a punt in five NFL seasons, but he was standing back there with Keith Ortego when Ortego caught the punt and handed the ball to Frazier on a reverse. Frazier was 26 and this was the third straight year he had led the team in interceptions. It was also the final year of his contract, so he was in position to get a good raise, or at least as much of a raise as his agent could wrestle from the stingy Bears. But now, on a trick play that the Bears hadn't run all season, Frazier blew out his left knee.

When his injury put an end to his career, it became controversial for two reasons. For one thing, Frazier was hurt on that reverse before ever getting touched by anyone from New England.

"I planted my foot in the Astroturf at the Superdome, and boom, I tore my knee up," remembers Frazier. "I needed major reconstructive knee surgery."

Thus the hazardous first generation of Astroturf had damaged another player. In addition, some people questioned why the play had been called in the first place.

"The game was in hand," says linebacker Brian Cabral. "We didn't need to run a reverse. There was no sense in that. We had practiced it, but never ran it. So it was a why-not type of deal. Why not have some fun? Unfortunately, it was at Leslie Frazier's expense. He had a career-ending knee injury."

Says rookie linebacker Jim Morrissey, "I thought Buddy Ryan was going to hyperventilate on that play. He was so upset he could barely breathe."

In the subsequent second-guessing associated with the loss of one of the NFL's best young cornerbacks, some people wondered *who* had called the trick play. Was it head coach Mike Ditka or special teams coach Steve Kazor? Ditka had brought Kazor with him from Dallas, where Kazor had been a scout but never a coach. Given that special teams were Ditka's passion, some of the Bears saw Kazor as mostly a figurehead.

Ditka takes responsibility, sort of.

"Leslie Frazier was a helluva player," says Ditka. "We kinda got cute there with the reverse stuff, and he got hurt. That was stupid, it really was. And I knew what we were going to do, because the special teams coach—who was a good coach— came over and told me we were gonna do this. I said, 'Well, I'd rather not run the reverse.' He said, 'It'll work.'

"Well, you know, we ran it, and there was no reason to run it. But we did. If he wouldn't have got hurt, nobody would have said anything. But he got hurt. And it did cross my mind before we ran it, *Why are we doing this? We don't need it. We don't need to fool people right now. We can smack them in the mouth.*"

The truth is, no one's to blame for Frazier's injury, except perhaps the makers of the first Astroturf. The Bears were winning the game 20–3, but it was the second quarter, and the outcome was hardly decided. Furthermore, Leslie Frazier, who is now the defensive coordinator for the Vikings, says he was excited to run the play.

"We practiced it during the season," Frazier says. "We practiced it for 19 weeks prior to the Super Bowl, and I re- member telling our special teams coach, 'If you guys ever call that play, I'm gonna score.' It's just one of those things.

It's just pro football. And I will tell you this: if I didn't get injured, I probably wouldn't be a coach today. Because I found myself looking at things that I never would have looked at if I was healthy and still playing football. So it opened the door to something I really enjoyed. So I think it worked out pretty good."

After Butler kicked his third field goal, the Bears jogged off the field leading 23–3 at halftime. The statistics at intermission were staggering. The Patriots had minus 5 yards rushing, minus 14 yards passing, minus 19 total yards. Rookie linebacker Jim Morrissey, who had defied the odds by making the Bears in the first place as an 11th-round draft pick, figured he had just won his first Super Bowl.

"I wanted to walk in the locker room yelling and screaming, but I didn't do it, based on my status," he says. "I just remember thinking, *Wow, we're walking in here at halftime, and we already know we're winning this game.*"

To the annoyance of the New England fans, "The Super Bowl Shuffle" was shown on the big screen in the stadium at halftime. Prince performed on the field, and during his song "Baby, I'm a Star" he was accompanied by the Honey Bears. The Chicago fans in the crowd gave them an ovation tinged with some sadness. The Honey Bears had been around since 1976, when George Halas decided he wanted professional cheerleaders on the sidelines. Yet now, with the franchise about to win its first Super Bowl, the Honey Bears were giving their final performance ever.

"I was told by Mr. Halas that as long as he was alive there would be cheerleaders," says Cathy Core, who founded and choreographed the Honey Bears. "In 1985 I was told by the Bears they were no longer interested in cheerleaders. They said they wanted to go back to blood-and-guts football and that didn't mix with the fluff on the sidelines. That wasn't a rational reason to me. Other NFL teams were bringing on cheerleaders, and the Bears were getting rid of them."

The Bears had announced their decision shortly before they played Miami on *Monday Night Football,* creating some hard feelings in a city that had grown fond of the Honey Bears, who not only entertained no matter how freezing it was at Soldier Field, but often made personal appearances, including fund-raisers for local charities.

"The unbeaten Bears may be heading toward their first Super Bowl, but their cheerleaders soon will be prancing into the unemployment line," wrote Rick Lorenz in the *Chicago Tribune.* "General Manager Jerry Vanisi told A-Plus Talent Agency, which provides 32 Honey Bears for each home game, that its contract will not be renewed after this season."

According to a statement from the front office, "the concept of cheerleading has outlived its time." But since this statement came from *Chicago's* front office, well, you can guess the rest.

"The front office was very tight, and there were stories that they didn't want to spend the money," says Core. "That was not true. It wasn't the money. As soon as we heard they were thinking of dissolving us, we had corporate sponsorships lined up and ready to go. What were the girls making anyway? A big ten dollars a game. We may have ended up with them making 20 dollars a game.

"It's still a mystery. I don't know if it will ever come out what the real agenda was. I think it was because Virginia McCaskey [Mike McCaskey's mother and George Halas's daughter] never really wanted them, and she made her wishes known and they acted on them. I was told she thought having dancers was maybe a little too risqué or immoral. She was the matriarch, and I really think everyone else's hands were tied."

As for the general feelings of the players, "We thought it was cruel when they were fired," says Duerson. "To us, the cheerleaders were part of the team."

Singletary had a similar reaction. In his 1986 book *Calling the Shots,* he wrote, "I can't imagine football without cheerleaders, even in pro ball. Seems our fans feel the same way. In some radio poll, the vote was 3–1 to keep them, but the only vote that really counts is McCaskey's."

Regardless of who made the decision, or why it was made, the Honey Bears' dismissal was another public relations hit for McCaskey. Twenty-five years later, Chicago is only one of six NFL teams without a cheerleading squad. Core now manages the Chicago Bulls' cheerleading group, the Luvabulls. But, she says, Chicago fans still want to talk about the final season of the city's *first* professional cheerleading group.

"The fans were outraged," says Core. "There were stories in the newspapers and on TV. But what are you going to do? It's not like the fans are going to stop buying tickets. Then the fans got caught up in the Super Bowl, and people forgot about it until the next season. Then they were asking, 'Where are the Honey Bears?' What do you mean, where are the Honey Bears? They got rid of us last year!"

Meanwhile, inside the Chicago locker room at halftime, McMahon encouraged his teammates to run up the score. Specifically, he says, "I told them we needed 60."

Evidently, Ditka felt the same way. The first time the Bears had the ball in the third quarter, they were backed up first-and-ten on their own four-yard line when McMahon threw from his end zone and hit Gault 60 yards downfield.

This dynamic play said a lot about Gault, who was having a big postseason after vanishing for stretches during the regular season. His tremendous speed allowed him to sprint by the secondary. But he was pulled down by the back of his jersey, on what the players call a "finger-tip tackle," which a more physical receiver would have run through for a touchdown.

Still, it took only nine plays for the Bears to drive 96 yards on their first third-quarter possession. They went up 30–3 on McMahon's second short touchdown run of the game.

By then, the quirky QB was more than halfway through his headbands. He had brought 15 with him to the sidelines and was changing them after every few series or so. First McMahon wore JDF CURE in honor of the Juvenile Diabetes Foundation. Then he wore POW-MIA, for the unaccounted-for soldiers in Vietnam. He wore several other headbands for charities, as well as a PLUTO headband in the third quarter. Dick Enberg thought this was a reference to McMahon's personality— "He's into outer space, well, that only figures"—but this one was in honor of Dan "Pluto" Plater, a teammate from Brigham Young who had given up football because of an illness.

Going into the game, the *Chicago Sun-Times* had predicted that McMahon might wear a headband that said BRAIN-DAMAGED. Though the ones he wore on Sunday were mostly for excellent causes, they reminded everyone what a character he had been throughout the postseason. What sometimes got overlooked was how crucial McMahon had been to his team. While everyone rhapsodized about Chicago's defense, in three postseason games the Bears scored 91 points and McMahon completed 39 of 66 passes for 636 yards with no interceptions. In the Super Bowl, he could have won MVP based on his 12-for-20, 256-yard passing performance and his two touchdown runs. Instead, the voters gave the award to

Richard Dent, who had one and a half sacks and forced two fumbles.

With the game already a 30–3 rout in the third quarter, the NBC announcers started to wonder aloud if Payton would score a touchdown. The leading rusher in NFL history, and the most beloved player in franchise history, Payton still hadn't reached the end zone in the showcase game he'd been waiting 11 years for.

Said Enberg in the third quarter, "And now that the Bears seem to be on a touchdown tirade, I think the fans, even the Patriot fans, who might be succumbing to all this, would want Payton to have a touchdown. If there's gonna be another Bear to score, I think everyone's rooting for this man."

At the partisan Superdome, this was true, literally. Throughout the second half, the crowd kept chanting, "Walter, Walter, Walter."

New England had entered the game keying on him, so he didn't have much running room all day, which showed in his final line of 22 carries for 61 yards. But that doesn't change the fact that there were at least two occasions when Payton could have scored in the second half. The first came when McMahon instead scored his second TD to put the Bears ahead 30–3. With first-and-goal from the one, Ditka inserted the Fridge into the backfield. Payton then went in motion into the right flat, and McMahon leaped over the pile for the six points. It was a pretty clever play, the Bears using Payton *and* the Fridge as decoys. But first-and-goal at the one—was it time to be clever, or time to take care of Payton, the soul of the Bears?

The next circumstance was even more egregious. Chicago led 37–3 late in the third quarter when McMahon hit Dennis Gentry for 27 yards near the right sideline. It appeared he might have scored, but the officials said Gentry stepped out of bounds at the one. And now the NBC announcers were certain. At least they were at first.

"And I wonder who's going to get the call on this one-yard line," said Olsen.

"Well, Walter Payton doesn't have one," said Enberg. "They're sending in Perry. Or are they?"

"Yep, they are," said Olsen.

Once again, it was first-and-goal at the one. Meaning, once again the Bears had four plays to give it to Payton. But McMahon handed off to Perry, who surged into the end zone easily.

"That one registered 3.8!" said Enberg. "Another Super Bowl record! The first refrigerator to score!" said Enberg.

"And the largest running back ever to score a touchdown," said Olsen.

"And Walter Payton, I guess they figure they got a whole quarter to go," said Enberg.

Well, not really. With the score 43–3, the Bears were already close to pulling their starters.

Up until then, McMahon had two short touchdown runs. Suhey had one. And now Perry had one. Perry, swept up in the moment, stood up from the Astroturf and power-spiked the ball. The Refrigerator didn't do anything wrong. They gave him the ball and he scored. And, sure, in random America, people loved it. The Fridge became an even bigger hero. But there were millions of football fans who felt they had just watched something a bit unseemly. It wasn't like Walter Payton needed anyone's *help*. But to score, he needed the rock.

The questions popped up in Chicago and around the NFL for years. What was Ditka thinking, giving it there to Perry instead of Payton? Was he still trying to make Perry a rock star? And when Ditka didn't call Payton's number, why didn't

McMahon get it done? Hadn't he been changing the plays Ditka had been sending in all season?

"That was bad, I guess," says Ditka. "You know who the leading rusher was in that game? Matt Suhey. If you look at the films, I had him [Payton] break the backfield quite a bit of the time, and we just handed the ball to Matt. Because every time he left the backfield, two people left with him. So basically what I am saying is, it was a hell of a game plan. We understood what they were trying to do, and we understood how we were going to negate what they were trying to do.

"But should he have had the ball at the goal line? Absolutely. Was it a mistake on my part? Yeah. I really didn't think about it at the time. Somebody said they said something to me on the sidelines and I said, 'It doesn't matter, we're winning.' And I guess it should have mattered to me. I should have thought a little bit more about it. But the play we ran when Perry scored? How many times did we run that damn thing that year? A lot!

"I told him before he passed that that was my fault. I just didn't think about it. I can honestly tell you that it never once crossed my mind who scored anything."

Says McMahon, "A lot has been said and written about that, and Walter never said a word to me about it. Whether or not he was upset, if people remember back, the Patriots' biggest concern was Walter Payton. And everywhere he went, there were four or five guys all over him. Walter opened it up for a lot of other guys. Matt Suhey had a nice day. Emery Moorehead got some balls. Kenny Margerum caught some balls.

"The first time that I scored, it was a reaction play. It was either Walter or me, and I came around the corner and the guy went right to Walter and there was nothing I could do. I turned it up. Then we came in at halftime talking about let's really run the score up, and then by the end of the third or the middle of the third the starters were out of the game already. So we had no more opportunities."

In Payton's 2000 book *Never Die Easy,* his coauthor and friend Don Yeager wrote, "Walter, as much as anyone, was overjoyed with the title and what it meant for the city of Chicago. But there was a tinge of hurt he carried with him after the game over not scoring a touchdown on the world's biggest stage, the Super Bowl."

Added Payton himself, "It would have been great to score one, they would have had your name down as scoring a touchdown in the Super Bowl. In the days and weeks after the game, yes, I was bothered it."

"Walter was disappointed," says Leslie Frazier. "Everyone was disappointed. He and I talked about it. Long after that Super Bowl, he was disappointed."

Says center Jay Hilgenberg, one of Payton's veteran blockers, "I didn't even realize it until the next day, tell you the truth. I had no idea he didn't score. And at the time when I heard about it, I thought, *Yeah, it's too bad, but next year we'll get him two or three touchdowns.* In my wildest dreams, I felt we would go on a roll for a couple Super Bowls."

Just how anticlimactic was the fourth quarter? And just how desperate did Enberg and Olsen get? In one of Enberg's attempts to try to make garbage time lively, he related a story about the time George Halas met Calvin Coolidge.

With the score a ridiculous 44–3 in the fourth quarter, the Bears sent in their subs and Grogan threw an eight-yard TD pass to Irving Fryer. A few minutes later, rarely used Henry Waechter sacked Grogan in the end zone for a safety. The

Bears led 46–10, and the only remaining drama unfolded on their sidelines. Wearing his trademark blue blazer and smiling enormously, team president Mike McCaskey had walked down to the field in the fourth quarter to bask in the impending Super Bowl title. But now McCaskey found himself surrounded by members of the defense telling him to do something to keep Buddy Ryan from leaving.

Hampton, as usual, was in the middle of it. "I said to him, 'You like this? You like the way this is going? Well, the one thing you can do to make sure this continues is make Buddy Ryan an offer he can't refuse to keep him here.' Of course, McCaskey, in his goofball way, kind of rolled his eyes and said, 'Well, we'll see.' Much like you ask your mom for a new airplane and she rolls her eyes and says, 'Well, we'll see.' Anyway, it was the least we could do for Buddy."

As the last few seconds ticked off the clock, the cakewalk finally ended with Chicago thrashing New England 46–10.

After 22 years, the Bears were once again the world champions. And not just any world champions. No other Super Bowl team had ever scored that many points. No other Super Bowl team had ever won by such a big margin. No other Super Bowl team had ever carried *two* coaches off the field. And yes, again, it was instigated by Dan Hampton, who, in case you haven't noticed, in some respects was the Jim McMahon of the defense.

Says Hampton, "Late in the game I went up to Steve McMichael, and I said, 'At the end of this deal, Dent and I are carrying Buddy off the field. You and Fridge better get your daddy Ditka.' See, Buddy loved me and Dent. And McMichael and Fridge were kind of like Ditka's pets. So Buddy always made fun of them. Buddy knew McMichael was important, but he would say stuff to him like, 'I don't care if *you* go out and get drunk, Steve. Just don't take the players with you.'

"Anyway, I told McMichael, 'You and Fridge better get your daddy and put him up on your shoulders so he doesn't pout. But Dent and I are gonna carry Buddy off.' And that was what we did when the game ended. We put Buddy up on our shoulders and carried him off."

Some reporters later noted that Ryan's ride lasted longer. But Ditka didn't look like he *wanted* to be up there. And after a moment or two, he ordered McMichael and Fridge to put him down so he could shake hands with Raymond Berry.

Once everyone had hugged and screamed out on the field, the Bears made their way back to the winning locker room, where the rookie Jim Morrissey was ready to get busy with the champagne. But bummer of all bummers, says Morrissey, "they didn't let us have champagne in there. We were all looking for the champagne. It was someone's decision not to have champagne. So that was one thing. But what I remember most is that it didn't seem like a group that was overly overjoyed. The celebration wasn't what you might think it would be for a Super Bowl champion. It was more business-like."

"I don't think I played the entire fourth quarter," says the Chicago native Gary Fencik. "So we kind of celebrated before the game was over on the sidelines. So the locker room was great, but it was like, okay, I already said all the words. And then being from Chicago, well, wouldn't you like the game to be more competitive? No. For once in my life, I didn't have to worry. This time the foregone-conclusion game was perfect."

Back up north, in jumping-for-joy Chicago, the city felt the same way Fencik did. Before the game even ended, there were impromptu car parades on Rush Street. On the sidewalks at bitterly cold Daley Plaza "The Super Bowl Shuffle" played on a giant screen as thousands of gleeful fans mimicked the corny dance moves. People across the city were shedding tears over a professional football game, and nobody felt even faintly embarrassed.

Of course, the '85 Bears, being the '85 Bears, still had all kinds of issues. Ryan was out the door, but just hadn't announced it yet. Payton was happy to win, but let down about not scoring. McCaskey was hugging and hogging the Super Bowl trophy to the extent that, McMahon says, "we were still teasing him in the mid-nineties over whether or not he still slept with that thing in his bed. He was running around the locker room with it like he was the guy who won the damn thing."

For Iron Mike Ditka, though, it was a poignant moment to be savored.

"A lot of dreams have been fulfilled, and a lot of frustrations have ended," he told NBC's Bob Costas after the game.

As the 46-year-old Ditka became the first Chicago coach to win a Super Bowl, he says he was also thinking about playing tight end for Halas on the 1963 NFL champions, and about the day he got hired at the Halas kitchen table in 1982.

"I was very proud because I felt I fulfilled what Halas hired me for," says Ditka. "And I thought the Old Man would have been very proud of this Super Bowl team. I told him in '83 before he died about a lot of the players we brought in. McMahon, he didn't really understand. I told him about Covert. I tried to explain to him that we were putting in the kind of people that he would like on offense and defense. Of course, he passed in '83, so he never got a chance to see it all come to be."

In New Orleans that night, no one felt like going out because it had been a long week and because they were leaving in the morning. And anyway, the front office had promised a postgame party in one of the ballrooms in the team's hotel. It just wasn't the party the players expected.

"It didn't last very long, and they cut out the booze pretty early," says assistant PR director Brian Harlan. "That didn't set a very good tone going into the next year either."

"The Bears were going to have this party after the game," remembers Kurt Becker. "They were making a big deal about this party, and you could have so many tickets and so many guests and blah-blah-blah. Well, you know how late it is by the time the Super Bowl gets done. By the time we got to the party it was 10 o'clock at night. Now, we just won the world championship, and all these food trays are empty, and this guy makes an announcement that they're gonna close the bar in a half-hour. So Hampton gets up on the microphone and pleads our case. He says at least leave the bar open a little longer. So they do, but not for much longer. So when that was over, we all go upstairs to our rooms, and we called the hotel, and we ordered the most unbelievable party you've ever thrown on a hotel room floor you could ever imagine, with cases of beer and food and this and that. So it was pretty good."

It didn't work out all that great for McMahon, though. After he saw his parents at the official party downstairs, he went up to his room, where he called the front desk. McMahon says, "I said, 'Can you send up some of those trays of beers that you guys have sitting around down there?' And they did, but I got charged for it. I got a $700 bill for beer."

On that fast-arriving Monday morning, a team-record nine of the Bears flew directly to Hawaii for the Pro Bowl: Payton, McMahon, Covert, and Hilgenberg from the offense,

Singletary, Hampton, Dent, Duerson, and Wilson from the defense. The rest of the team flew home to euphoric Chicago, where the parade was held the same day for the new NFL Super Bowl champions.

Originally the game plan was for the team to ride in 30 open convertibles from O'Hare Airport all the way to downtown. But there is cold and there is arctic, so the Bears ended up riding in chartered buses. At first they were flying along, with Chicago police cars blocking every on-ramp so the Bears could have a straight shot into the city. But as the buses entered the Loop on their way to the victory rally in Daley Plaza, there were an estimated 500,000 fans clogging LaSalle Street.

"That was amazing," says Tim Wrightman. "You remember how cold it was? It was amazing that many people came out in that weather."

It was 6 degrees above zero with a windchill factor of 25 below. As the frigid-but-jubilant people spilled onto LaSalle, the buses were no longer moving when Butler asked his driver if he could open a hatch in the bus's ceiling.

"The guy said, 'I don't care, we're not going anywhere,' " recalls Butler. "So I got up there and popped the top, and I stuck my head out, and the first thing that popped in my mind was 1968 or something when the astronauts came back to their ticker-tape parade. There were people out the windows, hanging off streetlamps, and I stuck my head back down, and I told all the guys, 'We gotta get up here!' We all start getting out on top of those buses, and then people are throwing bottles of champagne, they're throwing cameras up to take pictures of them. That was the coolest thing that ever happened to me as a Chicago Bear. That was when I understood how big we were, and how much we meant to the city."

"This is a football town. They love their Bears," says Keith

Van Horne, who grew up in California. "And that was a cool time. That year was a special year. That'll never happen again, for any team. It was special in the sense of the characters on the team and just the season itself. It was a once-in-a-lifetime thing. I was fortunate enough to be part of it, and to be part of the history of Chicago. The great city of Chicago."

CHAPTER 12

||||||||||||||||||||||||||||||||||||||||||||||||||||||||||||||||||||||||||||||

DID SOMEONE SAY DYNASTY?

There would be no trip to the White House for the new NFL world champions. On January 28, 1986, two days after Super Bowl XX, America went numb when the space shuttle *Challenger* exploded 73 seconds after takeoff and all seven crew members died. Thousands of children watched the disaster live on TV sets at their schools because one of the crew was Christa McAuliffe, a New Hampshire high school teacher and the charter member of NASA's Teacher in Space Project. When it had first been announced, the teacher project was dismissed by NASA's harshest critics as a way to deflect attention from recent congressional charges that the shuttle program was too wildly expensive. But McAuliffe herself had turned out to be so genuine and inspiring, even the worst political cynics had found themselves pulling for "the first citizen in space."

President Reagan had planned to give his State of the Union Address that evening. But he rescheduled it, telling the country instead from the Oval Office, "Today is a day for mourning and remembering. Nancy and I are pained to the core by the tragedy of the shuttle *Challenger.* We know we share this pain with all of the people in our country. This is truly a national loss."

The following afternoon the Philadelphia Eagles confirmed what everybody suspected: Buddy Ryan was their new head coach. Beaming owner Norman Braman referred to Ryan at a crowded news conference as "the next Vince Lombardi of the National Football League." When one reporter asked Ryan how Mike Ditka had reacted to his decision, Ryan said, "Mike who?"

The next day Ditka told the Associated Press, "Never again in history will an assistant get as much credit as Buddy did." AP also quoted Ditka as saying he was "elated" Ryan was gone, a word that Ditka said he never used. Still, Ryan replied, "Well, he's a jerk, so what difference does it make?"

In February 1986, the Bears replaced Ryan with Vince Tobin, the defensive coordinator for the New Orleans Saints and the younger brother of Chicago's personnel director, Bill Tobin. Vince Tobin, at Ditka's urging, began to install a more conventional 3-4 defense, which included the returning Todd Bell and Al Harris, who didn't receive even close to the money they had been seeking. Early that September, in his annual NFL preview, Paul Zimmerman predicted in *Sports Illustrated* that the 1986 Bears would go 13–3 and win the NFC Central. But Zimmerman noted ominously, "There's nothing major yet. It's just a sense I get that some of the edge is off."

Not in game two of the '86 season, it wasn't. As Ditka and Ryan stalked opposite sidelines, the Bears and Eagles played an intensely emotional game at Soldier Field. McMahon sat out with a troublesome right shoulder. And with second-year man Tomczak starting instead of the more experienced Fuller, the game went into overtime tied 10–10.

"I wasn't even on our kickoff team," says Dave Duerson, whom Ryan had never forgiven for simply replacing Todd Bell. "But I grabbed Steve Kazor and told him, 'I'm going down in the five spot.' I hit their return man, he fumbled, Ditka immediately sent Butler on the field, and he kicked a field goal and we won 13–10. Ditka ran up and embraced me, and we walked off the field together. I don't think Ditka could have been any happier about the way the whole thing came down. He beat his archrival, his nemesis, and the guy who Buddy was hardest on made the play to win the game."

By the second week of October, the defending Super Bowl champs were 6–0 and had won 24 of their last 25 games. But uncertainty engulfed the quarterback position. Back in the summer of 1985, after recovering from his lacerated kidney, McMahon had arrived at training camp in especially good condition. But in 1986, after an off-season of many Moose-heads, much golf, and a number of lucrative speaking engagements around the country, he had arrived at camp about 25 pounds fatter than his normal playing weight of 190. Now his bad throwing shoulder was yanking him in and out of the starting lineup. Thus, on October 14, in one of Ditka's most polarizing personnel decisions, the Bears acquired the rights to quarterback Doug Flutie.

"Ditka was trying to catch lightning in a bottle," says Dan Hampton. "Everything he had done the year before with the Fridge was magic. With Flutie, I think Ditka was flailing at the piñata. But Ditka was also trying to jar McMahon back to his senses and make him realize, 'Hey, you're not the rock star. You need to get to work here.' "

The Bears picked up Flutie in a trade with the Rams, who held his NFL rights after his previous team, the New Jersey Generals, had recently folded with the rest of the USFL. Personnel director Bill Tobin and president Mike McCaskey never wanted to sign the five-foot-nine Flutie, famous mostly for his scrambling, his last-second heroics against the

University of Miami, and his Heisman Trophy Award while starring at Boston College. Ditka and Vanisi were the ones who wanted Flutie, and the head coach and general manager won the day. In doing so, they fractured the '86 Bears, and this time it wasn't the offense vs. the defense.

Linebacker Otis Wilson said in a team meeting, "What do we need *him* for?"

Offensive tackle Keith Van Horne chimed in, "What's this Flutie shit?"

The most outspoken critic, in public, was McMahon. At Chicago's first practice after the trade was announced, McMahon made a mockery of it by wearing a red jersey with Flutie's BC number 22 on it. That same day McMahon told reporters, "I know it's not sitting well with a bunch of players."

Replied Ditka, "I frankly don't give a damn. Wasn't that a line in a movie?"

McMahon said, "Ditka talks about being loyal to ballplayers who go through training camp. Tell me where the loyalty is."

Ditka said, "If you put loyalty ahead of talent, you've got some problems."

This remark understandably stung Tomczak, who told the press his initial reaction to the trade was "disappointment. What if your employer goes and brings somebody in?"

Here's what some of the '86 Bears say today about what the *New York Times* called the Flutie Flap:

Keith Van Horne: "It was nothing against Doug Flutie. It's just that he didn't have enough time to assimilate with the offense, and they threw him in there expecting the Flutie miracle to happen. When Flutie struggled, Vanisi said something like we didn't try as hard because our friend McMahon wasn't in there, which was a totally ridiculous comment. I wrote a letter to Vanisi saying, 'You're just covering your ass because you made a mistake.' "

Dave Duerson: "That move backfired in a number of ways. Ditka would have Flutie over to his house for dinner. He had never invited anybody to his house, and that included Walter. So that created dissension in the locker room."

Mike Tomczak: "Anytime your job feels threatened, you got to look at yourself first and say, am I getting the job done. I felt I was playing well enough. I was starting to gain control of that team, and the defense respected me because I wasn't putting them into bad spots. But nobody asked my opinion, so I accepted it and moved on. McMahon voiced his displeasure more openly. He referred to Flutie as 'Bambi.' There was some animosity in the quarterback meetings."

Mike Ditka: "It was a good move. Flutie was a good football player. Our football team didn't handle it as well as it should have, period. I'll never apologize for bringing Doug Flutie in. It was a great experience for me because I was able to be associated with what I consider a winner, a guy who achieved a lot in his life and worked his ass off. That thing never bothered me. People criticized that, and that's a lot of bullshit there too."

Jim McMahon: "I saw no reason for it. We had a proven veteran backup in Steve Fuller. Tomczak was the second-year guy, but he had gotten some playing time. So we already had two guys who had been in the system and had won games for us, and that's why I was pissed off. I also thought they were maybe trying to get rid of me. After my book came out, McCaskey told Ditka to fire me right then. I guess Ditka didn't feel that Tomczak was ready yet."

His autobiography—*McMahon! The Bear Truth About Chicago's Brashest Bear*—had hit bookstores in late September.

Thanks to talented *Tribune* columnist Bob Verdi, the instant *New York Times* best-seller was breezy and concrete at the same time. Thanks to the edgy McMahon, it joined Jim Bouton's *Ball Four* as one of the most candid books ever written by a professional athlete. It was so candid, in fact, that Butler warned McMahon after reading the book, and before it was in the stores, about the possible fallout:

"We were in the back of the bus after a preseason game in Pittsburgh," says Butler. "Jim was reading his book, with him wearing those sunglasses on the cover. He hands it to me, and he says, 'Read chapter nine.' So I started reading it, and he said, 'What do you think?' I said, 'It was nice playing with you, man.' Because it was about McCaskey. I said, 'Dude, it's your boss. And your boss is a lot of things, but he's still your boss.' "

Says McMahon, "Verdi even said, 'You really don't want me to put this in there.'

"I said, 'Write it. Write it like I said it.' "

In addition to hammering McCaskey for the Hiroshi incident, these were among the potshots McMahon took at the team president: "Michael McCaskey doesn't have any qualifications to operate the Bears except his name. . . .

"Most of us just laugh to keep from strangling him. The Bears who won Super Bowl XX were not a happy bunch of players. Michael McCaskey might think we won because of him. He'd be offended to learn that most of us felt we won in spite of him. . . .

"If he had his choice, he'd have forty-five players with no personality, no individuality at all. Michael McCaskey would like a bunch of robots. Then, everything would go along peacefully. You might not win many games, but at least there wouldn't be any headbands."

Less than a month after McMahon's book came out, Chicago signed Flutie. That was Ditka's idea, not McCaskey's. But the following week, when the Bears cut injured receiver Ken Margerum, there was citywide speculation that this was McCaskey's revenge for McMahon's withering tome.

"Ken Margerum was Jim McMahon's best friend," says Butler. "And on our team, Ken was that player who keeps up the enthusiasm, who always hustles his ass off. So there seemed to be an agenda on not so much bringing in Flutie, but on who was let go. And it was certainly talked about among the players, because Ken was one of ours."

On October 19, with Flutie soon to arrive and Fuller starting, the 6–0 Bears floundered on offense in a 23–7 loss to Minnesota. The Rams beat them two games later, 20–17, on *Monday Night Football.* The next week Flutie began seeing spot action, proving to be inconsistent in a system he barely knew yet. By the time the 12th game arrived, McMahon had already missed six, and the quarterback situation was still fluid. But when Green Bay came that week to Soldier Field, the Bears were somehow 9–2, McMahon was starting again, and another Super Bowl ring seemed feasible. Then everything changed in an instant after one of the most vicious cheap shots in NFL history.

It was November 23, 1986. Like several of his Green Bay teammates that Sunday, noseguard Charles Martin wore a towel in his waistband with the uniform numbers of Bears players on it. Included on Martin's hit list was McMahon's number 9. When McMahon threw an interception in the second quarter, Martin picked him up and body-slammed him out of the 1986 season. His already damaged right shoulder was soon found to have a torn rotator cuff and myriad other problems. Since McMahon and his agent Steve Zucker didn't entirely trust the team's own doctors, they flew to Los Angeles, where the noted Dr. Frank Jobe performed major reconstructive surgery.

The Bears won their next four games to finish the regular season 14–2, but it was about as ugly as 14–2 can get. They barely squeaked by in five of their victories. Their schedule was a cream puff because the NFL Central stunk. The offense had struggled to score with its four revolving quarterbacks. And even though Vince Tobin's bend-but-don't-break 3-4 defense had allowed the fewest points ever in a 16-game season (187, 11.7 per game), a bunch of the Bears felt something vital was missing.

"I know what the argument was," says center Jay Hilgenberg. "Vince Tobin said the statistics were better in '86 than they were in '85. But Buddy Ryan brought an edge to those guys, an aggressive attitude. I think that was kind of lost in '86."

"It *wasn't* the same," says Hampton. "It wasn't the same type of defense that knocked balls loose, knocked quarterbacks out, got fumbles for our offense to get easy scoring opportunities."

Ditka had given Flutie his first NFL start against Dallas in the regular-season finale. Flutie had done a nice job, throwing touchdown passes of 58 and 33 yards in a 24–10 victory. After a bye week for winning the NFC Central, Ditka again started Flutie in Chicago's playoff opener against the wild-card Redskins at Soldier Field. It was a risky move given that Flutie had been in the league *eight weeks*. Nevertheless, the Bears were heavily favored since they had home-field advantage, they had destroyed Washington 45–10 the previous season, and the Redskins entered this game hampered by injuries.

Joe Gibbs had his team better prepared to play than Ditka had his. Flutie appeared overwhelmed, completing just 11 of

31 passes for 134 yards, only 37 in the second half. In the third quarter, Flutie threw an interception that Ditka blamed on Gault for running the wrong route. Regardless, the errant play set up a touchdown that put Washington ahead 14–13. The Bears never scored again, losing 27–13, but it wasn't all the fault of Flutie and the offense. The defense also broke down in the second half, allowing 20 points while making journeyman quarterback Jay Schroeder resemble Johnny Unitas.

The shocking upset at home in their playoff opener ended any talk of a dynasty.

Then, in 1987, the Bears went 13–2 in the strike-shortened regular season, but Ditka stoked the resentment building toward him in the locker room. Striking for the second time in five years, this time the players walked out after two games. The next week all games were canceled. When the games resumed one week later, with the NFL owners now using replacement players, Ditka infamously called the Chicago stand-ins "the real Bears."

Ditka insists he was never anti-union. He just empathized with the replacement players, who he says were branded as scabs "for wanting to earn some money and live out a dream." But at that turbulent time in NFL history, some of his players charged Ditka with metamorphosing into a company man.

"He said to the media, 'These are the real Bears,' " remembers Hampton. "It's like Grandpa throws out Grandma and takes up with a stripper and starts saying how much she means to him. Ditka was doing what he thought he had to do to placate management, i.e., McCaskey. But some players were offended. I was offended."

Says Duerson, one of the '86 union reps, "When we came back from the strike, Ditka kept four scab players. Then he told us in the locker room, 'You better not touch these guys.' "

Meanwhile, says Ron Rivera, "Buddy Ryan got rid of all his scab players in Philly. He didn't even want to coach them. And I remember a few meetings where some of our guys were saying, 'Look at what Buddy did. *He* didn't keep his players.' "

In the 1987 playoffs, the Bears were bounced again (21–17) in their opening game, and again by Washington at Soldier Field. By the start of the 1988 season, Payton had retired. Gault had been traded to the Raiders. Marshall had signed with the Redskins after the NFL players had won limited free agency and the Bears had refused to match Washington's offer. Ditka had benched the Fridge after he had blown up to nearly 400 pounds. McCaskey had fired general manager Vanisi, Ditka's best friend and one of the few Bears left hired by Halas.

Still, the '88 Bears stopped bickering, finished 12–4, and won their first playoff game against Ryan's Eagles. But they were dismantled at home by San Francisco in the NFC championship. Chicago traded McMahon to San Diego that summer, and that winter the '89 Bears slid down to 6–10. Two pretty good seasons preceded an awful one, with the '92 Bears going 5–11. Then on January 5, 1993, Michael McCaskey went down in Chicago history as The Man Who Fired Mike Ditka. And even though all the writers there saw it coming, and even though they knew Ditka was hardly a saint, they barbecued the man who gave him the ax.

Wrote Bob Verdi in his *Tribune* column, "When George Halas is finished spinning out of control in his grave, rest assured he shall ask the Great Scorer for permission to call one more play. Should the wish be granted, Papa Bear surely will grab grandson Michael McCaskey by the earlobes and drop-kick him, end over end, through the nearest goal posts."

Wrote Brian Hewitt in the *Sun-Times,* "The overwhelming temptation in addressing the question: 'What Must the Bears Do Next?' is to suggest Michael McCaskey fire Michael McCaskey.

"But that's blue sky. It's too easy. And it isn't going to happen.

"Nor is McCaskey, the team president and chief executive officer, about to sell the franchise. Which is too bad."

As usual in Chicago, the *Tribune*'s iconic Mike Royko had the printed reaction with the most weight. Noting that Ditka had gotten "tears in his eyes and a lump in his throat" at his farewell press conference, Royko suggested that Ditka should instead have said: "I have good news and I have bad news. The bad news is that I've just been fired by this weenie. The good news is that I don't have to work for this weenie anymore."

Royko also referred to McCaskey as a "cupcake" and a "Twinkie" and an "Ivy League stiff" and a "glorified book-keeper." And now that both Ditka *and* McMahon were gone, Royko (as Ditka) wrote that McCaskey is "going to rebuild this team in his image. From the Chicago Bears to the Chicago Poodles."

Says Mike Ditka today, "In 1985 I had no problem with Michael McCaskey. To this day I don't have any problem with anybody. Their problem became with me. And the problem was very simple. When we won, I became the Bears. And yeah, maybe I became bigger than I should have been. I don't know. It happened. I'm not gonna apologize. The Bears have won two championships in 60 years, and I played on one of the teams and coached the other one. I'll be damned if I'm gonna apologize for that. I think I know what it takes to build a championship team. If people don't understand that, fine. I had my days in the sun. I was fortunate. I came, I saw, I conquered, and I left. How I left? Maybe it wasn't pleasant. But I lived through it."

All of this is to say, the 1985 Chicago Bears never went on to win any more championships. Surely they had enough talent. In the first two rounds of the 1985 playoffs, they embarrassed the Giants and Rams by an aggregate score of 45–0. They doled out a historic 46–10 Super Bowl beating, after which New England guard Ron Wooten said, "It kind of felt like we were the team that the Globetrotters play all the time." And nobody can say they failed to win any more titles because they got old and arthritic. The 1985 Bears were the NFL's youngest team, with an average age of 25.1.

So what really happened, guys?

How in the world did you manage to win just one ring?

Jim McMahon: "The stuff with the scabs and Flutie was typical of what went on after '85. Ditka was making comments like he could win with anyone because he was such a great coach. I don't think that helped."

Mike Singletary: "Ditka and Ryan split up. That was a sad scene. Some of our guys thought their relationship was funny. I never thought it was funny. I saw two men who I loved not able to express how much they respected each other. They allowed the media and pride to kill them and the team. If they had come together, it would have been very frightening to see what the Bears could have done—much better than the '85 season. I look at two great men even today, and they're still very stubborn, still set in their ways, and it's kinda cute, but at the end of the day it's kinda sad. It was kinda like having a mom and dad divorce."

Brian Cabral: "Ditka handed out T-shirts in '86 that said ARE YOU SATISFIED? I think there were a lot of satisfied people."

Tom Thayer: "The outside influences. Who was getting the endorsements? Who wasn't getting endorsements? We were the youngest team in the NFL, and maybe it was unfortunate that we weren't a more mature group of guys. But it affected Ditka as much as it affected the players. No one on that team was exempt from it."

Keith Van Horne: "I remember coming into a team meeting and Ditka's yelling at us, you forgot what it takes to win and what it takes to get here and you're all worried about your endorsements and your commercials instead of focusing on what's important. So that was our chew-out that morning. Then I went home that night, and on channel 2, 5, and 7, Ditka had three different commercials, and not for the same product. I think that sorta encapsulates a little bit what happened to that team."

Mike Ditka: "That's all bullshit. I lost focus and this and that. Nah, I never lost focus. I could do radio shows and a TV show and never lose focus on what I was there for and what my job was. People can say anything they want to, but that's all bullshit."

Kevin Butler: "Free agency started. Wilber Marshall left. The Bears didn't want to pay him. Shit was coming out on Willie Gault and "The Super Bowl Shuffle," and they wanted to get rid of him. There was disharmony throughout the organization."

Mike Ditka: "Gault was gone. Marshall was gone. McMichael was gone. McMahon was gone. And I will coach whoever is there. I will play the hand I am dealt.

"But one thing I know for sure, you can't win by subtraction. We brought those people in there for a purpose, and you defeat that purpose when you purposely let them go. In most of the cases it was about money. With McMahon, it was about conflicts and personalities with the owner. Well, if you don't understand the game, and how to keep people happy, and how to keep a championship team intact, you got a problem. I think that's what happened with our ownership. I really believe that."

Jim Morrissey: "I think '86 and '87 weren't Super Bowl years because McMahon wasn't there for the playoffs. And that's not bashing anybody who played that position. That's just saying our leader on offense was not there. I think that was big."

Dan Hampton: "Like the fall of Rome. It happens. But to try and win it again without the same style of defense that Buddy had? And to try and win it again without our best quarterback healthy? That's hard to do in that league."

Jim McMahon: "Who knows? We had a hell of a run. We won a lot of games in those five years. Too bad we don't have those seven-game playoffs. One bad day and you're done."

Mike Ditka: "We won more games than anyone in the NFL for a span there. I give a lot of credit to our competition because while you're climbing that ladder, it's not as hard as once you get to the top. Then everyone tries to knock you off that ladder. You don't sneak up on anybody once you win the Super Bowl."

Ron Rivera: "I still believe we were the best Super Bowl team ever. Unfortunately, we were also the best team ever to win just one."

It's the American way to always want more, more, more. But when done in an epic way, even something done once can be eternal.

The 1985 Bears had magnetic leaders: McMahon, Payton, Hampton, Singletary, Fencik. They had a pair of alpha dogs,

Ditka and Ryan, who delivered when it counted despite their dysfunction. They had a never-before, never-since pop sensation in the Fridge. They were in the NFL, but un-NFL, presenting themselves as characters, not robots. In subsequent years, its critics would dub it the No Fun League, too stodgy, too corporate, too neutered, with too few cultural differences between the franchises. But in 1985, it was evident how much fun the Chicago Bears had. *Sports Illustrated* later called them "the last NFL team actually allowed to smile."

For a single season, the 1985 Bears may have been the greatest pro football team ever. But their reign on top was brief. They never became the Steelers of the 1970s, the 49ers of the 1980s, the Cowboys of the 1990s. In Chicago itself, they never resembled Michael Jordan's Bulls, who won six championships in eight seasons between 1991 and 1998.

But 25 years later, the fans still remember what the 1985 Bears meant to a city starving for a winner. Nor will the players ever forget the civic pride they unleashed. Ron Rivera returned to Chicago in 1986 and saw T-shirts saying, SECOND CITY TO WHO? Emery Moorehead says the only way the '85 Bears can ever lose their position as the most beloved team in Chicago's history is if the Cubs win the World Series. But as someone who grew up in the City of Big Shoulders, Moorehead says that just might never happen.

The immaturity, the infighting, the very human scent of missed opportunity—does it diminish the '85 Bears or make them more endearing and enduring?

If we're still talking about it, we know the answer.

ACKNOWLEDGMENTS

||||||||||||||||||||||||||||||||||||||||||||||||||||||||||||||||||||||||||||||||||||||||||||||||||||||

There are many kind people to thank. Above all, I thank the 1985 Chicago Bears who shared their memories of a remarkable season. This book could not have been written without their time and cooperation.

Anyone trying to illuminate the 1985 Bears is indebted to Walter Payton and Don Yaeger for their book, *Never Die Easy;* to Jim McMahon and Bob Verdi for their book, *McMahon!;* to Mike Singletary and Armen Keteyian for their book, *Calling the Shots;* to Keteyian for his book *Ditka;* to Scott Simon for his book *Home and Away;* to John Mullin for his book *The Rise and Self-Destruction of the Greatest Football Team in History;* to Mike Ditka and Don Pierson for their book, *Ditka: An Autobiography;* to Ditka and Rick Telander for their book, *In Life, First You Kick Ass;* to Steve McMichael and Phil Arvia for their book, *Tales from the Chicago Bears Sideline;* and to Roy Taylor for his comprehensive website www.BearsHistory.com.

The *Tribune* and the *Sun-Times,* the two great newspapers that I grew up on, were invaluable resources for their lively and excellent coverage of that historic season in Chicago. Another crucial resource was *Sports Illustrated,* which covered the '85 Bears with its trademark blend of substance and style.

I am deeply grateful to Scott Waxman, my literary agent, who liked this book idea from the beginning and kept encouraging me to sit down and write it.

I am especially thankful to my editor, Sean Desmond, who is smart, straightforward, and fun—all in all, pretty much the perfect editor. Thanks also to Sean's associate Stephanie Chan, who always kept things moving forward, and did it graciously.

I am thankful to my friends and colleagues at ESPN. I have been fortunate to work with so many gifted and hardworking journalists.

For their various contributions, I'd also like to say thank you to Denis Anthony, Jennifer Anthony, Kathleen Anthony, Bob Baer, Gary Delsohn, Eilene Delsohn, Penny Delsohn, Sharon Delsohn, Sheldon Gottlieb, Erik Kramer, Chris Mortensen, David Rubenstein, Scott Sohn, Jim Steiner, and Steve Zucker.

Extraordinary thanks to my daughters, Emma, Hannah, and Grace. You're amazing and I love you and admire you. It's a blessing to be around you every day.

Finally, my deepest thanks to my wife, Mary Kay Delsohn. You have been there for our whole family, and you have been there for me on everything I've ever published. You're my partner and best friend, and you even helped transcribe all those damn interview tapes. I believe that is what's called unconditional love.

INDEX

||||||||||||||||||||||||||||||||||||||||||||||||||||||||||||||||||||||||||||||||||||||||||||||||||||||||||||||||||||||||||||||

ABOUT THE AUTHOR

STEVE DELSOHN is the author or co-author of several notable sports books, including the *New York Times* bestseller *Out of Bounds* with NFL great Jim Brown. He is currently a reporter for ESPN television. As a teenager growing up in the Windy City, Delsohn sold hot dogs at Chicago Bears games.